PROTECTING THE CULTURAL HERITAGE

National Legislations and International Conventions

PROTECTING THE CULTURAL HERITAGE

National Legislations and International Conventions

Sachindra Sekhar Biswas

Aryan Books International
New Delhi

PROTECTING THE CULTURAL HERITAGE

ISBN-978-81-7305-150-0

First Published in 1999 by:

Aryan Books International

Pooja Apartments, 4B, Ansari Road, New Delhi-110 002 (India)

Tel.: 23287589, 23255799; Fax: 91-11-23270385

E-mail: aryanbooks@gmail.com

www.aryanbooks.co.in

Designed and Printed in India by

ABI Prints & Publishing Co., New Delhi

Dedicated to
The Golden Jubilee Celebration
of
India's Independence
&
The Establishment of UNESCO-ICOM
(International Council of Museums)

Preface

To ensure protection and preservation of cultural heritage, various Acts, Rules and Regulations have been framed and notified, which are often referred to by Government personnels, professionals, non-governmental agencies and others. Corrigendums and Amendments have also been issued from time to time, which are usually filed and invariably remain unnoticed. This creates problem when the issues under reference are referred to in the court of law.

It is therefore long felt that a Compendium on the National Legislations and International conventions may be prepared to facilitate their application in the functional issue. The present volume, thus has been prepared in a comprehensive manner including all the Acts and Rules issued by the competent authorities in respect of protecting and preserving the cultural heritage and regulating the business and export of antiquities and art treasures of the country, so that they are available at a single place for the use of all concerned. International conventions in this regard have also been included in this work to know and understand the international implication of laws specially in case of restitution of cultural properties to their country of origin. The ICOM Code of Ethics has also been included in the volume to make aware the cultural institutions and professionals, so that their actions in the regard are lawful. I hope that the volume will serve the rightful purpose and be of use to agencies and persons concerned with the cultural heritage management.

I, however, wish to say that there might be amendments of the rules etc. during the process of preparation of the volume and its publication, and as such there might be omissions. Some errors also might have crept inadvertently in the process of publication. The faults are mine and I sincerely regret for any such ornissions and commissions, if any, in the volume.

S.S. Biswas

Acknowledgements

The author of the volume sincerely offers his thanks to Archaeological Survey of India and UNESCO-ICOM for their active support and co-operation for making available relevant records which are incorporated in this volume. My thanks are offered to Smt. J. Kedareswari, Deputy Keeper, Salar Jung Museum, Hyderabad, Miss Tulshimanjuri Ganguli, Asstt. Curator, Rabindra Bharti Museum, Calcutta, Prof. Anupa Pande of the National Museum Institute, New Delhi, Shri Virendra Pandey Asstt. to ICOM-ASPAC and Shri Janardan of National Museum, New Delhi who lent their valuable services in making this volume a successful one. I am also thankful to my son Shri Rupanjan and Mrs. Geetali Mullick for preparing the Index.

Last but not the least, I wish to thank Shri Vikas Arya for taking personal interest in publishing the book.

Contents

List of Illustrations

List of Abbreviations Used

A.O. 1937	:	Government of India (Adaptation of Indian Laws) Order, 1937 as modified by the Government of India (Adaptation of Indian Laws) Supplementary Order, 1937
A.O. 1948	:	Indian Independence (Adaptation of Central Acts and Ordinances) Order, 1948
Govt.	:	Government
L.G.	:	Local Government
G.G. in C.	:	Governor General in Council
Mad.	:	Madras
C.P.	:	Central Provinces
Subs.	:	Substituted
Rep.	:	Repealed
S.	:	Section

PART I
NATIONAL LEGISLATIONS

1. Introduction

Protection and preservation of our cultural property against the dangers of damage and destruction and, in particular, against damages resulting from theft, vandalism, clandestine excavations and illicit traffic is our sacred duty, which we owe to posterity. Cultural heritage along with environment is very essential to the well being and to the enjoyment of man's basic rights—even the right to life itself. Hence, there is a strong need to undertake all measures possible to stop the impoverishment of the cultural heritage of our country, in addition to inculcating a strong sense of public awareness and pride in one's own heritage. However, such protection cannot be effectively provided without reference to law, which defines the legal status of property to be protected and renders obligatory respect of the many and varied measures taken for the preservation and transmission to future generations of the tangible and most valuable heritage of our culture.

Like several parts of Asia and Europe which are face to face with new threats and perils of theft, illicit traffic and vandalism, India, too, is forced to turn its attention to these immediate problems which are sure to impede the development activities in connection with museums. Diversion of resources, limited as they always are, to combat these risks and threats is naturally a setback to the growth of museums, specially when the main burden of financial responsibilities falls on the government.

Incentives for theft, vandalism and damage are each day increasing by the soaring prices paid for 'collector's items', the growing lack of respect for cultural property—particularly religious property—which was traditionally revered in most countries, the extension of the means of communication on all fronts and the development of mass tourism. Quite germane to all these are, the problems of reserve collection in Indian museums and the Indian architecture. In most museums, reserve collections do not receive equal attention as the displayed exhibits, so far their care, preservation, classification and safety are concerned. The manner in which antiquities are stored or stacked in many museums makes it extremely hard to detect theft if it happens to take place. Reserve collection in capacious accommodation arranged as visual store may prevent surreptitious removal of museum objects.

The entire humanity was never so anxious, as it is today, to preserve and protect the world's cultural and natural heritage. Documents published by UNESCO further reveal and stress this fact. Some of the Recommendations and Conventions brought out by this world body after 1950 are as follows:

(i) Convention for, Protection of Cultural Property in the Event of Armed Conflict (1953).

(ii) Recommendation of International Principles Applicable to Archaeological Excavations (1956).

(iii) Recommendation on the Most Effective Means of Rendering Museums to everyone (1960).

(iv) Recommendation on the Means of Prohibiting and Preventing the Illicit Import, Export and Transfer of Ownership of Cultural Property (1964).

(v) Convention on the Means of Prohibiting and Preventing the Illicit Import, Export and Transfer of Ownership of Cultural Property (1970).

(vi) Recommendation for the Protection of Movable Cultural Property (1979).

In addition, the ICOM has issued documents like the "ICOM Ethical Acquisition Code" and the "Guidelines for Loans" which have relevance in the protection of cultural property.

Indian museums rely on government for their support and development, and the country's antiquarian laws and other legislative measures help immensely in establishment of new museums and in augmenting and safeguarding the holdings of the existing ones. Indian legislation divides cultural property into ancient monuments, archaeological sites, antiquities and art treasures. The first two categories refer essentially to immovable property and the others to movable property. In order to be brought under the protection of the law, monuments have to be declared to be of national importance. Movable cultural property may only be considered to be an antiquity if it is of a minimum age (75 in the case of manuscripts and documents and 100 for other objects). Art treasures are not subject to this condition but they must be the subject of a declaration by the Central Government published in the official Gazette. Thus, in exercise of the powers conferred by clause (6) of sub-section (1) of section 2 of the Antiquities and Art Treasures Act, 1972, the Central Government has declared paintings including drawings, sketches, diagrams and the like and the objects of plastic art by Rabindranath Tagore, Amrit Sher-Gil, Jamini Roy, Nandlal Bose, Ravi Varma, Gaganendranath Tagore, Abanindranath Tagore, Sailoj Mukherjee and N. Roerich as art-treasure for the purpose of this Act. These are all human works of art, not being antiquities and have artistic and aesthetic value.

In the field of national legislation, the earliest attempt was the passing of Bengal Regulations XIX of 1810, sections (iii) and (iv) of which were repeated verbatim in the Madras Regulations VII of 1817. After a lapse of more than half a century, the next legislative measure was the Act XX of 1863 which invested the government with the authority "to prevent injury to and preserve buildings remarkable for their antiquity or for the historical or architectural value". The next law that was enacted and is still in force is the Indian Treasure Trove Act 1878 which marks the shift in emphasis from monuments to antiquities. This Act was directed, no doubt, to combat treasure-hunting, besides regulating the lawful disposal of treasures found in accidental digging.

James Burgess who succeeded Sir Alexander Cunninghum as the Director-General of Archaeological Survey of India (A.S.I) showed greater awareness about legislative measures as tools to protect cultural legacy from decay and despoilation. At his initiative, the government issued two directives, one forbidding any person or agency to undertake excavation without prior consent of the Archaeological Survey and the other debarring officers from disposing of antiquities found or acquired without the permission of the government.

Not until 1904 was the Ancient Monuments Preservation Act to be passed, which came into force, "to provide for the preservation of ancient monuments, for the exercise of control over traffic in antiquities and over excavation in certain places and for the protection and acquisition in certain cases of ancient monuments and of objects of archaeological, historical or artistic interest." This Act has been broad-based by the passing of the Ancient Monuments and Archaeological Sites and Remains Act 1958, but not repealed.

No legislative measure was carried out thereafter till India won Independence. On 18th April, 1947 when Mortimer Wheeler was the Director-General, A.S.I., the Indian legislature passed the Antiquities (Export Control) Act, 1947. Under this Act, no antiquity, a term given a comprehensive definition here, can be exported without a licence issued by the Director-General. In terms of this Act, antiquity does not include any object which is less than one hundred years old and the Antiquities (Export Control) Rule,

1947 includes provision for giving certificate as to whether an object is an antiquity or not. An attempt was made in 1965 to introduce an amendment to the Antiquities (Export Control) Act, 1947 but it did not meet with success.

Fortunately, with the promulgation of the Constitution of India from 26th January 1950, the allocation of functions was given a permanent shape. The allocation as per the Seventh schedule of the Constitution is as follows:

List I (Union List), item 67: Ancient and historical monuments and records, and archaeological sites and remains declared by or under law by Parliament to be of national importance.

List II (State List), item 12: Libraries, museums and other similar institutions controlled or financed by the states; ancient and historical monuments and records other than those declared by or under law made by Parliament to be of national importance. (The Indian Treasure Trove Act, 1878 also included in the State List).

List III (Concurrent List), item 40: Archaeological sites and remains other than those declared by or under law made by Parliament to be of national importance.

Thus in fulfilment of the provisions of the Constitution, the Ancient and Historical Monuments and Archaeological Sites and Remains (Declaration of National Importance) Act, 1951 was enacted on 28th November 1951. According to this Act, all ancient and historical monuments and all archaeological sites and remains declared under Ancient Monuments Preservation Act, 1904, were re-declared as monuments and archaeological sites of national importance. About 450 monuments and sites in the Part B States were included in this national list. Subsequently by section 126 of the States Reorganisation Act, 1956, some more monuments and archaeological sites were declared as of national importance.

With a view to bringing the Ancient Monuments Preservation Act, 1904 in line with the constitutional provisions and also to conform it with the new developments in the changed situation, the Ancient Monuments and Archaeological Sites and Remains Act, 1958 was enacted on 28th August 1958 and the Act along with the Ancient Monuments and Archaeological Sites and Remains Rules, 1959 came into force from 15 October 1959. Similarly, as the provisions of the Antiquities (Export Control) Act, 1947 were found inadequate to cope with the alarmingly high incidence of theft and illicit traffic in antiquities, a new Act—The Antiquities and Art Treasures Act, 1972—was passed on 9 September 1972. Unlike the Act of 1958 it repeals the Antiquities (Export Control) Act, 1947. Both the Act and the Antiquities and Art Treasures Rules, 1973 deal with a new category i.e., "art-treasures" which are not antiquities within the meaning of the same legislation. The object of this Act is threefold: to regulate the export trade in antiquities and art treasures, to provide for the prevention of smuggling of, and fraudulent dealings in antiquities, and to provide for the compulsory acquisition of antiquities and art treasures for preservation in public places. Besides the Act also provides the government, power to take any other steps which are necessary for the preservation of the antiquities and art treasures of the country. One of the objects of the Act through the registration and licensing of dealers of antiquities is to prepare a National Register of Antiquities.

Though the Antiquities and the Art Treasures Act, along with its rule was enforced from 5 April 1976, an Ordinance amending certain provisions of the Act was promulgated on 4 June 1976. The Antiquities and Art Treasures (Amendment) Ordinance, 1976 was made into an Act later in the same year without effecting any change in the provisions of the Ordinance or incorporating any new clause. So far as the legislative measures pertaining to monuments and antiquities are concerned, this is the last in the long list which commenced from 1810 onwards.

The international community, through its appropriate organs, defines standards of protection invites all member states to observe: Convention and Protocol for the Protection of Cultural Property in the Event of Armed Conflict (The Hague, 1954), Instruments of Ratification of the Convention and of the Protocol deposited on 16 June 1958. The Convention and the Protocol entered into force with respect to India on 16th September, 1958. Convention on the Means of Prohibiting and Preventing the Illicit Import, Export and Transfer of Ownership of Cultural Property (Paris, 1970). Instrument of Ratification of the Convention deposited on 24 January 1977. The convention entered into force with respect to India on 24 April 1977. Recommendation for the protection of Moveable Cultural Property, 1978. Final Act of the Diplomatic Conference for the Adoption of the Draft Unidroit Convention on the International Return of Stolen or Illegally exported Cultural objects.

The INC-ICOM, 1993, News Edition focused on museum security and its aspects. As a natural sequel to this volume, I was prompted to embark upon the publication of the present compendium on national legislations and international standards of protection intended for museum professionals, art and antique dealers, private collectors, protection, customs and police services and any one else required to have a knowledge of the legal status of cultural property of our country. In addition, a chapter on How's and Why's of Antiquities Regulation has also been included. This knowledge, I hope, would go a long way in fostering national and international co-operation in the prevention and repression of offences concerning cultural property.

2. The Indian Treasure Trove Act 1878*

An Act to amend the law relating to Treasure trove
(as modified up to the 1st September, 1949)

Whereas it is expedient to amend the law relating to Treasure Trove, it is hereby enacted as follows :

PRELIMINARY

1. Short title

This Act may be called the Indian Treasure Trove Act, 1878.

Extent: It extends to[2] (all the Provinces of India).

* * * * * *[3]

2. (Repeal of enactments.) Rep. by the Amending Act, 1891 (XII of 1891).

3. Interpretation clause

In this Act—

"treasure" means anything of any value hidden in the soil, or in anything affixed thereto.

"collector" means (1) any Revenue-officer in independent charge of a district, and (2) any officer appointed by the[4] (provincial Government) to perform the function of a Collector under this Act.

When any person is entitled, under any reservation in an instrument of transfer of any land or thing affixed thereto, to treasure in such land or thing, he shall, for the purposes of this Act, be deemed to be the owner of such land or thing.

---

* Act No. VI of 1878 (13th February, 1878)

PROCEDURE ON FINDING TREASURE

4. Notice by finder of treasure

Wherever any treasure exceeding in amount or value ten rupees is found, the finder shall, as soon as practicable, give to the Collector notice in writing:

(a) of the nature and amount or approximate value of such treasure,

(b) of the place in which it was found,

(c) of the date of the finding,

and either deposit the treasure in the nearest Government Treasury, or give the Collector such security as/the Collector thinks fit, to produce the treasure at such time and place as he may from time to time require.

5. Notification requiring claimants to appear

On receiving a notice under section 4, the Collector shall, after making such enquiry (if any) as he thinks fit, take the following steps (namely):

(a) he shall publish a notification in such manner as the 1 (provincial Government) from time to time prescribes in this behalf, to the effect that, on a certain date (mentioning it) certain treasure (mentioning its nature, amount and approximate value) was found in a certain place (mentioning it); and requiring all persons claiming the treasure, or any part thereof, to appear personally or by agent before the Collector on a day and at a place therein mentioned, such day not being earlier than four months, or later than six months, after the date of the publication of such notification;

(b) when the place in which the treasure appears to the Collector to have been found was at the date of the finding in the possession of some person other than the finder, the Collector shall also serve on such person a special notice in writing to the same effect.

6. Forfeiture of right on failure to appear

Any person having any right to such treasure or any part thereof, as owner of the place in which it was found or otherwise, and not appearing as required by the notification issued under section 5, shall forfeit such right.

7. Matters to be enquired into and determined by the Collector

On the day notified under section 5, the Collector shall cause the treasure to be produced before him, and shall enquire as to and determine—

(a) the person by whom, the place in which, and the circumstances under which, such treasure was found; and

(b) as far as is possible, the person by whom, and the circumstances under which, such treasure was hidden.

8. Time to be allowed for suit by person claiming the treasure

If, upon an enquiry made under section 1, the Collector has reason to believe that the treasure was hidden, within one hundred years before the date of the finding, by a person appearing as required by the said notification and claiming such treasure, or by some other person under whom such person claims, the Collector shall make an order adjourning the hearing of the case for such period as he feels sufficient, to allow of a suit being instituted in the Civil Court by the claimant, to establish his right.

9. Treasure may be declared ownerless

If upon much enquiry the Collector sees no reason to believe that the treasure was hidden; or

If, where a period is fixed under section 8, no suit is constituted as aforesaid within such period to the knowledge of the Collector; or

(These words were substituted for the words "Local Government" by the Government of India (Adaptation of Indian Laws) Order, 1937).

If such suit is instituted within-such period, and the plaintiff's is finally rejected, the Collector may declare the treasure to be ownerless.

Appeal against such declaration—Any person aggrieved by a declaration made under this section may appeal against the same within two months from the date thereof to the Chief Controlling Revenue authority.

Subject to such appeal, every such declaration shall be final and conclusive.

10. Proceedings subsequent to declaration

When a declaration has been made in respect of any treasure under section 9, such treasure shall, in accordance with the provisions hereinafter contained, either be desired to the finder thereof, or be divided between him and the owner of the place in which it has been found in manner hereinafter provided.

11. When no other person claims as owner of place, treasure to be given to finder

When a declaration has been made in respect of any treasure as aforesaid and no person other than the finder of such treasure has appeared as required by the notification published under section 5 and claimed a share of the treasure as owner of the place in which it has been found, the Collector shall deliver such treasure to the finder thereof.

12. When only one such person claims and his claim is not disputed, treasure to be divided, and shares to be delivered in respect of any treasure, and only one person other than the finder of such treasure has so appeared and claimed, and the claim of such person is not disputed by the finder, the Collector shall proceed to divide the treasure between the finder and the person so claiming to the following rule (namely):-

If the finder and the person so claiming have not entered into any agreement then in force as to the disposal of the treasure, three-fourths of the treasure shall be allotted to such person who have entered into any such agreement, the treasure shall be disposed of in accordance therewith:

Provided that the Collector may, in any case, if he thinks fit, instead of dividing any treasure as directed by this section:

(a) allot to either party the whole or more than his share of such treasure, on such party paying to the Collector for the other party such sum of money as the Collector may fix as the equivalent of the share of such other party, or of the excess so allotted, as the case may be; or

(b) sell such treasure or any portion thereof by public-auction and divide the sale-proceeds between the parties according to the rule hereinbefore prescribed:

Provided also that, when the Collector has by his declaration under section 9 rejected any claim made under this Act any person other than the said finder or person claiming as owner of the place in which the treasure was found, such division shall not be made until after the expiration of two months without appeal having been presented under section 9 by the person whose claim has been so rejected, or when an appeal has been so presented after such appeal has been dismissed.

When the Collector has made a division under this section he shall deliver to the parties the portions of such treasure, or the money in lieu thereof, to which they are respectively sited under such division.

13. In case of dispute as to ownership of place, proceedings to be stayed

When a declaration has been made as aforesaid in respect of any treasure, and two or more persons have appeared as aforesaid and each of them claimed as owner of the place where such and claimed as disputed by the finder of such treasure, the Collector shall retain such treasure and shall make an order staying his proceedings with a view to the matter being enquired into and determined by a Civil Court.

14. Statement of such dispute

Any person who has so appeared and claimed may, within one month from the date of such order, institute a suit in the Civil Court to obtain a decree declaring his right; and in every such suit the finder of the treasure and all persons disputing such claim before the Collector shall be made defendants.

15. And division thereupon

If any such suit is instituted and the plaintiff's claim is finally established therein, the Collector shall, subject to the provisions of section 12, divide the treasure between him and the finder.

If no such suit is instituted as aforesaid, or if the claims of the plaintiffs in all such finally rejected, the Collector shall deliver the treasure to the finder.

16. Power to acquire the treasure on behalf of Government

The Collector may, at any time after making a declaration under section 9, and before delivering or dividing the treasure as hereinbefore provided, declare by writing under his hand his intention to acquire on behalf of the Government the treasure, or any specified portion thereof, by payment to the persons entitled thereto of a sum equal to the value of the materials of such treasure or portion, together with one-fifth of such value, and may place such sum in deposit in his treasury to the credit of such persons; and thereupon such treasure or portion shall be deemed to be the property of Government, and the money so deposited shall be debit with, as far as may be, as if it were such treasure or portion.

17. Decision of Collector final, and no suit to lie against him for acts done bona fide

No decision passed or act done by the Collector under this Act shall be called in question by any Civil Court, and no suit or other proceeding shall lie against him for anything done in good faith in exercise of the powers hereby conferred.

18. Collector to exercise any power of Civil Court

A collector making any enquiry under this Act may exercise any power conferred by the Code of Civil Procedure[5] on a Civil Court for the trial of suits.

19. Power to make rules

The[6] (Provincial Government) may from time to time, make rules consistent with this Act to regulate proceedings hereunder.

Such rules shall, on being published in the[7] (*Official Gazette*), have the force of law.

PENALTIES

20. Penalty on finder failing to give notice, etc.

If the finder of any treasure fails to give the notice or does not make the deposit or give the security, required by section 4, or alters or attempts to alter such treasure so as to conceal its identity, the share of such treasure, or the money in lieu thereof which he would otherwise be entitled, shall vest in Her Majesty.

And he shall, on conviction before a Magistrate, be punished with imprisonment for a term which may extend to one year, or with fine, or with both.

21. Penalty on owner for offence under section 20

If the owner of the place in which any treasure is found abets, within the limits of the Indian Penal Code (Act XLV of 1860), any offence under section 20, the share of such treasure or the money in lieu thereof to which he would otherwise be entitled, Magistrate, be punished with imprisonment which may extend to six months, or with fine, or with both.

SCHEDULE

Repealed by the Amending Act 1891 (XII of 1891).

NOTES AND REFERENCES

1. For the Statement of Objects and Reasons, see *Gazette of India*, 1878, Pt.V, p.1463, discussions in Council, see *ibid.* Supplement pp. 1288 and 1326; *ibid.* 1878, pp. 207 and 287.

    This Act has been declared to be in force in Santhal Parganas by the Santhal Parganas Settlement Regulation (3 of 1872), s. 3. Khondmals District by the Khondmals Laws Regulation, 1936 (4 of 1936), s. 3 and Sch. and Angul District by the Angul Laws Regulation, 1936 (5 of 1936) s. 3 and Sch.

It has also been declared, by notification under s. 3(a) of the Scheduled Districts of Hazaribagh, Lohardaga and Manbhum and Pargana Dhalbhum, and the Kolhan in the District of Singhbhum—see *Gazette of India,* 1881, Pt. I, p. 504. (The District of Lohardaga included at that time the present District of Palamau, which was separated in 1894; Lohardaga is now called the Ranchi District; see *Calcutta Gazette,* 1899, Pt. I, p. 44).

2. These words were substituted for the words "the whole of British India" by the Indian Independence (Adaptation of Central Act and Ordinances) Order, 1948.

3. The words "And it shall come into force at once" were called by the Repealing and Amending Act, 1914 (10 of 1914).

4. These words were substituted for the words "Local" by the Government of India (Adaptation of Indian Order, 1937).

5. See now the Code of Civil Procedure, 1908 (Act 5 of 1908)

6. These words were substituted for the words "Local Government" by the Government of India (Adaptation of Indian Laws) Order 1937.

7. These words were substituted for the words "Local Gazette", *ibid.*

3. The Ancient Monuments Preservation Act, 1904*

An Act to provide for the preservation of monuments and objects of archaeological, historical, or artistic interest

(As modified up to 1st September, 1949)

Whereas it is expedient to provide for the preservation of ancient monuments, for the exercise of control over traffic in antiquities and over excavation in certain places, and for the protection and acquisition in certain cases of ancient monuments and of objects of archaeological, historical or artistic interest; it is hereby enacted as follows :

1. Short title and extent

(1) This Act may be called the Ancient Monuments Preservation Act, 1904.

(2) It extends to[2] [all the Provinces of India], inclusive of [3]* * *, the Santhal Parganas and the Pargana of Spirit.

2. Definitions

In this Act, unless there is anything repugnant in the subject or context, —

(1) "ancient monument" means any structure, erection or monument, or any tumulus or place of interment, or any cave, rock-sculpture, inscription or monolith, which is of historical, archaeological or artistic interest, or any remains thereof, and includes—

(a) the site of an ancient monument;

(b) such portion of land adjoining the site of an ancient monument as may be required for fencing or covering in or otherwise preserving such monument; and

---

* Act No. VII of 1904 [18th March, 1904]

(c) the means of access to and convenient inspection of an ancient monument;

(2) "antiquities" include any moveable objects which [4][the Central Government], by reason of their historical or archaeological associations, may think a necessary to protect against injury, removal or dispersion;

(3) "commissioner" includes any officer authorised by [5][the Central Government] to perform the duties of a Commissioner under this Act;

(4) "maintain" and "maintenance" include the fencing, covering in, remaining, restoring and cleaning of a protected monument, and the doing of any act which may be necessary for the purpose of maintaining a protected monument or of securing convenient access thereto;

(5) "land" includes a revenue-free estate, a revenue-paying estate, and a permanent transferable tenure, whether such an estate or tenure be subject to incumbrances or not; and

(6) "owner" includes a joint owner invested with powers of management on behalf of himself and other joint owners, and any manager or trustee exercising powers of management over an ancient monument, and the successor in title of any such owner and the successor in office of any such manager or trustee.

Provided that nothing in this Act shall be deemed to extend the powers which may lawfully be exercised by such manager or trustee.

3. Protected Monuments

(1) The Central Government may, by notification in the [7][*Official Gazette*], declare an ancient monument to be a protected monument within the meaning of this Act.

(2) A copy of every notification published under sub-section (1) shall be fixed up in a conspicuous place on or near the monument, together with an intimation that any objections to the issue of the notification received by the [6][Central Government] within one month from the date when it is so fixed up will be taken into consideration.

(3) On the expiry of the said period of one month, the [6][Central Government] after considering the objections, if any, shall confirm or withdraw the notification.

(4) A notification published under this section shall, unless and until it

is withdrawn, be conclusive evidence of the fact that the monument to which it relates is an ancient monument within the meaning of this Act.

ANCIENT MONUMENTS

4. Acquisition of rights in or guardianship of an ancient monument

(1) The Collector, with the sanction of the [6][Central Government], may purchase or take a case of any protected monument.

(2) The Collector, with the like sanction, may accept a gift or bequest of any protected monument.

(3) The owner of any protected monument may, by written instrument, constitute the Commissioner as the guardian of the monument, and the Commissioner may, with the sanction of the [6][Central Government], accept such guardianship.

(4) When the Commissioner has accepted the guardianship of a monument under sub-section (3), the owner shall, except as expressly provided in this Act, have the same estate, right, title and interest in and to the monument as if the Commissioner had not been constituted guardian thereof.

(5) When the Commissioner has accepted the guardianship of a monument under sub-section (3), the provisions of this Act relating to agreements executed under section 5 shall apply to the written instrument executed under the said sub-section.

(6) Where a protected monument is without an owner, the Commissioner may assume the guardianship of the monument.

5. Preservation of ancient monument by agreement

(1) The Collector may with the previous sanction of [8][the Central Government], propose to the owner to enter into an agreement with [9][the Central Government] for the preservation of any protected monument in his district.

(2) An agreement under this section may provide for the following matters, or for such of them as it may be found expedient to include in the agreement:

(a) the maintenance of the monument;

(b) the custody of the monument, and the duties of any person who may be employed to watch it;

(c) the restriction of the owner's right to destroy, remove, alter or deface the monument or to build on or near the site of the monument;

(d) the facilities of access to be permitted to the public or to any portion of the public and to persons deputed by the owner or the Collector to inspect or maintain the monument;

(e) the notice to be given to [10][the Central Government] in case the land on which the monument is situated is offered for sale by the owner, and the right to be reserved to [1][the Central Government] to purchase such land, or any specified portion of such land, at its market-value;

(f) the payment of any expenses incurred by the owner or by [10][the Central Government] in connection with the preservation of the monument;

(g) the proprietary or other rights which are to vest in His Majesty in respect of the monument when any expenses are incurred by [10][the Central Government] in connection with the preservation of the monument;

(h) the appointment of an authority to decide any dispute arising out of the agreement; and

(i) any matter connected with the preservation of the monument which is a proper subject of agreement between the owner and [10][the Central Government].

* * * * * * * * *[11]

(4) The terms of an agreement under this section may be altered from time to time with the sanction of [12][the Central Government] and with the consent of the owner.

(5) With the previous sanction of [12][the Central Government], the Collector may terminate an agreement under this section on giving six months' notice in writing to the owner.

(6) The owner may terminate an agreement under this section on giving six months' notice to the Collector.

(7) An agreement under this section shall be binding on any person claiming to be owner of the monument to which it relates, through or under a party by whom or on whose behalf the agreement was executed.

(8) Any rights acquired by [13][the Central Government] in respect of expenses incurred in protecting or preserving a monument shall not be affected by the termination of an agreement under this section.

6. Owners under disability or not in possession

(1) If the owner is unable by reason of infancy or other disability, to act for himself, the person legally competent to act on his behalf may exercise the powers conferred upon an owner by section 5.

(2) In the case of village-property, the headman or other village-officer exercising powers of management over such property may exercise the powers conferred upon an owner by section 5.

(3) Nothing in this section shall be deemed to empower any person not being of the same religion as the persons on whose behalf he is acting to make or execute an agreement relating to a protected monument which or any part of which is periodically used for the religious worship or observances of that religion.

7. Enforcement of agreement

(1) If the Collector apprehends that the owner or occupier of a monument intends to destroy, remove, alter, deface, or imperil the monument or to build on or near the site thereof in contravention of the terms of an agreement for its preservation under section 5, the Collector may make an order prohibiting any such contravention of the agreement.

(2) If an owner or other person who is bound by an agreement for the preservation or maintenance of a monument under section 5 refuses to do any act which is in the opinion of the Collector necessary to such preservation or maintenance, or neglects to do any such act within such reasonable time as may be fixed by the Collector, the Collector may authorize any person to do any such act, and the expense of doing any such act or such portion of the expense as the owner may be liable to pay under the agreement may be recovered from the owner as if it were an arrear of land-revenue.

(3) A person aggrieved by an order made under this section may appeal to the Commissioner, who may cancel or modify it and whose decision shall be final.

8. Purchasers at certain sales and persons claiming through owner bound by instrument executed by owner

Every person who purchases, at a sale for arrears of land-revenue or any other public demand, or at a sale made under the Bengal Patni Taluks Regulation, 1819 (Ben. Reg. VIII of 1819) an estate or tenure in which is situated a monument in respect of which any instrument has been executed by the owner for the time being, under section 4 or section 5, and every person claiming any title to a monument from, through or under an owner who executed any such instrument, shall be bound by such instrument.

9. Application of endowment to repair of an ancient monument

(1) If any owner or other person competent to enter into an agreement under section 5 for the preservation of a protected monument, refuses or fails to enter into such an agreement when proposed to him by the Collector, and if any endowment has been created for the purpose of keeping such monument in repair, or for that purpose among others, the Collector may institute a suit in the Court of the District Judge, or, if the estimated cost of repairing the monument does not exceed one thousand rupees, may make an application to the District Judge for the proper application of such endowment or part thereof.

(2) On the hearing of an application under sub-section (1), the District Judge may summon and examine the owner and any person whose evidence appears to him necessary, and may pass an order for the proper application of the endowment or of any part thereof, and any such order may be executed as if it were the decree of a Civil Court.

10. Compulsory purchase of ancient monument

(1) If the [14][Central Government], apprehends that a protected monument is in danger of being destroyed, injured or allowed to fall into decay, [15][the Central Government may direct the Provincial Government to acquire it] under the provisions of the Land Acquisition Act, 1894 (I of 1894), as if the preservation of a protected monument were a "public purpose" within the meaning of that Act.

(2) The powers of compulsory purchase conferred by sub-section (1) shall not be exercised in the case of:

(a) any monument which or any part of which is periodically used for religious observances; or

(b) any monument which is the subject of a subsisting agreement executed under section 5.

(3) In any case other than the cases referred to in sub-section (2) the said powers of compulsory purchase shall not be exercised unless the owner or other person competent to enter into an agreement under section 5 has failed, within such reasonable period as the Collector may fix in this behalf, to enter into an agreement proposed to him under the said section or has

terminated or given notice of his intention to terminate such an agreement.

[16][10A.Power of Central Government to control mining, etc., near ancient monument]

(1) If the [14][Central Government] is of opinion that mining, quarrying, excavating, blasting and other operations of a like nature should be restricted or regulated for the purpose of protecting or preserving any ancient monument, the [14][Central Government] may, by notification in the [17][*Official Gazette*], make rules—

(a) fixing the boundaries of the area to which the rules are to apply,

(b) forbidding the carrying on of mining, quarrying, excavating, blasting or any operation of a like nature except in accordance with the rules and with the terms of a licence, and

(c) prescribing the authority by which, and the terms on which, licences may be granted to carry on any of the said operations.

(2) The power to make rules given by this section is subject to the condition of the rules being made after previous publication.

(3) A rule made under this section may provide that any person committing a breach thereof shall be punishable with fine which may extend to two hundred rupees.

(4) If any owner or occupier of land included in a notification under sub-section (1) proves to the satisfaction of the [14][Central Government] that he has sustained loss by reason of such land being so included, the [14][Central Government] shall pay compensation in respect of such loss.

11. Maintenance of certain protected monuments

(1) The Commissioner shall maintain every monument in respect of which the Government has acquired any of the rights mentioned in section 4 or which the Government has acquired under section 10.

(2) When the Commissioner has accepted the guardianship of a monument under section 4, he shall, for the purpose of maintaining such monument, have access to the monument at all reasonable times, by himself and by his agents, subordinates and workmen, for the purpose of inspecting this monu-ment, and for the purpose of bringing such materials and doing such acts as he may consider necessary or desirable for the maintenance thereof.

12. Voluntary contributions

The Commissioner may receive voluntary contributions towards the cost of maintaining a protected monument and may give orders as to the management and application of any funds so received by him.

Provided that no contribution received under this section shall be applied to any purpose other than the purpose for which it was contributed.

13. Protection of place of worship from misuse, pollution or desecration

(1) A place of worship or shrine maintained by the Government under this Act shall not be used for any purpose inconsistent with its character.

(2) Where the Collector has, under section 4, purchased or taken a lease of any protected monument, or has accepted a gift or bequest, or the Commissioner has, under the same section, accepted the guardianship thereof, and such monument, or any part thereof, is periodically used for religious worship or observances by any community, the Collector shall make due provision for the protection of such monument, or such part thereof, from pollution or desecration—

(a) by prohibiting the entry therein, except in accordance with conditions prescribed with the concurrence of the persons in religious charge of the said monument or part thereof, of any person not entitled so to enter by the religious usages of the community by which the monument or part thereof is used, or

(b) by taking such other action as he may think necessary in this behalf.

14. Relinquishment of Government rights in a monument

With the sanction of [18][the Central Government], the Commissioner may:

(a) where rights have been acquired by [19][the Central Government] in respect of any monument under this Act by virtue of any sale, lease, gift or will, relinquish the rights so acquired to the person who would for the time being be the owner of the monument if such rights had not been acquired; or

(b) relinquish any guardianship of a monument which he has accepted under this Act.

15. Right of access to certain protected monuments

(1) Subject to such rules as may after previous publication be made by

[18][the Central Government], the public shall have a right of access to any monument maintained by [20][the Central Government] under this Act.

(2) In making any rule under sub-section (1) [18][the Central Government] may provide that a breach of it shall be punishable with fine which may extend to twenty rupees.

16. Penalties

Any person other than the owner destroys, removes, injures, alters, defaces or imperils a protected monument, and any other who destroys, removes, injures, alters, defaces or imperils a monument, maintained by [21][the Central Government] under this Act or in respect of which an agreement has been executed under section 5, and any owner or occupier who contravenes an order made under section 7, sub-section (1), shall be punishable with fine which may extend to five thousand rupees, or with imprisonment which may extend to three months, or with both.

TRAFFIC IN ANTIQUITIES

17. Power to Central Government to control traffic in antiquities

(1) If the [22][Central Government] apprehends that antiquities are being sold or removed to the detriment of India or of any neighbouring country, [23][it] may, by [24] notification in the [25][*Official Gazette*], prohibit or restrict the bringing or taking by sea or by land of any antiquities or class of antiquities described in the notification into or out of [26][the Provinces] or any specified part of [26][the Provinces].

(2) Any person who brings or takes or attempts to bring or take any such antiquities into or out of [26][the Provinces] or any part of [26][the Provinces] in contravention of a notification issued under sub-section (1), shall be punishable with fine which may extend to five hundred rupees.

(3) Antiquities in respect of which an offence referred to in sub-section (2) has been committed shall be liable to confiscation.

(4) An officer of Customs, or an officer of Police of a grade not lower than Sub-Inspector, duly empowered by the [27][Central Government] in this behalf, may search any vessel, cart or other means of conveyance and may open any baggage or package of goods, if he has reason to believe that goods in respect of which an offence has been committed under sub-section (2) are contained therein.

(5) A person who complains that the power of search mentioned in sub-section (4) has been vexatiously or improperly exercised may address his complaint to the [27][Central Government], and the [27][Central Government] shall pass such order and may award such compensation, if any, as appears to it to be just.

PROTECTION OF SCULPTURES, CARVINGS, IMAGES, BAS-RELIEFS, INSCRIPTIONS OR LIKE OBJECTS

18. Power to Central Government to control moving of sculptures, carvings or like objects

(1) If [28][the Central Government] considers that any sculptures, carvings, images, bas-reliefs, inscriptions or other like objects ought not to be moved from the place where they are without the sanction of [29][the Central Government], [30][the Central Government] may by notification[31] in the [32][*Official Gazette*], direct that any such object or any class of such objects shall not be moved unless with the written permission of the Collector.

(2) A person applying for the permission mentioned in sub-section (1) shall specify the object or objects which he proposes to move, and shall furnish, in regard to such object or objects, any information which the Collector may require.

(3) If the Collector refuses to grant such permission, the applicant may appeal to the Commissioner, whose decision shall be final.

(4) Any person who moves any object in contravention of a notification issued under sub-section (1), shall be punishable with fine which may extend to five hundred rupees.

(5) If the owner of any property proves to the satisfaction of [30][the Central Government] that he has suffered any loss or damage by reason of the inclusion of such property in a notification published under sub-section (1), [30][the Central Government] shall either—

(a) exempt such property from the said notification;

(b) purchase such property, if it be moveable, at its market value; or

(c) pay compensation for any loss or damage sustained by the owner of such property, if it be immoveable.

19. Purchase of sculptures, carvings or like objects by the Government

(1) If [30][the Central Government] apprehends that any object mentioned

in a notification issued under section 18, sub-section (1), is in danger of being destroyed, removed, injured or allowed to fall into decay, [30][the Central Government] may pass orders for the compulsory purchase of such objects at its market-value, and the Collector shall thereupon give notice to the owner of the object to be purchased.

(2) The power of compulsory purchase given by this section shall not extend to—

(a) any image or symbol actually used for the purpose of any religious observance; or

(b) anything which the owner desires to retain on any reasonable ground personal to himself or to any of his ancestors or to any member of his family.

[33]ARCHAEOLOGICAL EXCAVATION

[34]20. Power of Central Government to notify areas as protected

(1) If the [34][Central Government] [35]* * is of opinion that excavation for archaeological purposes in any area should be restricted and regulated in the interests of archaeological research, the [34][Central Government] may, by notification in the [36][*Official Gazette*] specifying the boundaries of the area, declare it to be a protected area.

(2) From the date of such notification all antiquities buried in the protected area shall be the property of [37][the Crown] and shall be deemed to be in the possession of until ownership thereof is transferred; but in all other respects the rights of any owner or occupier of land in such area shall not be affected.

[38]20A. Power to enter upon and make excavations in a protected area

(1) Any officer of the Archaeological Department or any person holding a licence under section 20B may, with the written permission of the Collector, enter upon and make excavations in any protected area.

(2) Where, in the exercise of the power conferred by sub-section (1), the rights of any person are infringed by the occupation or disturbance of the surface of any land, [39][the Central Government] shall pay to that compensation for the infringement.]

[38]20B. Power of Central Government to make rules regulating archaeological excavation in protected areas

(1) The [40][Central Government] may make rules—

(a) prescribing the authorities by whom licences to excavate for archaeological purposes in a protected area may be granted;

(b) regulating the conditions on which such licences may be granted, the form of such licences, and the taking of security from licensees;

(c) prescribing the manner in which antiquities found by a licensee shall be divided between [37][the Central Government] and the licensee; and

(d) generally to carry out the purposes of section 20.

(2) The power to make rules given by this section is subject to the condition of the rules being made after previous publication.

(3) Such rules may be general for all protected areas for the time being, or may be special for any particular protected area or areas.

(4) Such rules may provide that any person committing a breach of any rule or of any condition of a licence shall be punishable with fine which may extend to five thousand rupees, and may further provide that where the breach has been by the agent or servant of a licensee the licensee himself shall be punishable.]

[38]20C. Power to acquire a protected area

If the [40][Central Government] is of opinion that a protected area contains an ancient monument or antiquities of national interest and value [5][it] may direct the [41][Provincial Government] to acquire such area, or any part thereof, and the [42][Provincial Government] may thereupon acquire such area or part under the Land Acquisition Act, 1894 (I of 1894), as for a public purpose].

21. Assessment of market-value or compensation

(1) The market-value of any property which Government is empowered to purchase at such value under this Act, or the [43]* * compensation to be paid by Government in respect of anything done under this Act, shall, where any dispute arises [44][in respect] of such market-value or compensation, be ascertained in the manner provided by the Land Acquisition Act, 1894, sections 3, 8 to 34, 45 to 47, 51 and 52 so far as they can be made applicable:

Provided that when making an inquiry under the said Land Acquisition Act, 1894, the Collector shall be assisted by two assessors, one of whom shall be a competent person nominated by the Collector, and one a person nominated by the owner or, in case the owner fails to nominate an assessor within such reasonable time as may be fixed by the Collector in this behalf, by the Collector.

22. Jurisdiction

A Magistrate of the third class shall not have jurisdiction to try any person charged with an offence against this Act.

23. Power to make rules

(1) The [45][Central Government] [46]* * may make rules[47] for carrying out any of the purposes of this Act.

(2) The power to make rules given by this section is subject to the condition of the rules being made after previous publication.

24. Protection to public servants acting under the Act

No suit for compensation and no criminal proceeding shall lie against any public servant in respect of any act done, or in good faith intended to be done, in the exercise of any power conferred by this Act.

NOTES AND REFERENCES

1. For Statement of Objects and Reasons, see *Gazette of India*, 1903, Pt.V, p.513; for Report of the Select Committee, see *ibid.*, 1904, Pt.V, page 57; and for Proceedings in Council, see *ibid.*, 1903, Pt.VI, pp. 166, 191; *ibid.*, 1904, Pt.VI, pp. 20 and 76.

   This Act has been declared to be in force in the Khondmals District by the Khondmals Laws Regulation, 1936 (4 of 1936), s. 3 and Sch.; and in the Angul District by the Angul Laws Regulation, 1936 (5 of 1936), s. 3 and Sch.

   It has been extended to Berar by the Laws Act, 1941 (4 of 1941).
2. Subs. by the A.O. 1948, for "the whole of British India".
3. The words "British Baluchistan" were rep. by the A.O. 1948.
4. Subs. by the A.O. 1937, for "the Govt.".
5. Subs. by the A.O. 1937, for "the L.G.".
6. Subs. by the A.O. 1937, for "L.G.".
7. Subs. by the A.O. 1937, for "local *Official Gazette*".
8. Subs. by the A.O. 1937, for "the L.G.".
9. Subs. by the A.O. 1937, for "the Secretary of State for India in Council".
10. Subs. by the A.O. 1937, for "the Govt.".
11. Sub-section (3) was rep. by the A.O. 1937.
12. Subs. by the A.O. 1937, for "the L.G.".

13. Subs. by the A.O. 1937, for "Govt.".

14. Subs. by the A.O. 1937, for "L.G.".

15. Subs. by the A.O. 1937, for "the L.G. may proceed to acquire it".

16. S. 10A ins. by the Ancient Monuments Preservation (Amendment) Act, 1932 (18 of 1932), s. 2.

17. Subs. by the A.O. 1937, for "local *Official Gazette*".

18. Subs. by the A.O. 1937, for "the L.G.".

19. Subs. by the A.O. 1937, for "Govt.".

20. Subs. by the A.O. 1937, for "Govt.".

21. Subs. by the A.O. 1937, for "Govt.".

22. Subs. by the A.O. 1937, for "G. G. in C.".

23. Subs. by the A.O. 1937, for "he".

24. See notification No. 110, dated 28th May, 1917, Gazette of India, 1917, Part I, p.989, and notification No. 1385, dated 8th July 1924, Gazette of India, 1924. Pt. I, p.614; Gen. R. & O., Vol. III.

25. Subs. by the A.O. 1937, for "Gazette of India".

26. Subs. by the A.O. 1948, for "British India".

27. Subs. by the A.O. 1937, for "L. G.".

28. Subs. by the A.O. 1937, for "the L. G.".

29. Subs. by the A.O. 1937, for "the Govt.".

30. Subs. by the A.O. 1937, for "the L.G.".

31. For notification under this section, issued before the 1st April, 1937, by the Government of - (1) Bengal, see Calcutta Gazette, 1908, Pt. I, p. 1248, and *ibid.*, 1909, Pt. I, p. 23; and p. 957 as to Gaya District.

    (2) Central Provinces, see C.P. Gazette, 1906, Pt. III, p. 616.

32. Subs. by the A.O., 1937, for "local *Official Gazette*".

33. This heading and Ss. 20, 20A, 20B and 20C were subs. by the Ancient Monuments Preservation (Amendment) Act, 1932 (18 of 1932), s. 3, for the original heading and s. 20.

34. Subs. by the A.O. 1937, for "G.G. in C.".

35. The words "after consulting the L.G." rep. by the A.O. 1937.

36. Subs. by the A.O. 1937, for "Gazette of India".

37. Subs. by the A.O. 1937, for "Govt.".

38. See footnote 4 on pre-page.

39. Subs. by the A.O. 1937, for "the Govt.".

40. Subs. by the A.O. 1937, for "G.G. in C.".

41. Subs. by the A.O. 1937, for "he".

42. Subs. by the A.O. 1937, for "L.G.".

43. The words "amount of " rep. by the Ancient Monuments Preservation (Amendment) Act, 1932 (18 of 1932), s. 4.

44. Subs. by s. 4, *ibid.*, for "touching the amount".

45. Subs. by the A.O. 1937, for "G.G. in C.".

46. The words "or the L.G." rep. by the A.O. 1937.

47. For rules made by the Mad. Govt. before the 1st April 1937, for the decipherment, publication, and custody of Indian inscriptions on stone and copper, see Mad. R. and O.

4. The Antiquities (Export Control) Act, 1947*

An Act to control the export of the antiquities export of objects of antiquitarian or historical interest or significance;

It is hereby enacted as follows:-

1. Short title and extent

(1) This Act may be called the Antiquities (Export Control) Act, 1947.

(2) It extends to the whole of British India.

2. Interpretation

In this Act, unless there is anything repugnant in the subject or context,

(a) "antiquity" includes—

(i) any coin, sculpture, manuscript, epigraph, or other work of art or craftsmanship,

(ii) any article, object or thing detached from a building or cave,

(iii) any article, object or thing illustrative of science, art, culture, literature, religion, customs, morals or politics in bygone ages,

(iv) any article, object or thing declared by the Central Government by notification in the *Official Gazette* to be an antiquity for the purpose of this Act,

which has been in existence for not less than one hundred years;

(b) "export" means export from British India by sea, land or air.

---

* Act No. XXXI of 1947
(Passed by the Indian Legislature)
(Received the assent of the Governor General on the 18th April, 1947)

3. Prohibition of export

No person shall export any antiquity except under the authority of a licence granted by the Central Government.

4. Application of Act VIII of 1878

All antiquities the export of which is prohibited under section shall be deemed to be goods of which the export has been prohibited under section 19 of the Sea Customs Act, 1878, and all the prohibitions of that Act shall have effect accordingly, except that, the prohibitions of section 183 of that Act notwithstanding, any confiscation authorised under that Act shall be made, unless the Central Government, on application to it in such behalf, otherwise directs.

5. Penalty and procedure

(1) If any person exports or attempts to export an antiquity in contravention of section 3, he shall, without prejudice to any confiscation or penalty to which he may be liable under the provisions of the Sea Customs Act, 1878 (VII of 1878) as applied by section 4, be punishable with imprisonment for a term which may extend to one month, or with fine which may extend to five thousand rupees, or with both.

(2) No court shall take cognizance of an offence punishable under this section except upon complaint in writing made by an officer generally or specially authorised in this behalf by the Central Government, and no Court inferior to that of Presidency Magistrate or the Magistrate of the first class shall try any such offence.

6. Power to determine whether or not an article is an antiquity

If any question arises whether any article, object or thing is or is not an antiquity for the purposes of this Act, it shall be referred to the Director-General of Archaeology in India, and his decision thereon shall be final.

7. Power to make rules

(1) The Central Government may, by notification in the *Official Gazette*, make rules to carry out the purposes of this Act.

(2) In particular and without prejudice to the generality of the foregoing power, such rules may prescribe the procedure for granting licences for the export of antiquities, and fix the fees payable for applications therefor.

8. Protection of action taken under this Act

No suit, prosecution or other legal proceeding shall lie against any person for anything in good faith done or intended to be done under this Act.

9. Application of other laws not barred

The provisions of this Act shall be in addition to, and not in derogation of, the provisions of the Ancient Monuments Preservation Act, 1904 (VII of 1904) or any other law for the time being in force.

5. The Antiquities (Export Control) Rules, 1947

(New Delhi, the 18th June, 1947)

No. F.12-46-47, Arch

In exercise of the powers conferred by section 7 of the Antiquities (Export Control) Act, 1947, the Central Government is pleased to make the following rules:-

1. These rules may be called the "Antiquities (Export Control) Rules, 1947."

2. In these rules—

(a) "Act" means the Antiquities (Export Control) Act, 1947.

(b) "The Director-General" means the Director-General of Archaeology in India.

(c) "Form" means a form in the Schedule to the Rules.

3. (a) Any person having in this possession any article, object or thing of the nature described in the sub-clauses n(i), (ii), (iii) or (iv) of clauses (a) of section 2 of the Act may, if he intends to export it, apply to the Director-General for a decision whether it is an antiquity for the purposes of the Act.

(b) Such application shall be accompanied by a full description of the article, object or thing.

(c) The Director-General may, before giving his decision, require the article, object or thing to be produced to him, or to any person authorised by him, for the purposes of inspection.

(d) The decision of the Director-General shall be given in form A.

4. If a Customs Officer has any doubt as to whether any article, object

or thing which is intended or about to be exported is an antiquity for the purposes of this Act, he may refer the question for the decision of the Director-General together with a full description of the article, object or thing; and the decision of the Director-General shall be given in form A.

5. (a) An application for a licence for the export of an antiquity shall be made in writing in form B and submitted through the Director-General.

(b) Every such application shall be accompanied by a fee of Rs. 10/-
.

For the proviso of sub-rule (2) or rule 5 of the said Rules, following proviso shall be substituted, namely:-

"Provided that no fee shall be payable in respect of an application made:-

(i) by a person on his own behalf for the export of an antiquity which has been allotted to him in accordance with rules made under section 20-B of the Ancient Monuments Preservation Act, 1904, or

(ii) for the export of an antiquity which is the personal property of a diplomatic officer of a foreign or Commonwealth Mission in India." or of a Consular post or Consular Officers in India.

6. The Director-General may, by an order in writing, call for such further information as he may specify, and a photograph of the antiquity, and require the antiquity to be produced to him or to any person authorised by him for the purposes of inspection.

7. The licence granted by the Central Government for the export of an antiquity shall be in form C.

8. Any antiquity confiscated under section 4 of the Act shall not be sold or disposed of by the Collector of Customs except under order of the Government of India.

6. The Ancient Monuments and Archaeological Sites and Remains Act, 1958*

An Act to provide for the preservation of ancient and historical monuments and archaeological excavations and for the protection of sculptures, carvings and other like objects.

Be it enacted by Parliament in the Ninth Year of the Republic of India as follows:

Short title, extent and commencement

PRELIMINARY

1. Short title, extent and commencement

(1) This Act may be called the Ancient Monuments and Archaeological Sites and Remains Act, 1958.

(2) It extends to the whole of India, but sections 22, 24, 25 and 26 shall not apply to the State of Jammu and Kashmir.

(3) It shall come into force on such date as the Central Government may, by notification in the *Official Gazette*, appoint.

2. Definitions

In this Act, unless the context otherwise requires,—

(a) "ancient monument" means any structure, erection or monument or any tumulus or place of interment, or any cave, rock-sculpture, inscription or monolith, which is of historical, archaeological or artistic interest and which has been in existence for not less than one hundred years, and includes—

---

* Act No. 24 of 1958 [28th August, 1958]

(i) the remains of an ancient monument,

(ii) the site of an ancient monument,

(iii) such portion of land adjoining the site of an ancient monument as may be required for fencing or covering in or otherwise preserving such monument, and

(iv) the means of access to, and convenient inspection of, an ancient monument;

(b) "antiquity" includes—

(i) any coin, sculpture, manuscript, epigraph, or other work of art or craftsmanship,

(ii) any article, object or thing detached from a building or cave,

(iii) any article, object or thing illustrative of science, art, crafts, literature, religion, customs, morals or politics in bygone ages,

(iv) any article, object or thing of historical interest, and

(v) any article, object or thing declared by the Central Government, by notification in the *Official Gazette*, to be an antiquity for the purposes of this Act,

which has been in existence for not less than one hundred years;

(c) "archaeological officer" means an officer of the Department of Archaeology of Government of India not lower in rank than Assistant Superintendent of Archaeology;

(d) "archaeological sites and remains" means any area which contains or is reasonably believed to contain ruins or relics of historical or archaeological importance which have been in existence for not less than one hundred years, and includes—

(i) such portion of land adjoining the area as may be required for fencing or covering in or otherwise preserving it, and

(ii) the means of access to, and convenient inspection of the area;

(e) "Director-General" means the Director-General of Archaeology, and includes any officer authorised by the Central Government to perform the duties of the Director-General;

(f) "maintain", with its grammatical variations and cognate expressions, includes the fencing, covering in, repairing, restoring and cleansing of a protected monument, and the doing of any act which may be necessary for the purpose of preserving a protected monument or of securing convenient access thereto;

(g) "owner" includes—

(i) a joint owner invested with powers of management on behalf of himself and other joint owners and the successor-in-title of any such owner; and

(ii) any manager or trustee exercising powers of management and the successor-in-office of any such manager or trustee;

(h) "prescribed" means prescribed by rules made under this Act;

(i) "protected area" means any archaeological site and remains which is declared to be of national importance by or under this Act;

(j) "protected monument" means an ancient monument which is declared to be of national importance by or under this Act.

ANCIENT MONUMENT AND ARCHAEOLOGICAL SITES AND REMAINS OF NATIONAL IMPORTANCE

3. Certain ancient monuments, etc., deemed to be of national importance

All ancient and historical monuments and all Archaeological Sites and Remains (Declaration of National Importance) Act, 1951(71 of 151), or by section 126 of the States Reorganisation Act, 1956 (31 of 1956), to be of national importance shall be deemed to be ancient and historical monuments or archaeological sites and remains declared to be of national importance for the purposes of this Act.

4. Power of Central Government to declare ancient monument, etc., to be of national importance

(1) Where the Central Government is of opinion that any ancient monument or archaeological site and remains not included in section 3 is of national importance, it may, by notification in the *Official Gazette*, give two months' notice of its intention to declare such ancient monument or archaeological site and remains to be of national importance; and a copy of every such notification shall be affixed in a conspicuous place near the monument or site and remains, as the case may be.

(2) Any person interested in any such ancient monument or archaeological site and remains may, within two months after the issue of the notification, object to the declaration of the monument, or the archaeological site and remains, to be of national importance.

(3) On the expiry of the said period of two months, the Central Government may, after considering the objections, if any, received by it, declare by notification in the *Official Gazette*, the ancient monument or the archaeological site and remains, as the case may be, to be of national importance.

(4) A notification published under sub-section (3) shall, unless and until it is withdrawn, be conclusive evidence of the fact that the ancient monument or the archaeological site and remains to which it relates is of national importance for the purposes of this Act.

PROTECTED MONUMENTS

5. Acquisition of rights in a protected monument

(1) The Director-General may, with the sanction of the Central Government, purchase, or take a lease of, or accept a gift or bequest of, any protected monument.

(2) Where a protected monument is without an owner, the Director-General may, by notification in the *Official Gazette* assume the guardianship of the monument.

(3) The owner of any protected monument may, by written instrument, constitute the Director-General as the guardian of the monument, and the Director-General may, with the sanction of the Central Government, accept such guardianship.

(4) When the Director-General has accepted the guardianship of a monument under sub-section (3), the owner shall, except as expressly provided in this Act, have the same estate, right, title and interest in and to the monument as if the Director-General had not been constituted a guardian thereof.

(5) When the Director-General has accepted the guardianship of a monument under sub-section (3), the provisions of this Act relating to agreements executed under section 6 shall apply to the written to agreements executed under the said sub-section.

(6) Nothing in this section shall affect the use of any protected monument for customary religious observances.

6. Preservation of protected monument by agreement

(1) The Collector, when so directed by the Central Government, shall propose to the owner of the protected monument to enter into an agreement with the Central Government within a specified period for the maintenance of the monument.

(2) An agreement under this section may provide for all or any of the following matters, namely—

(a) the maintenance of the monument;

(b) the custody of the monument and the duties any person who may be employed to watch it;

(c) the restriction of the owner's right—

(i) to use the monument for any purpose,

(ii) to charge any fee for entry into, or inspection of, the monument,

(iii) to destroy, remove, alter or deface the monument, or

(iv) to build on or near the site of the monument;

(d) the facilities of access to be permitted to the public or any section thereof or to archaeological officers or to persons deputed by the owner or any archaeological officer or the Collector to inspect or maintain the monument;

(e) the notice to be given to the Central Government in case the land on which the monument is situated or any adjoining land is offered for sale by the owner, and the right to be reserved to the Central Government to purchase such land, or any specified portion of such land, at its market value;

(f) the payment of any expenses incurred by the owner or by the Central Government in connection with the maintenance of the monument;

(g) the proprietary or other rights which are to vest in the Central Government in respect of the monument when any expenses are incurred by the Central Government in connection with the maintenance of the monument;

(h) the appointment of any authority to decide any dispute arising out of the agreement; and

(i) any matter connected with the maintenance of the monument which is a proper subject of agreement between the owner and the Central Government.

(3) The Central Government or the owner may, at any time after the expiration of three years from the date of execution of an agreement under this section, terminate it on giving six months' notice in writing to the other party :

Provided that where the agreement is terminated by the owner, he shall pay to the Central Government the expenses, if any, incurred by it on the maintenance of the monument during the five years immediately preceding the termination of the agreement or, if the agreement has been in force for a shorter period, during the period the agreement was in force.

(4) An agreement under this section shall be binding on any person claiming to be the owner of the monument to which it relates, from, through or under a party by whom or on whose behalf the agreement was executed.

7. Owner under disability or not in possession

(1) If the owner of the protected monument is unable, by reason of infancy or other disability, to act for himself, the person legally competent to act on his behalf may exercise the powers conferred upon an owner by section 6.

(2) In the case of village property, the headman or other village officer exercising powers of management over such property may exercise the powers conferred upon an owner by section 6.

(3) Nothing in this section shall be deemed to empower any person not being of the same religion as the person on whose behalf he is acting to make or execute an agreement relating to a protected monument which or any part of which is periodically used for the religious worship or observances of that religion.

8. Application of endownment to repair a protected monument

(1) If any owner or other person competent to enter into an agreement under section 6 for the maintenance of a protected monument refuses or fails to enter into such an agreement, and if any endowment has been created for the purpose of keeping such monument in repair or for the purpose among others, the Central Government may institute a suit in the court of the District Judge, or, if the estimated cost of repairing the monument does not exceed

one thousand rupees, may make an application to the District Judge, for the proper application of such endowment or part thereof.

(2) On the hearing of an application under sub-section (1), the District Judge may summon and examine the owner and any person whose evidence appears to him necessary and may pass an order for the proper application of the endowment or of any part thereof, and any such order may be executed as if it were a decree of a civil court.

9. Failure or refusal to enter into an agreement

(1) If any owner or other person competent to enter into an agreement under section 6 for the maintenance of a protected monument refuses or fails to enter into such an agreement, the Central Government may make an order providing for all or any of the matters specified in sub-section (2) of section 6 and such order shall be binding on the owner or such other person.

(2) Where an order made under sub-section (1) provides that the monument shall be maintained by the owner or other person competent to enter into an agreement, all reasonable expenses for the maintenance of the monument shall be payable by the Central Government.

(3) No order under sub-section (1) shall be made unless the owner or other person has been given an opportunity of making a representation in writing against the proposed order.

10. Power to make order prohibiting contravention of agreement under section 6

(1) If the Director-General apprehends that the owner or occupier of a protected monument intends to destroy, remove, alter, deface, imperil or misuse the monument or to build on or near the site thereof in contravention of the terms of an agreement under section 6, the Director-General may, after giving the owner or occupier an opportunity of making a representation in writing, make an order prohibiting any such contravention of the agreement.

Provided that no such opportunity may be given in any case where the Director-General, for reasons to be recorded, is satisfied that it is not expedient or practicable to do so.

(2) Any person aggrieved by an order under this section may appeal to the Central Government within such time and in such manner as may be prescribed and the decision of the Central Government shall be final.

11. Enforcement of agreements

(1) If an owner or other person who is bound by an agreement for the maintenance of a monument under section 6 refuses or fails within such reasonable time as the Director-General may fix, to do any act which in the opinion of the Director-General is necessary for the maintenance of the monument, the Director-General may authorise any person to do any such act, and the owner or other person shall be liable to pay the expenses of doing any such act or such portion of the expenses as the owner may be liable to pay under the agreement.

(2) If any dispute arises regarding the amount of expenses payable by the owner or other person under sub-section (1), it shall be referred to the Central Government whose decision shall be final.

12. Purchasers at certain sales and persons claiming through owner bound by instrument executed by owner

Every person who purchases, at a sale for arrears of land revenue or any other public demand, any land on which is situated a monument in respect of which any instrument has been executed by the owner for the time being under section 5 or section 6, and every person claiming any title to a monument from, through or under, an owner who executed any such instrument, shall be bound by such instrument.

13. Acquisition of protected monuments

If the Central Government apprehends that a protected monument is in danger of being destroyed, injured, misused, or allowed to fall into decay, it may acquire the protected monument under the provisions of the Land Acquisition Act, 1894 [1 of 1894], as if the maintenance of the protected monument were a public purpose within the meaning of that Act.

14. Maintenance of certain protected monuments

(1) The Central Government shall maintain every monument which has been acquired under section 13 or in respect of which any of the rights mentioned in section 5 have been acquired.

(2) When the Director-General has assumed the guardianship of a monument under section 5, he shall, for the purpose of maintaining such monument, have access to the monument at all reasonable times, by himself and by the agents, subordinates and workmen, for the purpose of inspecting

the monument and for the purpose of bringing such materials and doing such acts as he may consider necessary or desirable for the maintenance thereof.

15. Voluntary contributions.

The Director-General may receive voluntary contributions towards the cost of maintaining a protected monument and may give orders as to the management and application of any funds so received by him:

Provided that no contribution under this section shall be applied to any purpose other than the purpose for which it was contributed.

16. Protection of place of worship from misuse, pollution or desecration.

(1) A protected monument maintained by the Central Government under this Act which is a place of worship or shrine shall not be used for any purpose inconsistent with its character.

(2) Where the Central Government has acquired a protected monument under section 13, or taken a lease or accepted a gift or bequest or assumed guardianship of, a protected monument under section 5, and such monument or any part thereof is used for religious worship or observances by any community, the Collector shall make due provision for the protection of such monument or part thereof, from pollution or desecration—

(a) by prohibiting the entry therein, except in accordance with the conditions prescribed with the concurrence of the persons, if any, in religious charge of the said monument or part thereof, of any person not entitled so to enter by the religious usages of the community by which the monument or part thereof is used, or

(b) by taking such other action as he may think necessary in this behalf.

17. Relinquishment of Government rights in a monument.

With the sanction of the Central Government, the Director-General may,—

(a) where rights have been acquired by the Director-General in respect of any monument under this Act by virtue of any sale, lease, gift or will, relinquish, by notification in the *Official Gazette*, the rights so acquired to the person who would for the time being be the owner of the monument if such rights had not been acquired; or

(b) relinquish any guardianship of a monument which he had assumed under this Act.

18. Right of access to protected monuments

Subject to any rules made under this Act, the public shall have a right of access to any protected monument.

PROTECTED AREAS

19. Restrictions on enjoyment of property rights in protected areas

(1) No person, including the owner or occupier of a protected area, shall construct any building within the protected area or carry on any mining, quarrying, excavating, blasting or any operation of a like nature in such area, utilise such area or any part thereof in any other manner without the permission of the Central Government:

Provided that nothing in this sub-section shall be deemed to prohibit the use of any such area or carry on any mining, quarrying, excavating, blasting or any operation of a like nature in such area, or utilise such area or any part thereof in any other manner without the permission of the Central Government:

Provided that nothing in this sub-section shall be deemed to prohibit the use of any such area or part thereof for purposes of cultivation if such cultivation does not involve the digging of not more than one foot of soil from the surface.

(2) The Central Government may, by order, direct that any building constructed by any person within a protected area in contravention of the provisions of sub-section (1) shall be removed within a specified period and, if the person refuses or fails to comply with the order, the Collector may cause the building to be removed and the person shall be liable to pay the cost of such removal.

20. Power to acquire a protected area

If the Central Government is of opinion that any protected area contains an ancient monument or antiquities of national interest and value, it may acquire such area under the provisions of Land Acquisition Act, 1894, as if the acquisition were for a public purpose within the meaning of that Act.

ARCHAEOLOGICAL EXCAVATIONS

21. Excavations in protected areas

An archaeological officer or an officer authorised by him in this behalf or any person holding a licence granted in this behalf under this Act (hereinafter referred to as the licensee) may, after giving notice in writing to the Collector and the owner, enter upon and make excavations in any protected area.

22. Excavations in areas other than protected areas

Where an archaeological officer has reason to believe that an area not being a protected area contains ruins or relics of historical or archaeological importance, he or an officer authorised by him in this behalf may, after giving notice in writing to the Collector and the owner, enter upon and make excavations in the area.

23. Compulsory purchase of antiquities etc., discovered during excavation operation

(1) Where, as a result of any excavations made in any area under section 21 or section 22, any antiquities are discovered, the archaeological officer or the licensee, as the case may be, shall—

(a) as soon as practicable, examine such antiquities and submit a report to the Central Government in such manner and containing such particulars as may be prescribed;

(b) at the conclusion of the excavation operations, give notice in writing to the owner of the land from which such antiquities have been discovered, of the nature of such antiquities.

(2) Until an order for the compulsory purchase of any such antiquities is made under sub-section (3), the archaeological officer or the licensee, as the case may be, shall keep them in such safe custody as he may deem fit.

(3) On receipt of a report under sub-section (1), the Central Government may make an order for the compulsory purchase of any such antiquities at their market value.

(4) When an order for the compulsory purchase of any antiquities is made under sub-section (3), such antiquities shall vest in the Central Government with effect from the date of the order.

24. Excavations, etc., for archaeological purposes

No State Government shall undertake or authorise any person to undertake any excavation or other like operation for archaeological purposes in any area which is not a protected area except with the previous approval of the Central Government and in accordance with such rules or directions, if any, as the Central Government may make or give in this behalf.

PROTECTION OF ANTIQUITIES

25. Power of Central Government to control moving of antiquities

(1) If the Central Government considers that any antiquities or class of antiquities ought not to be moved from the place where they are without the sanction of the Central Government, the Central Government may, by notification in the *Official Gazette*, direct that any such antiquity or any class of such antiquities shall not to be moved except with the written permission of the Director-General.

(2) Every application for permission under sub-section (1) shall be in such form and contain such particulars as may be prescribed.

(3) Any person aggrieved by an order refusing permission may appeal to the Central Government whose decision shall be final.

26. Purchase of antiquity by Central Government

(1) If the Central Government apprehends that any antiquity mentioned in a notification issued under sub-section (1) of section 25 is in danger of being destroyed, removed, injured, misused or allowed to fall into decay or is of opinion that, by reason of its historical or archaeological importance, it is desirable to preserve such antiquity in a public place, the Central Government may make an order for compulsory purchase of such antiquity at its market value and the Collector shall thereupon give notice to the owner of the antiquity to be purchased.

(2) Where a notice of compulsory purchase is issued under sub-section (1) in respect of any antiquity shall vest in the Central Government with effect from the date of the notice.

(3) The power of compulsory purchase given by this section shall not extend to any image or symbol actually used for *bona fide* religious observances.

PRINCIPLES OF COMPENSATION

27. Compensation for loss or damage

Any owner or occupier of land who has sustained any loss or damage or any diminution of profits from the land by reason of any entry on, or excavations in, such land or the exercise of any other power conferred by this Act shall be paid compensation by the Central Government for such loss, damage or diminution of profits.

28. Assessment of market value or compensation

(1) The market value of any property which the Central Government is empowered to purchase at such value under this Act or such the compensation to paid by the Central Government in respect of anything done under this Act shall, where any dispute arises in respect of such market value or compensation, be ascertained in the manner provided in sections 3, 5, 8 to 34, 45 to 47, 51 and 52 of the Land Acquisition Act, 1894 [1 of 1894], so far as they can be made applicable :

Provided that, when making an enquiry under this said Land Acquisition Act, the Collector shall be assisted by two assessors, one of whom shall be competent person nominated by the Central Government and one a person nominated by the owner, or, in case the owner fails to nominate an assessor within such reasonable time as may be fixed by the Collector in this behalf, by the Collector.

(2) Notwithstanding anything contained in sub-section (1) or in the Land Acquisition Act, 1894 (1 of 1894), in determining the market value of any antiquity in respect of which an order for compulsory purchase is made under sub-section (1) of section 26, any increase in the value of the antiquity by reason of its being of historical or archaeological importance shall not be taken into consideration.

MISCELLANEOUS

29. Delegation of powers

The Central Government may, by notification in the *Official Gazette*, direct that any powers conferred on it by or under this Act shall, subject to such conditions as may be specified in the direction, be exercisable also by—

(a) such officer or authority subordinate to the Central Government, or

(b) such State Government or such officer or authority subordinate to the State Government

as may be specified in the direction.

30. Penalties

(1) Whoever—

(i) destroys, removes, injures, alters, defaces, imperils or misuses a protected monument, or

(ii) being the owner or occupier of a protected monument, contravenes an order made under sub-section (1) of section 9 or under sub-section (1) of section 10, or

(iii) removes from a protected monument any sculpture, carving, image, bas-relief, inscription, or other like object, or

(iv) does any act in contravention of sub-section (1) of section 19,

shall be punishable with imprisonment which may extend to three months, or with fine which may extend to five thousand rupees, or with both.

(2) Any person who moves any antiquity in contravention of a notification issued under sub-section (1) of section 25 shall be punishable with fine which may extend to five thousand rupees; and the court convicting a person of any such contravention may by order direct such person to restore the antiquity to the place from which it was removed.

31. Jurisdiction to try offences

No court inferior to that of a Presidency Magistrate or Magistrate of the first class shall try any offence under this Act.

32. Certain of fences to be cognizable

Notwithstanding anything contained in the Code of Criminal Procedure, 1898 [5 of 1898], an offence under clause (i) or clause (iii) of sub-section (1) of section 30, shall be deemed to be a cognizable offence within the meaning of that Code.

33. Special provision regarding fine

Notwithstanding anything contained in section 32 of the Code of Criminal Procedure, 1898 (5 of 1898), it shall be lawful for any Magistrate of the first class specially empowered by the State Government in this behalf and for any Presidency Magistrate to pass a sentence of fine exceeding two thousand rupees on any person convicted of an offence which under this Act is punishable with fine exceeding two thousand rupees.

34. Recovery of amounts due to the Government

Any amount due to the Government from any person under this Act may, on a certificate issued by the Director-General or an archaeological officer authorised by him in this behalf be recovered in the same manner as an arrear of land revenue.

35. Ancient monuments etc., which have ceased to be of national importance

If the Central Government is of opinion that any ancient and historical monument or archaeological site and remains declared to be of national importance by or under this Act has ceased to be of national importance, it may, by notification in the *Official Gazette*, declare that the ancient and historical monument or archaeological site and remains, as the case may be, has ceased to be of national importance for the purposes of this Act.

36. Power to correct mistakes, etc.

Any clerical mistake, patent error or arising from accidental slip or omission in the description of any ancient monument or archaeological site and remains declared to be of national importance by or under this Act may, at any time, be corrected by the Central Government by notification in the *Official Gazette*.

37. Protection of action taken under the Act

No suit for compensation and no criminal proceeding shall lie against any public servant in respect of any act done or in good faith intended to be done in the exercise of any power conferred by this Act.

38. Power to make rules

(1) The Central Government may, by notification in the *Official Gazette* and subject to the condition of previous publication, make rules for carrying out the purposes of this Act.

(2) In particular, and without prejudice to the generality of the foregoing power, such rules may provide for all or any of the following matters, namely:

(a) the prohibition or the regulation by licensing or otherwise of mining, quarrying, excavating, blasting or any operation of a like nature near a protected monument or the construction of buildings on land adjoining such monument and the removal of unauthorised buildings;

(b) the grant of licences and permissions to make excavations for archaeological purposes in protected areas, the authorities by whom, and the restrictions and conditions subject to which, such licences may be granted, the taking of securities from licensees and the fees that may be charged for such licences;

(c) the right of access of the public to a protected monument and the fee, if any, to be charged therefor;

(d) the form and contents of the report of an archaeological officer or a licensee under clause (a) of sub-section (1) of section 23;

(e) the form in which applications for permission under section 19 or section 25 may be made of particulars which they should contain;

(f) the form and manner of preferring appeals under this Act and the time within which they may be preferred;

(g) the manner of service of any order or notice under this Act;

(h) any other matter which is to be or may be prescribed.

(3) Any rule made under this section may provide that a breach thereof shall be punishable,—

(i) in the case of a rule made with reference to clause (a) of sub-section (2), with imprisonment which may extend to five thousand rupees, or with both;

(ii) in the case of a rule made with reference to clause (b) of sub-section (2), with fine which may extend to five thousand rupees;

(iii) in the case of a rule made with reference to clause (c) of sub-section (2), with fine which may extend to five hundred rupees.

(4) All rules made under this section shall be laid for not less than thirty days before each House of Parliament as soon as possible after they are made, and shall be subject to such modifications as Parliament may make during the session in which they are so laid or the session immediately following.

39. Repeals and saving

(1) The Ancient and Historical Monuments and Archaeological Sites and Remains (Declaration of National Importance) Act, 1951 [71 of 1951], and section 126 of the States Reorganisation Act, 1956 [37 of 1956], are hereby repealed.

(2) The Ancient Monuments Preservation Act, 1904, shall cease to have effect in the relation to ancient and historical monuments and archaeological sites and remains declared by or under this Act to be of national importance, except as respects things done or omitted to be done before the commencement of this Act.

G.R. RAJAGOPAL,
Secy. to the Government of India

7. The Ancient Monuments and Archaeological Sites and Remains Rules, 1959

CHAPTER I

PRELIMINARY

1. Short title, extent and commencement

(1) These rules may be called the Ancient Monuments and Archaeological Sites and Remains Rules, 1959.

(2) They extend to the whole of India, but rules 24, 25, 26, and 30 shall not apply to the State of Jammu and Kashmir.

(3) They shall come into force on the 15th day of October, 1959.

2. Definitions

In these rules, unless the context otherwise required,—

(a) "construction" means the construction of any structure and includes additions to or alternations of an existing building;

(b) "copying", together with its grammatical variations and cognate expressions, means the preparation of copies by drawing or by photography or by mould or by squeezing and includes the preparation of a cinematographic film with the aid of a hand-camera which is capable of taking films of not more than eight millimetres and which does not require the use of a stand or involve any special previous arrangement;

(c) "filming", together with its grammatical variations and cognate expressions, means the preparation of a cinematographic film with the aid of a camera which is capable of taking films of more than eight millimetres and which requires the use of a stand or involves other special previous arrangements;

(d) "form" means a form set out in the Third Schedule;

(e) "mining operation" means any operation for the purpose of searching for or obtaining minerals and includes quarrying, excavating, blasting and any operation of a like nature;

(f) "prohibited area" or "regulated area" means an area near or adjoining a protected monument which the Central Government has, by notification in the *Official Gazette*, declared to be a prohibited area or, as the case may be, a regulated area, for purpose of mining operation or construction or both.

(g) "Schedule" means a schedule to these rules; and

(h) "section" means a section of the Ancient Monuments and Archaeological Sites and Remains Act, 1958 (24 of 1958).

CHAPTER II

ACCESS TO PROTECTED MONUMENTS

3. Monuments governed by agreement

(1) Access to protected monuments in respect of which an agreement has been entered into between the owner and the Central Government under sections 6 or 7 shall be construed as affecting any such agreement or order.

(2) A copy of the relevant provisions of every such agreement or order shall be exhibited in a conspicuous part of the monument concerned.

4. Parts of monuments not open

The Director-General may, by order, direct that any specified part of a protected monument shall not be open, permanently or for a specified period, to any person other than an archaeological officer, his agents, subordinates and workmen and any other Government servant on duty at such part.

5. Monuments when kept open

(1) The protected monuments specified in the First Schedule shall remain open during the hours specified against them in that Schedule; protected monuments which are not so specified and to which neither rule 3 nor rule 4 applies shall remain open from sunrise to sunset:

Provided that an archaeological officer may, by notice to be exhibited in a conspicuous part of the monument, direct that a protected monument or part thereof shall be closed temporarily for such periods as may be specified in the notice.

(2) Nothing in this rule or in rule 6 shall apply to an archaeological officer, his agents, subordinates and workmen or to any other Government servant on duty at a protected monument.

6. Entrance fee

No person above the age of fifteen years shall enter any protected monument or part thereof specified in the Second Schedule except on payment of a fee of twenty naye paise :

Provided that the Director-General may, by order, direct that, on such occasions and for such periods as may be specified in the order, no fee shall be charged for entry into a protected monument or part thereof.

7. Holding of meetings etc. in monuments

(1) No protected monuments shall be used for the purpose of holding any meetings, reception, party, conference or entertainment except under and in accordance with a permission in writing granted by the Central Government.

(2) Nothing in sub-rule (1) shall apply to any meeting, reception, party, conference or entertainment which is held in pursuance of a recognised religious usage or custom.

8. Prohibition of certain acts within monuments

No person shall, within a protected monument,—

(a) do any act which causes or is likely to cause damage or injury to any part of the monument; or

(b) discharge any fire-arms; or

(c) cook or consume food except in areas, if any, permitted to be used for that purpose; or

(d) hawk or sell any goods or wares or canvass any custom for such goods or wares or display any advertisement in any form or show a visitor round for monetary consideration, except under the authority of, or under and in accordance with the conditions of a licence granted by, an archaeo-logical officer; or

(e) beg for alms; or

(f) violate any practice, usage or custom applicable to or observed in the monument; or

(g) bring, for any purpose other than the maintenance of the monument,

(i) any animal, or

(ii) any vehicle except in areas reserved for the parking thereof.

9. Penalty

Whoever—

(i) unlawfully enters any protected monument or part thereof at a time when, under these rules, it is not to be kept open, or

(ii) unlawfully enters any protected monument in respect of which an order has been made under rule 4 or rule 5, or

(iii) contravenes any of the provisions of rule 6 or rule 7 or rule 8, shall be punishable with fine which may extend to five hundred rupees.

CHAPTER III

CONSTRUCTION AND OTHER OPERATIONS IN PROTECTED AREAS

10. Permission required for construction etc.

(1) No person shall undertake any construction or mining operation within a protected area except under and in accordance with a permission granted in this behalf by the Central Government.

(2) Every application for permission under sub-rule (1) shall be made to the Central Government in Form I at least three months before the date of commencement of the construction of operation.

11. Licence required for excavation

No person other than an archaeological officer or an officer authorised by him in this behalf shall undertake any excavation for archaeological purposes in any protected area except under and in accordance with the terms and conditions of a licence granted under rule 13.

12. Application for licence

Every application for a licence shall be in Form II and be made to the Director-General at least three months before the proposed date of the commencement of the excavation operations.

13. Grant or refusal of licence

(1) On receipt of an application under rule 12, the Director-General may grant a licence in Form III if he is satisfied that, having regard to the status of the applicant, the competence of the director of excavation operations, the adequacy of the staff to be employed and other relevant factors, the licence may be granted to the applicant:

Provided that no licence shall be granted unless the applicant has furnished security of such amount not exceeding rupees ten thousand as the Director-General may, having regard to the circumstances of each case, require.

(2) The Director-General, by order, may, for reasons to be recorded in writing, refuse to grant a licence in any particular case.

14. Period of licence

Every licence shall be in force for such period not exceeding three years as may be specified in the licence:

Provided that the Director-General may, on application made to him at least one month before the expiry of a licence, extend its period by one year at a time so that the aggregate period does not exceed five years.

15. Cancellation of licence

The Director-General may, by order, cancel a licence granted under rule 13 if he is satisfied that the conduct of the excavation operations has not been satisfactory or in accordance with the conditions of the licence, or if any further security demanded under rule 18 has not been deposited within the specified time:

Provided that no licence shall be cancelled unless the licensee has been given an opportunity to make his objections.

16. Conditions of licence

Every licence shall be subject to the following conditions, namely:

(a) the licence shall not be transferable;

(b) the licensee shall give to the Director-General, the Collector and the owner of the land to be excavated at least fifteen days' notice in writing of the commencement of the excavation operations;

(c) the licensee shall produce the licence before the District Magistrate or the District Superintendent of Police concerned or an archaeological officer, if so required.

(d) the excavation operations shall be conducted under the supervision of the director named in the licence who shall be present at the excavation operations for at least three-fourths of the period of the operations;

(e) the licensee shall not, without the permission of the Director-General, dismantle or disturb any structures found during the excavation operations and shall make adequate arrangements for the safety of such structures and of the excavated antiquities till they are taken charge of by the Director-General;

(f) the licensee shall not subject any antiquities recovered during the excavation operations to any chemical or electrolytic process of cleaning without the written permission of the Director-General;

(g) an archaeological officer or his representative may inspect the excavation operations or any antiquities recovered during the operations and make notes on or copy or film the excavated structures and antiquities.

(h) at the conclusion of the excavation operations, the licensee shall give notice in writing to the owner of the land specifying the nature of the antiquities, if any, recovered during the operations;

(i) the licensee shall, within three months of the completion of the excavation operations, submit to the Director-General a summary report of the results of the excavation, and where the operations are carried on for a period of more than three months such report shall be submitted every quarter, and it shall be open to the Director-General to publish the report in his reports or reviews; and

(j) the licensee shall as soon as practicable submit a report in Form IV to the Central Government through the Director-General on the antiquities recovered during the excavation operations.

17. Recovery from security

The Director-General may, by order, direct the deduction, from the security furnished by a licensee under rule 13, of—

(a) the value of any antiquities recovered during the excavation operations and lost or destroyed while in the custody of the licensee; and

(b) any compensation payable by the Central Government under section 27 to the owner or occupier of the land excavated by the licensee.

18. Demand of further security

Where, during the currency of a licence, any amount has been recovered under rule 17, the Director-General may require the licensee, within such time as he may specify, to deposit such further sum as security as is equivalent to the amount so recovered.

19. Appeal

Any person aggrieved by an order of the Director-General under rule 13 or rule 15 or rule 17 may prefer an appeal to Central Government, and the decision of that Government on such appeal shall be final.

20. Return of security

On expiration or earlier cancellation of a licence, the security deposited by the licensee or the balance thereof remaining after deduction of any amount under rule 17 shall be returned to him.

21. Publication of the result of excavation

Save as otherwise provided in rule 16, the Director-General shall not, without the consent of the licensee, publish the results of the excavation unless the licensee has failed to publish the results within the period specified by the Director-General in this behalf.

22. Retention of antiquities by licensee

The Central Government may, by order, subject to such terms and conditions as may be specified, permit the licensee to retain such of the antiquities recovered during the excavation operations as may be specified therein :

Provided that human relics of historical importance and antiquities, which in the opinion of the Central Government are of national importance, shall not be permitted to be retained by the licensee.

23. Penalty

Whoever—

(i) unlawfully undertakes any excavation for archaeological purposes in any protected area, or

(ii) contravenes any of the conditions of a licence, shall be punishable with fine which may extend to five thousand rupees.

CHAPTER IV

EXCAVATION IN UNPROTECTED AREAS

24. Intimation to the Central Government

Every State Government intending to undertake or authorise any person to undertake any archaeological excavation or other like operation in any area which is not a protected area shall intimate its intention to the Central Government at least three months prior to the proposed date of the commencement of the excavation or operation specifying the following details, namely:

(i) name, location and other details of the site;

(ii) nature of antiquities previously found;

(iii) details of previous exploration, if any;

(iv) purpose of the excavation or operation;

(v) proposed extent of the excavation or operation (a plan of the site in triplicate showing in red outline the extent of the proposed excavation or operation should be attached);

(vi) proposed duration of the excavation or operation;

(vii) amount of the proposed expenditure on the excavation or operation; and

(viii) name and status of the director of the excavation or operation.

25. Approval by the Central Government

After considering the proposal, the Central Government may modify it or to abandon it altogether.

26. Deputation of an archaeological officer

The Central Government may depute an archaeological officer to inspect the excavation or operation while it is in process and render such advice as he deems necessary.

CHAPTER V

REPORT ON EXCAVATED ANTIQUITIES BY AN ARCHAEOLOGICAL OFFICER

27. Form of report by an archaeological officer

Where, as a result of an excavation made by an archaeological officer in any area under sections 21 or 22, any antiquities are discovered, the archaeological officer shall, as soon as practicable, submit a report in Form V to the Central Government through the Director-General on the antiquities recovered during the excavation.

CHAPTER VI

MOVING OF ANTIQUITIES FROM CERTAIN AREAS

28. Application for moving antiquities

Every application for permission to move any antiquities or any class of antiquities in respect of which a notification has been issued under sub-section (1) of section 25 shall be made in Form VI to the Director-General at least three months before the proposed date of the moving.

29. Grant or refusal of permission

On receipt of an application under rule necessary, grant permission for the moving of all or any of the antiquities or, for reasons to be recorded, refuse such permission.

30. Appeal

Any person aggrieved by an order of the Director-General under rule 29 may prefer an appeal to the Central Government, and the decision of that Government on such appeal shall be final.

CHAPTER VII

MINING OPERATION AND CONSTRUCTION NEAR PROTECTED MONUMENTS

31. Notice of intention to declare a prohibited or regulated area

(1) Before declaring an area near or adjoining a protected monument to be a prohibited area or a regulated area for purposes of mining operation or construction or both, the Central Government shall, by notification in the *Official Gazette*, give one month's notice of its intention to do so; and a copy of such notification shall be affixed in a conspicuous place near the area.

(2) Every such notification shall specify the limits of the area which is to be so declared and shall also call for objections, if any, from interested persons.

32. Declaration of prohibited or regulated area

After the expiry of one month from the date of the notification under rule 31 and after considering the objections, if any, received within the said period, the Central Government may declare, by notification in the *Official Gazette,* the area specified in the notification under rule 31, or any part of such area, to be a prohibited area or, as the case may be, a regulated area for purposes of mining operation or construction or both.

33. Effect of declaration of prohibited or regulated area

No person other than an archaeological officer shall undertake any mining operation or any construction,—

(a) in a prohibited area, or

(b) in a regulated area, except under and in accordance with the terms and conditions of a licence granted by the Director-General.

34. Application for licence

Every person intending to undertake any mining operation or any construction in a regulated area shall apply to the Director-General in Form VII at least three months before the date of commencement of such operation or construction.

35. Grant or refusal of licence

(1) On receipt of an application under rule 34, the Director-General may grant a licence, or if he is satisfied that the licence asked for should not be granted, may, for reasons to be recorded, refuse to grant a licence.

(2) Every licence granted under sub-rule (1) shall be in Form VII and be subject to the following conditions, namely:

(a) the licence shall not be transferable;

(b) it shall be valid for the period specified therein; and

(c) any other condition relating to the manner of carrying out the mining operation or the construction which the Director-General may specify in the licence for ensuring the safety and appearance of, and the maintenance of the approach and access to the protected monument.

36. Cancellation of licence

The Director-General may, by order, cancel a licence granted under rule 35 if he is satisfied that any of its conditions has been violated :

Provided that no licence shall be cancelled unless the licensee has been given an opportunity to make his objections.

37. Appeal

Any person aggrieved by an order of the Director-General made under rule 35 or rule 36 may prefer an appeal to the Central Government, and the decision of that Government on such appeal shall be final.

38. Removal of unauthorised buildings

(1) The Central Government may, by order, direct the owner or occupier of an unauthorised building in a prohibited area or in a regulated area or of a building or part thereof which has been constructed in contravention of any of the conditions of a licence granted under rule 35 to remove such building or part thereof within a period specified in that order.

(2) If the owner or occupier refuses or fails to comply with an order made under sub-rule (1), the Central Government may direct the District Magistrate to cause the building or part thereof to be removed, and the owner or occupier shall be liable to pay the cost of such removal.

39. Penalty

Whoever—

(i) unlawfully undertakes any mining operation or construction in a prohibited area or in a regulated area, or

(ii) contravenes any of the conditions of a licence, or

(iii) fails or refuses to comply with an order made under sub-rule (1) of rule 38,

shall be punishable with imprisonment which may extend to three months or with fine which may extend to five thousand rupees or with both.

CHAPTER VIII

COPYING AND FILMING OF PROTECTED MONUMENTS

40. Permission required for copying certain monuments

The Director-General may, by order, direct that no person other than an archaeological officer or an officer authorised by an archaeological officer in this behalf shall copy any specified monument or part thereof except under and in accordance with the terms and conditions of a permission in writing granted by an archaeological officer.

41. Conditions of copying other monuments

(1) Any person may copy a protected monument in respect of which no order under rule 40 has been made.

(2) Nothing in sub-rule (1) shall be construed as authorising any person other than an archaeological officer or an officer authorised by him in this behalf, while copying any such monuments, to—

(a) bring into or use within the precincts of such monument a camerastand, stool, chair, table, large drawing-board, easel or any such appliance, or

(b) erect any scaffolding within such precincts, or

(c) use within such precincts any artificial light other than a flash-light synchronised with the exposure of a camera, or

(d) apply any extraneous matter, such as water, oil, grease or any moulding material, on such monument or part thereof, or

(e) prepare a direct tracing or mould or squeeze of such monument or part thereof,

except under and in accordance with the terms and conditions of a permission in writing granted by an archaeological officer.

42. Licence required for filming

No person other than an archaeological officer or an officer authorised by him in this behalf shall undertake any filming operation at a protected monument or part thereof except under and in accordance with the terms and conditions of a licence granted under rule 44.

43. Application for licence

Every person intending to undertake any filming operation at a protected monument shall apply to the Director-General in Form IX at least three months before the proposed date of the commencement of such operation.

44. Grant or refusal of licence

(1) On receipt of an application under rule 43, the Director-General may grant a licence or, if he is satisfied that the licence asked for should not be granted, may, for reasons to the recorded, refuse to grant a licence:

Provided that the Director-General shall not grant any licence to film the interior of any protected monument, that is to say such part of any protected monument as is covered by a roof of any description, except when the film is for the purpose of education or of publicising the monument.

(2) Every licence granted under sub-rule 10 shall be in Form X and be subject to the following conditions, namely:

(a) the licence shall not be transferable and shall be valid for the period specified therein;

(b) nothing shall be done by the licensee or any member of his party which has, or may have, the effect of exposing any part of the monument or attached lawn or garden to the risk of damage;

(c) the filming operation shall be restricted to that part of the monument in respect of which the licence has been granted;

(d) no extraneous matter, such as water, oil, grease or the like, shall be applied on any part of the monument;

(e) the generating plant for electric power, wherever required, shall be placed away from the monument or the attached lawn or garden;

(f) the filming operation shall not obstruct or hamper the movement of persons who may lawfully be within the precincts of the monument; and

(g) any other condition which the Director-General, by order, may after giving notice to the licensee, cancel a licence granted under rule 44 if he is satisfied that any of its conditions has been violated.

46. Appeal

Any person aggrieved by an order of the Director-General made under rule 44 or rule 45 may prefer an appeal to the Central Government, and the decision of that Government on such appeal shall be final.

47. Certain rules not affected

Nothing in rule 41 and no precision of a permission granted under rule 40 or of a licence granted under rule 44 shall affect the operation of rules 3, 4, 5, 6, 7, 8 and 9.

48. Penalty

Whoever copies or films any protected monument or does any other act in contravention of any provision of this chapter or of any permission or licence granted thereunder shall be punishable with fine which may extend to five hundred rupees.

CHAPTER IX

MISCELLANEOUS

49. Manner of preferring an appeal

(1) Every appeal to the Central Government under the Ancient Monuments and Archaeological Sites and Remains Act, 1958, or under these rules shall be in writing and shall be preferred within one month of the date of receipt of the order appealed against.

(2) Every such appeal shall be accompanied by a copy of the order appealed against.

50. Service of orders and notices

Every order or notice made or issued under the Ancient Monuments and Archaeological Sites and Remains Act, 1958 or these rules shall—

(a) in the case of any order or notice of a general nature or affecting a class of persons, be published in the *Official Gazette*; and

(b) in the case of any order or notice affecting a corporation or firm, be served in the manner provided for the service of summons in rule 2 of order XXIX or rule 3 of order XXX, as the case may be, in the First Schedule to the Code of Civil Procedure, 1908; and

(c) in the case of any order or notice affecting an individual person, be served on such person—

(i) by delivering or tendering it to the person concerned, or

(ii) if it cannot be so delivered or tendered, by delivering or tendering it to any adult male member of the family of such person or by affixing a copy thereof on the outer door or some conspicuous part of the premises in which that person is known to have last resided or carried on business or personally worked for gain, or

(iii) by sending it by registered post, acknowledgement due.

Third Schedule

FORM I

Application for Permission for Construction/Mining Operation within a Protected Area

(vide rule 10)

1. Name and address of applicant[1]
2. Name of the protected area within which construction/mining operation is proposed

   Locality ________________ District ____________ State ___________
3. Nature and details of the proposed construction/mining operation in respect of which permission is sought

(In the case of construction, a site-plan in triplicate showing in red outline the location of the building in relation to the protected area and the plan and elevation of the building should be attached; and the colour, external appearance and method of the screening of the building and the depth down to which the soil will be excavated for the appurtenances of the building should be specified.

In the case of mining operation, a site-plan in triplicate showing in red outline the extent of the operation in relation to the protected area should be attached; and details regarding the depth down to which the operation is to be carried out, the mode of the operation, the method of the muffing of sound, the kind and charge of blasting material and the depth and number of blast-holes to be fired at a time should be specified.)

4. Purpose of the proposed construction/mining operation.
5. Approximate duration and date of commencement of the proposed construction/mining operation.

I declare that the above information is correct. I also undertake to observe the provisions of the Ancient Monuments and Archaeological Sites and Remains Act, 1958, and the rules made thereunder.

Station ____

Seal of the organisation ___________________________

Date ________________ Signature of the applicant[2]

---

1. If the application is on behalf of an organisation, the name thereof should be given.
2. If the application is on behalf of an organisation, the signature should be that of the head of that organisation.

FORM II

Application for Licence to Excavate in a Protected Area

(vide rule 12)

1. Name and address of applicant[1]
2. Name of the site

   Locality________________ District_____________ State ____________
3. Extent of the proposed excavation (a plan of the site in triplicate showing in red outline the extent of the proposed excavation should be attached).
4. Approximate duration and date of commencement of the proposed excavation
5. Approximate expenditure on the proposed excavation
6. Name and status of the director of the proposed excavation
7. Details of photographic, surveying and other equipments available for the proposed excavation

I declare that the above information is correct. I also undertake to observe the provisions of the Ancient Monuments and Archaeological Sites and Remains Act, 1958, and the rules made thereunder.

Station ____

Seal of the institution ______________________________

Date ___________________

Signature of the applicant[2]

---

1. If the application is on behalf of an institution, the name thereof should be given.
2. If the application is on behalf of an institution, the signature should be that of the head of the institution, which term includes the Registrar of a university.

FORM III

Licence for Excavation in a Protected Area

(vide rule 13)

Whereas__________________has applied for a licence for carrying out excavation operations in the protected area known as________ at ________, District_________, State_______________, and has undertaken to observe the provisions of the Ancient Monuments and Archaeological Sites and Remains Act, 1958, and the rules made thereunder and has further deposited the sum of Rs. ... (Rupees————only) as required by the rules.

I, __________________, Director-General of Archaeology, do hereby grant this licence under sub-rule (1) of rule 13 of the said rules to the said— to carry out excavation operations in the area indicated in red outline on the plan attached hereto.

The licence is granted subject to the provisions of the said Act and rules and is further subject to the condition that________of________shall be the director of the excavation.

The licence is not transferable. It shall be valid for________commencing with________day of________19.

Station ____

Seal of the Department ____________________________________
of Archaeology of the Date
Government of India

Signature of the
Director-General of Archaeology

FORM IV

Report on Antiquities Excavated in a Protected Area

(vide rule 16)

Name of site ____________________

Locality ____________________

District____________________

State ____________________

Report for the period from _______19 __________ to ____________ 19.

Serial No.	Class of antiquities	Material	Number of antiquities[1]		Approximate age	Remarks
			Complete	Fragmentary		

Station ____________________

Date ____________________

Signature of the Licensee

1. In the case of potsherds, the approximate number should be stated.

FORM V

Report on Antiquities Excavated in a Protected Area

(vide rule 27)

Name of site ________________________________

Locality ________________________________

District ________________________________

State ________________________________

Report for the period from ________19 __________ to ____________ 19.

Serial No.	Class of antiquities	Material	Number of antiquities[1]		Approximate age	Remarks
			Complete	Fragmentary		

Station ________________________

Date ________________________

Signature of the Licensee

1. In the case of potsherds, the approximate number should be stated.

FORM VI

Application for the Moving of Antiquities

(vide rule 28)

1. Name and address of applicant[1]
2. Name of the place from which antiquities are to be moved
   Locality________________ District ____________ State ___________
3. Description of antiquities proposed to be moved
   (Photographs showing details of the antiquities should be attached)
4. Approximate date of the moving
5. Purpose of the moving
6. Whether the antiquities or any of them are objects of worship

I declare that the above information is correct.

Station ____

Seal of the organisation ______________________________

Date ____

Signature of the applicant[2]

1. If the application is on behalf of an organisation, the name thereof should be given.
2. If the application is on behalf of an organisation, the signature should be that of the head of that organisation.

FORM VII

Application for Licence for Mining Operation/Construction within a Regulated Area

(vide rule 34)

1. Name and address of applicant[1]
2. Name of the place from which antiquities are to be moved

   Locality ________________ District ____________ State ___________
3. Nature and details of the proposed mining operation/construction in respect of which permission is sought

(In the case of mining operation, a site-plan in triplicate showing in red outline the extent of the operation in relation to the monument and the regulated area should be attached; and the details regarding the depth down to which the operation is to be carried out, the mode of the operation, the method of the muffing of sound, the kind and charge of blasting material and the depth and number of blast-holes to be fired at a time should be specified.

In the case of construction, a site-plan in triplicate showing in red outline the location of the building in relation to the monument and the regulated area and the plan and elevation of the building should be attached; and the colour external appearance and method of the screening of the building and the depth down to which the soil will be excavated for the appurtenances of the building should be specified.)

4. Purpose of the proposed mining operation/construction
5. Approximate duration and date of commencement of the proposed mining operation/construction

I declare that the above information is correct. I also undertake to observe the provisions of the Ancient Monuments and Archaeological Sites and Remains Act, 1958, and the rules made thereunder.

Station ____________________________________

Seal of the organisation ____________________

Date __________________

Signature of the applicant[2]

---

1. If the application is on behalf of an organisation, the name thereof should be given.
2. If the application is on behalf of an organisation, the signature should be that of the head of that organisation.

FORM VIII

Licence for Mining Operation/Construction within a Regulated Area

(vide rule 35)

Whereas_________of_________has applied for a licence for _____ in the regulated area near or adjoining_________at_________,District____________, State____________, and has undertaken to observe the provisions of the Ancient Monuments and Archaeological Sites and Remains Act, 1958, and the rules made thereunder.

I,____________________, Director-General of Archaeology, do hereby grant this licence under sub-rule (1) of rule 35 of the said rules to the said ________ for ___________ in the area indicated in red outline on the plan attached hereto.

The licence is granted subject to the provisions of the said Act and rules and is further subject to the following conditions, namely:-

The licence is not transferable. It shall be valid for___________ commencing with________ day of________ 19.

Station ____

Seal of the Department ____
of Archaeology of the Date
Government of India

Signature of the
Director-General of Archaeology

FORM IX

Application for Licence of Filming Operation at a Protected Monument

(vide rule 43)

1. Name and address of applicant[1]
2. Name of the monument at which the proposed filming operation is to be carried out

   Locality ______________________

   District ______________________

   State ______________________
3. Part of the monument proposed to be filmed
4. Nature and purpose of the proposed filming operation and the context in which the monument is proposed to be filmed (relevant extract of the script should be attached in triplicate and details of the scenes to be filmed should be furnished in triplicate).
5. Number of persons in the cast
6. Approximate duration and date of commencement of proposed filming operation

I declare that the above information is correct. I also undertake to observe the provisions of the Ancient Monuments and Archaeological Sites and Remains Act, 1958, and the rules made thereunder.

Station ______________________

Seal of the organisation ______________________

Date ______________________

Signature of the applicant[2]

---

1. If the application is on behalf of an organisation, the name thereof should be given.
2. If the application is on behalf of an organisation, the signature should be that of the head of that organisation.

FORM X

Licence of Filming Operation at a Protected Monument

(vide rule 44)

Whereas_________of_________has applied for a licence for filming operation at the protected monument known as_________located at_________, District ______, State_________, and has undertaken to observe the provisions of the Ancient Monuments and Archaeological Sites and Remains Act, 1958, and the rules made thereunder.

I, _________, Director-General of Archaeology, do hereby grant this licence under rule 44 of the said rules to the said_________for the carrying out of filming operation, as per script and details of scenes attached hereto, in the following parts of the monuments, namely:-

The licence is granted subject to the provisions of the said Act and rules and is further subject to the following conditions, namely:-

The licence is not transferable. It shall be valid for_________commencing with day of_________19.

Station ____

Seal of the Department ______________________________
of Archaeology of the Date
Government of India

Signature of the
Director-General of Archaeology

The Schedules

First Schedule

Hours during which certain monuments or parts thereof will remain open

(vide rule 5)

S. No.	State	District	Locality	Name of monument	Parts of monument which shall remain open during hours other than from sunrise to sunset	Hours of opening
1	2	3	4	5	6	7
1.	Andhra Pradesh	Hyderabad	Hyderabad City	Char Minar	(i) Second storey and upwards	(i) From 9 a.m. to 5-30 p.m. or sunset whichever is earlier
2.	Bihar	Patna	Kumrahar	Site of Mauryan Palace	(ii) Remaining area whole	(ii) From sunrise to 10 p.m. From 9 a.m. to 5-30 p.m. or sunset whichever is earlier
3.	Bihar	Patna	Nalanda (Burgaon)	All mounds, structures and buildings enclosed in the acquired area	Fenced area containing excavated remains	From 9 a.m. to 5-30 p.m. or sunset whichever is earlier
4.	Bombay	Aurangabad	Ajanta	Ajanta Caves	Whole	From 9 a.m. to 5-30 p.m. or sunset whichever is earlier
5.	Bombay	Aurangabad	Aurangabad	Tomb of Rabia Daurani (Bibi-ka-Maqbara)	Garden	From sunrise to 10 p.m.

S. No.	State	District	Locality	Name of monument	Parts of monument which shall remain open during hours other than from sunrise to sunset	Hours of opening
1	2	3	4	5	6	7
6.	Bombay	Kolaba	Gharapuri	Elephanta Caves	Whole	From 9 a.m. to 5-30 p.m. or sunset whichever is earlier
7.	Bombay	Poona	Karla	Caves of temples and inscriptions	Whole	From 9 a.m. to 5-30 p.m. or sunset whichever is earlier
8.	Delhi	Delhi	Delhi Zail (Shahja nabad)	Delhi Fort	Archaeological area	From 9 a.m. to 5-30 p.m. or sunset whichever is earlier
9.	Delhi	Delhi	Mehrauli Zail	Group of buildings at Hauz Khas	Garden	From sunrise to 10 p.m.
10.	Delhi	Delhi	Delhi Zail	Humayun's Tomb	Garden	From sunrise to 10 p.m.
11.	Delhi	Delhi	Delhi Zail	Kotla Firoz Shah	Garden	From sunrise to 10 p.m.
12.	Delhi	Delhi	Delhi Zail	Tomb of Khan Khanan	Garden	From sunrise to 10 p.m.
13.	Delhi	Delhi	Delhi Zail	Tomb of Safdarjang	Garden	From sunrise to 10 p.m.
14.	Delhi	Delhi	Mehrauli Zail	Qutb archaeological area	(i) Minar of Qutbuddin	(i) From 9 a.m. to 5-30 p.m. or sunset whichever is earlier

S. No.	State	District	Locality	Name of monument	Parts of monument which shall remain open during hours other than from sunrise to sunset	Hours of opening
1	2	3	4	5	6	7
15.	Madhya Pradesh	Chattarpur	Khajuraho	Western group of Temples	(ii) Garden Whole, except the Matangesvara Temple	(ii) From sunrise to 10 p.m. From 9 a.m. to 5-30 p.m. or sunset whichever is earlier
16.	Madhya Pradesh	Dhar	Bagh	Buddhist Caves	Whole	From 9 a.m. to 5-30 p.m. or sunset whichever is earlier
17.	Madhya Pradesh	Raisen	Sanchi	Buddhist Monuments	Whole	From 9 a.m. to 5-30 p.m. or sunset whichever is earlie
18.	Madras	South Arcot	Gingee	Fortress including monuments on Krishnagiri and Rajagiri Hills	Whole	From 9 a.m. to 5-30 p.m. or sunset whichever is earlier
19.	Mysore	Bangalore	Bangalore	Tipu Sultan's Palace	Garden	From sunrise to 10 p.m.
20.	Mysore	Bijapur	Bijapur	Gol Gumbaz	(i) The Mausoleum	(i) From 9 a.m. to 5-30 p.m. or sunset whichever is earlier
21.	Mysore	Mandya	Seringapattam	Daria Daulat Bagh	(ii) Garden (i) Palace	(ii) From sunrise to 10 p.m. (i) From 9 a.m. to 5-30 p.m. or sunset whichever is earlier
22.	Mysore	Mysore	Somanathpur	Kesava Temple	(ii) Garden Whole	(ii) From sunrise to 10 p.m. From 9 a.m. to 5-30 p.m. or sunset whichever is earlier

S. No.	State	District	Locality	Name of monument	Parts of monument which shall remain open during hours other than from sunrise to sunset	Hours of opening
1	2	3	4	5	6	7
23.	Rajasthan	Ajmer	Ajmer	Marble pavilion and balustrade on the Anasagar Bund and the ruins of the marble Hamam behind the Anasagar Dam	Whole	From sunrise to 10 p.m.
24	Uttar Pradesh	Agra	Agra	Agra Fort	Archaeological area	From 9 a.m. to 5-30 p.m. or sunset whichever is earlier
25.	Uttar Pradesh	Agra	Agra	Itimad-ud-Daula's Tomb	Garden	From sunrise to 10 p.m.
26.	Uttar Pradesh	Agra	Agra	Taj Mahal	Garden	From sunrise to 10 p.m., except on full-moon nights and two nights preceding and following when the opening hours shall be from sunrise to midnight
27.	Uttar Pradesh	Agra	Sikandara	Akbar's Tomb	(i) Second storey and upwards of the Mausoleum. (ii) Garden	(i) From 9 a.m. to 5-30 p.m. or sunset whichever is earlier (ii) From sunrise to 10 p.m.
28.	Uttar Pradesh	Lucknow	Lucknow	Residency Buildings	(i) Model Rooms (ii) Garden	(i) From 9 a.m. to 5-30 p.m. or sunset whichever is earlier (ii) From sunrise to 10 p.m.

SECOND SCHEDULE

Monuments or parts thereof entry into which can be had only on payment of fee

(vide rule 6)

S. No. 1	State 2	District 3	Locality 4	Name of monument 5	Parts of monument for which payment of fee is required 6
1.	Andhra Pradesh	Hyderabad	Hyderabad City	Char Minar	Second storey and upwards
2.	Bihar	Patna	Kumrahar	Site of Mauryan Palace	Whole
3.	Bihar	Patna	Nalanda (Burgaon)	All mounds, structures and buildings enclosed in the acquired area	Fenced area containing excavated remains
4.	Bombay	Aurangabad	Ajanta	Ajanta Caves	Whole
5.	Bombay	Kolaba	Gharapuri	Elephanta Caves	Whole
6.	Bombay	Poona	Karla	Caves of temples and inscriptions	Whole
7.	Delhi	Delhi	Delhi Zail (Shahjahanabad)	Delhi Fort	Archaeological area
8.	Delhi	Delhi	Mehrauli Zail	Qutb archaeological area	Minar of Qutbuddin
9.	Madhya Pradesh	Chattarpur	Khajuraho	Western group of Temples	Whole, except the Matangesvara Temple

S. No.	State	District	Locality	Name of monument	Parts of monument for which payment of fee is required
1	2	3	4	5	6
10.	Madhya Pradesh	Dhar	Bagh	Buddhist Caves	Whole
11.	Madhya Pradesh	Raisen	Sanchi	Buddhist Monuments	Whole
12.	Madras	South Arcot	Gingee	Fortress including monuments on Krishnagiri and Rajagiri hills	Whole
13.	Mysore	Bijapur	Bijapur	Gol Gumbaz	The Mausoleum
14.	Mysore	Mandya	Seringapattam	Daria Daulat Bagh	Palace
15.	Mysore	Mysore	Somanathpur	Kesava Temple	Whole
16.	Uttar Pradesh	Agra	Agra	Agra Fort	Archaeological area
17.	Uttar Pradesh	Agra	Sikandara	Akbar's Tomb	Second storey and upwards of the Mausoleum
18.	Uttar Pradesh	Lucknow	Lucknow	Residency Buildings	Model Room

8. The Antiquities and Art Treasures Act, 1972*

An Acts to regulate the export trade in antiquities and art treasures, to provide for the prevention of smuggling of, and fraudulent dealings in, antiquities, to provide for the compulsory acquisition of antiquities and art treasures for preservation in public places and to provide for certain other matters connected therewith or incidental or ancillary thereto.

Be it enacted by Parliament in the Twenty-third Year of the Republic of India as follows:

1. Short title, extent and commencement

(1) This Act may be called the Antiquities and Art Treasures Act, 1972.[1]

(2) It extends to the whole of India.

(3) It shall come into force on such date as the Central Government may, by notification in the *Official Gazette*, appoint and different dates may be appointed for different provisions of this Act and for different States and any reference in any such provision to the commencement of this Act shall be construed as a reference to the coming into force of that provision.

2. Definitions

(1) In this Act, unless the context otherwise requires,—

(a) "antiquity" includes—

(I) (i) any coin, sculpture, painting, epigraph or other work of art or craftsmanship;

(ii) any article, object or thing detached from a building or cave;

---

* Act No. 52 of 1972 (as modified up to April 1975) [9th September 1972]

(iii) any article, object or thing illustrative of science, art, crafts, literature, religion, customs, morals or politics in bygone ages;

(iv) any article, object or thing of historical interest;

(v) any article, object or thing declared by the Central Government, by notification in the *Official Gazette*, to be an antiquity for the purposes of this Act, which has been in existence for not less than one hundred years; and

(II) (a) any manuscript, record or other document which is of scientific, historical, literary or aesthetic value and which has been in existence for not less than seventy-five years;

(b) "art treasure"[2] means any human work of art, not being an antiquity, declared by the Central Government by notification in the *Official Gazette*, to be an art treasure for the purposes of this Act having regard to its artistic or aesthetic value:

Provided that no declaration under this clause shall be made in respect of any such work of art so long as the author thereof is alive;

(c) "export" means taking out of India to a place outside India;

(d) "licensing officer" means an officer appointed as such under section 15;

(e) "registering officer" means an officer appointed as such under section 15;

(f) "prescribed" means prescribed by rules made under this Act.

(2) Any reference in this Act to any law which is not in force in any area shall, in relation to that area, may be construed as a reference to the corresponding law, if any in force in that area.

3. Regulation of export trade in antiquities and art treasures

(1) On and from the commencement of this Act, it shall not be lawful for any person, other than the Central Government or any authority or agency authorised by the Central Government in this behalf, to export any antiquity or art treasure.

(2) Whenever the Central Government or any authority or agency referred to in sub-section (1) intends to export any antiquity or art treasure such export shall be made only under and in accordance with the terms and conditions of a permit issued for the purpose by such authority as may be prescribed.

4. Application of Act 52 of 1962

The Customs Act, 1962, shall have effect in relation to all antiquities and art treasures, the export of which by any person (other than the Central Government or any authority or agency authorised by the Central Government) is prohibited under section 3 save insofar as that Act is inconsistent with the provisions of this Act and except that (notwithstanding anything contained in section 125 of that Act) any confiscation authorised under that Act shall be made unless the Central Government on an application made to it in this behalf, otherwise directs.

5. Antiquities to be sold only under a licence

[As from the date of expiry of a period of six months from the commencement of this Act],[4] no person shall, himself or by any other person on his behalf, vary on the business of selling or offering to sell any antiquity except under and in accordance with the terms and conditions of a licence granted under section 8.[3]

Explanation—In this section and in sections 7, 8, 12, 13, 14, 17 and 18 "antiquity" does not include ancient and historical records other than those declared by or under law made by Parliament to be of national importance.

6. Appointment of licensing officers

The Central Government may, by notified order,—

(a) appoint such persons, being gazetted officers of Government, as it thinks fit, to be licensing officers for the purposes of this Act;

(b) define the limits of the area within which a licensing officer shall exercise the powers conferred on licensing officers by or under this Act.

7. Application for licence

(1) Any person desiring to carry on, himself or by any other person on his behalf, the business of selling or offering to sell antiquities may make an application for the grant of a licence to the licensing officer having jurisdiction.

(2) Every application under sub-section (1) shall be made in such form and shall contain such particulars as may be prescribed.

8. Grant of licence

(1) On receipt of an application for the grant of a licence under section 7, the licensing officer may, after holding such enquiry as he deems fit, grant

a licence to the applicant having regard to the following factors, namely:

(a) the experience of the applicant with respect to trade in antiquities;

(b) the village, town or city where the applicant intends to carry on business;

(c) the number of persons already engaged in the business of selling, or offering for sale of, antiquities in the said village, town or city; and

(d) such other factors as may be prescribed :

Provided that no licence shall be granted to the applicant if he is convicted to an offence punishable under the Antiquities (Export Control) Act, 1947 (31 of 1947), unless a period of ten years has elapsed since the date of conviction.

(2) Every licence granted under this section shall be on payment of much fees as may be prescribed.

(3) Every licence granted under this section shall be for such period, subject to such conditions and in such form and shall contain such particulars, as may be prescribed.

(4) No application for the grant of a licence made under section 7 shall be rejected unless the applicant has been given a reasonable opportunity of being heard in the matter.

9. Renewal of licence

(1) A licence granted under section 8 may, on an application made by the licensee, be renewed by the licensing officer for such period and on payment of such fees as may be prescribed.

(2) No application made under this section shall be rejected unless the applicant has been given a reasonable opportunity of being heard in the matter.

10. Maintenance of records, photographs and registers by the licensees

(1) Every holder of a licence granted under section 8 or renewed under section 9 shall maintain such records, photographs and registers, in such a manner and containing such particulars, as may be prescribed.

(2) Every record, photograph and register maintained under sub-section (1) shall, at reasonable times, be open to inspection by the licensing officer or by any other gazetted officer of the Government authorised in writing by the licensing officer in this behalf.

11. Revocation, suspension and amendment of licences

(1) If the licensing officer is satisfied either on a reference made to him in this behalf or otherwise that,—

(a) a licence granted under section 8 has been obtained by misrepresentation of an essential fact, or

(b) the holder of a licence has, without reasonable cause, failed to comply with the conditions subject to which the licence has been granted or has contravened any of the provisions of this Act or the rules made thereunder;

then, without prejudice to any other penalty to which the holder of the licence may be liable under this Act, the licensing officer may, after giving the holder of the licence an opportunity of showing cause, revoke or suspend the licence.

(2) Subject to any rules that may be made in this behalf, the licensing officer may also vary or amend a licence granted under section 8.

12. Persons whose licences have been revoked may sell antiquities to other licensees

Notwithstanding anything contained in section 5, any person whose licence has been revoked under section 11 may, after making a declaration before the licensing officer, within such period, in such form and in such a manner, as may be prescribed, of all the antiquities in his ownership, control or possession immediately before such revocation, sell such antiquities to another person holding a valid licence under this Act:

Provided that no such antiquity shall be sold after the expiry of a period of six months for the date of revocation of the licence.

13. Power of Central Government to carry on the business of selling antiquities to the exclusion of others

(1) If the Central Government is of opinion that with a view to conserving antiquities or in the public interest it is necessary or expedient so to do, it may, be notification in the *Official Gazette*, declare that with effect on and from such date as may be specified in the notification, the Central Government or any authority or agency authorised by the Central Government in this behalf shall alone be entitled to carry on the business of selling or offering for sale of antiquities.

(2) On the issue of a notification under sub-section (1),—

(a) it shall not be lawful for any person, authority or agency, other than the Central Government or any authority or agency authorised by the Central Government to carry on the business of selling or offering for sale any antiquity on and from the date specified therein;

(b) the provisions of this Act, in so far as they relate to the licensing of persons carrying on the business of selling or offering for sale of antiquities shall cease to have effect except as respects things done or omitted to be done before such cesser of operation and section 6 of the General Clauses Act, 1897 (10 of 1897), shall apply upon such cesser of operation as if those provisions had been repealed by a Central Act:

Provided that every licence granted under section 8 and in force on the date aforesaid shall, notwithstanding that the period specified therein has not expired, cease to be in force.

(3) Every person whose licence has ceased to be in force under the proviso to clause (b) of sub-section (2) shall, within such period, in such form and in such manner as may be prescribed, make a declaration before the licensing officer of all the antiquities in his ownership, control or possession immediately before the date specified in the notification issued under sub-section (1).

14. Registration of Antiquities

(1) The Central Government may, from time to time, by notification in the *Official Gazette*, specify those antiquities which shall be registered under this Act.

(2) In specifying the antiquities Registration of Antiquites under sub-section (1), the Central Government shall have regard to the following factors, namely :

(i) the necessity for conserving the objects of art;

(ii) the need to preserve such objects within India for the better appreciation of the cultural heritage of India;

(iii) such other factors as will, or are likely to, contribute to the safeguarding of the cultural heritage of India.

(3) Every person who owns, controls or is in possession of any antiquity specified in the notification issued under sub-section (1) shall register such antiquity before the registering officer—

(a) in the case of a person who owns, controls or possesses such antiquity on the date of issue of such notification, within three months of such date; and

(b) in the case of another person, within fifteen days of the date on which he comes into ownership, control or possession of such antiquity, and obtains a certificate in token of such registration.

15. Appointment of registering officers

The Central Government may, by notified order,—

(a) appoint such persons, as it thinks fit, to be registering officers for the purposes of this Act; and

(b) define the limits of the area within which a registering officer shall exercise the powers conferred on registering officers by or under this Act.

16. Application for registration and grant of certificate of registration

(1)[5] Every person required to register any antiquity before the registering officer under section 14 shall make an application to the registering officer for the grant of certificate of registration.

(2) Every application under sub-section (1) shall, in the case of such antiquites or class of antiquites as the Central Government may, by notification in the *Official Gazette* specify, be accompanied by such photographs of the antiquity which is to be registered and by such number of copies, not exceeding six, as may be prescribed and shall be made in such form and shall contain such particulars as may be prescribed.[4]

(3) On receipt of an application under sub-section (1), the registering officer may, after holding such enquiry as he deems fit, grant a certificate of registration containing such particulars as may be prescribed.

(4) No application made under this section shall be rejected unless the applicant has been given a reasonable opportunity of being heard in the matter.

17. Transfer of ownership, etc. of antiquities to be intimated to the registering officer

Whenever any person transfers the ownership, control or possession of any antiquity specified in any notification issued under sub-section (1) of section 14 such person shall intimate, within such period and in such forms as may be prescribed, the fact of such transfer to the registering officer.

18. Provisions of sections 14, 16 and 17 not to apply in certain cases

Nothing in section 14 or section 16 or section 17 shall apply to any antiquity kept—

(i) in a museum; or

(ii) in an office; or

(iii) in an archive; or

(iv) in an educational or cultural institution,[5]

owned, controlled or managed by the Government[6] [or by any local authority or by any such body as the Central Government may, for reason to be recorded in writing, approve for the purpose of this section by General or special order].

19. Power of Central Government to compulsorily acquire antiquities and art treasures

(1) If the Central Government is of opinion that it is desirable to preserve any antiquity or art treasure in a public place, that Government may make an order for the compulsory acquisition of such antiquity or art treasure.

(2) On the making of an order under sub-section (1) the Collector of the district in which such antiquity or art treasure is kept shall give notice to the owner thereof intimating him of the decision of the Central Government to acquire the same and it shall be lawful for the Collector to take possession of such antiquity or art treasure, for which purpose the Collector may use such force as may be necessary.

(3) Where the owner of any antiquity or art treasure the possession of which has been taken over by the Collector under sub-section (2) objects to the taking over of such possession, he may, within a period of thirty days from the date on which such possession was taken over, make a representation to the Central Government putting forth his objections:

Provided that the Central Government may entertain the representation after the expiry of the said period of thirty days, if it is satisfied that the owner of such antiquity or art treasure was prevented by sufficient cause from making the representation in time.

(4) On receipt of any representation under sub-section (3), the Central Government, after making such inquiry as it deems fit and after giving to the objector an opportunity of being heard in the matter, shall, within a period

of ninety days from the date of receipt of the representation, either rescind or confirm the order made by it under sub-section (1).

(5) Where any order made by the Central Government under sub-section (1) is rescinded under sub-section (4) the antiquity or art treasure shall be returned to the owner thereof without delay and at the expense of the Central Government.

(6) Where the order made by the Central Government under sub-section (1) is confirmed under sub-section (4) the antiquity or art treasure shall vest in the Central Government with effect from the date on which the possession thereof has been taken over by the Collector under sub-section (2).

(7) The power of compulsory acquisition conferred by this section shall not extend to any object, being an antiquity or art treasure, used for *bona fide* religious observances.

Explanation—In this section, "public place" means any place which is open to the use of the public, whether on payment of fees or not, or whether it is actually used by the public or not.

20. Payment of compensation for antiquities and art treasures compulsorily acquired under section 19

(1) Where any antiquity or art treasure is compulsorily acquired under section 19, there shall be paid compensation, the amount of which shall be determined in the manner and in accordance with the principles hereinafter set out, that is to say,—

(a) where the amount of compensation can be fixed by agreement, it shall be paid in accordance with such agreement;

(b) where no such agreement can be reached, the Central Government shall appoint as arbitrator a person who is, or has been, or is qualified for appointment as, a Judge of a High Court;

(c) the Central Government may, in any particular case, nominate a person having expert knowledge as to the nature of the antiquity or art treasure compulsorily acquired to assist the arbitrator and where such nomination is made, the person to be compensated may also nominate an assessor for the same purpose;

(d) at the commencement of the proceedings before the arbitrator, the Central Government and the person to be compensated shall state what, in their respective opinion, is a fair amount of compensation;

(e) the arbitrator shall, after hearing the dispute, make an award determining the amount of compensation which appears to him to be just and specifying the person or persons to whom such compensation shall be paid and in making the award he shall have regard to the circumstances of each case and the provisions of sub-section (2);

(f) where there is any dispute as to the person or persons who are entitled to the compensation, the arbitrator shall decide such dispute and if the arbitrator finds that more persons than one are entitled to compensation, he shall apportion the amount thereof amongst such persons;

(g) nothing in the Arbitration Act, 1940 shall apply to arbitration under this section.

(2) While determining the compensation under sub-section (1), the arbitrator shall have regard to the following factors, namely:

(i) the date or the period to which the antiquity or art treasure belongs;

(ii) the artistic, aesthetic, historical, architectural, archaeological or anthropological importance of the antiquity or art treasure;

(iii) the rarity of the antiquity or art treasure;

(iv) such other matters as are relevant to the dispute.

(3) The arbitrator appointed under sub-section (1), while holding arbitration proceedings under this section, shall have all the powers of a civil court, while trying a suit, under the Code of Civil Procedure, 1908, (5 of 1908) in respect of the following matters, namely:

(a) summoning and enforcing the attendance of any person and examining him on oath;

(b) requiring the discovery and production of any document;

(c) reception of evidence on affidavits;

(d) requisitioning any public record from any court or office;

(e) issuing commissions for the examination of witnesses.

21. Appeals against decisions of licensing officers and registering officers

(1) Any person aggrieved by a decision of a licensing officer under section 8 or section 9 or section 11 or by a decision of a registering officer under section 16 may, within thirty days from the date on which the decision is

communicated to him, prefer an appeal to such authority as may be prescribed :

Provided that the appellate authority may entertain the appeal after the expiry of the said period of thirty days, if it is satisfied that the appellant was prevented by sufficient cause from filing the appeal in time.

(2) On receipt of an appeal under sub-section (1), the appellate authority shall, after giving the appellant an opportunity of being heard, pass such orders as it deems fit.

22. Appeals against awards of arbitrators

Any person aggrieved by an award of the arbitrator made under section 20 may, within thirty days from the date on which the award is communicated to him, prefer an appeal to the High Court within whose jurisdiction he resides:

Provided that the High Court may entertain the appeal after the expiry of the said period of thirty days if it is satisfied that the appellant was prevented by a sufficient cause from filing the appeal in time.

23. Powers of entry, search, seizure, etc.

(1) Any person, being an officer of Government, authorized in this behalf by the Central Government, may, with a view to securing compliance with the provisions of this Act or to satisfying himself that the provisions of this Act have been complied with—

(i) enter and search any place;

(ii) seize any antiquity or art treasure in respect of which he suspects that any provision of this Act has been, is being, or is about to be, contravened and thereafter take all measures necessary for securing the production of the antiquity or art treasure so seized in a court and for its safe custody, pending such production.

(2) The provisions of sections 102 and 103 of the Code of Criminal Procedure, 1898 (5 of 1898) relating to search and seizure shall, so far as may be, apply to searches and seizures under this section.

24. Power to determine whether or not an article, etc. is antiquity or art treasure

If any question arises whether any article, object or thing or manuscript, record or other document is or is not an antiquity or is or is not an art treasure for the purposes of this Act, it shall be referred to the Director-General, Archaeological Survey of India, or to an officer not below the rank of a Director in the Archaeological Survey of India authorized by the Director-General, Archaeological Survey of India and the decision of the Director-General, Archaeological Survey of India or such officer, as the case may be, on such question shall be final.

25. Penalty

(1) If any person, himself or by any other person on his behalf, exports or attempts to export any antiquity or art treasure in contravention of section 3, he shall, without prejudice to any confiscation or penalty to which he may be liable under the provisions of the Customs Act, 1962 (52 of 1962), as applied by section 4, be punishable with imprisonment for a term which shall not be less than six months but which may extend to three years and with fine.

(2) If any person contravenes the provisions of section 5 or section 12 or sub-section (2) or sub-section (3) of section 13 or section 14 or section 17, he shall be punishable with imprisonment for a term which may extend to six months or with fine or with both and the antiquity in respect of which the offence has been committed shall be liable to confiscation.

(3) If any person prevents any licensing officer from inspecting any record, photograph or register maintained under section 10 or prevents any officer authorised by the Central Government under sub-section (1) of section 23 from entering into or searching any place under that sub-section, he shall be punishable with imprisonment for a term which may extend to six months, or with fine, or with both.

26. Cognizance of offences

(1) No prosecution for an offence under sub-section (1) of section 25 shall be instituted except by or with the sanction of such officer of Government as may be prescribed in this behalf.

(2) No court shall take cognizance of an offence punishable under sub-section (2) or sub-section (3) of section 25 except upon complaint in writing made by an officer generally or specially authorised in this behalf by the Central Government.

(3) No court inferior to that of a Presidency Magistrate or a Magistrate of the First Class shall try any offence punishable under this Act.

27. Magistrate's power to impose enhanced penalties.

Notwithstanding anything contained in section 32 of the Code of Criminal Procedure, 1898 (5 of 1898), it shall be lawful for any Presidency Magistrate or any Magistrate of the First Class to pass any sentence under this Act in excess of his power under section 32 of the said Code.

28. Offences by companies

(1) Where an offence under this Act has been committed by a company, every person who at time the offence was committed was in charge of, or was responsible to, the company for the conduct of the business of the company, as well as the company, shall be deemed to be guilty of the offence and shall be liable to be proceeded against and punished accordingly:

Provided that nothing contained in this sub-section shall render any such person liable to any punishment under this Act if he proves that the offence was committed without his knowledge or that he exercised all due diligence to prevent the commission of such offence.

(2) Notwithstanding anything contained in sub-section (1), where an offence under this Act has been committed with the consent or connivance of, or is attributable to, any neglect on the part of any director, manager, secretary or other officer of the company, such director, manager, secretary or other officer shall also be deemed to be guilty of that offence and shall be liable to be proceeded against and punished accordingly.

Explanation. — For the purpose of this section,–

(a) "company" means any body corporate and includes a firm or other association or individuals; and

(b) "director", in relation to a firm, means a partner in the firm.

29. Protection of action taken in good faith

No suit, prosecution or other legal proceeding shall lie against the Government or any officer of the Government for anything which is in good faith done or is intended to be done under this Act.

30. Application of other laws not barred.

The provisions of this Act shall be in addition to, and not in derogation of, the provisions of the Ancient Monuments Preservation Act, 1904 (7 of 1904), or the Ancient Monuments and Archaeological Sites and Remains Act,

1958 (24 of 1958), or any other law for the time being in force.

31. Power to make rules

(1) The Central Government may, by notification in the *Official Gazette*, make rules for the purpose of giving effect to the provision of this Act.

(2) In particular and without prejudice to the generality of the foregoing power, such rules may provide for—

(a) the authority for issue of permit under sub-section (2) of section 3;

(b) the form in which an application for the grant of a licence may be made under sub-section (1) of section 7 and the particulars which such application shall contain;

(c) the factors to which regard may be had while granting a licence under sub-section (1) of section 8;

(d) the fees on payment of which, the period for which, the conditions subject to which and the form in which a licence may be granted under sub-section (1) of section 8 and the particulars which such licence shall contain;

(e) the fees on payment of which and the period for which a licence may be renewed under sub-section (1) of section 9;

(f) the records, photographs and registers which are to be maintained under section 10 and the manner in which such records, photographs and registers shall be maintained and the particulars which such records, photographs and registers shall contain;

(g) the nature of the photographs of the antiquity and the number of copies thereof which shall accompany an application for the grant of a certificate of registration to be made under sub-section (1) of section 16 and the form in which such application may be made and the particulars which such application shall contain;

(h) the particulars which a certificate of registration granted under sub-section (3) of section 16 shall contain;

(i) the authority to which an appeal may be preferred under sub-section (1) of section 21; and

(j) any other matter which has to be or may be prescribed.

(3) Every rule made under this Act shall be laid, as soon as may be after it is made, before each House of Parliament while it is in session for a total period of thirty days which may be comprised in one session or in two or more successive sessions, and if, before the expiry of the session immediately following the session or the successive sessions aforesaid, both Houses agree in making any modification in the rule or both Houses agree that the rule should not be made, the rule shall thereafter have effect only in such modified form or be of no effect, as the case may be; so, however, that any such modification or annulment shall be without prejudice to the validity of anything previously done under that rule.

32. Repeal

(1) The Antiquities (Export Control) Act, 1947 (3 of 1947) is hereby repealed.

(2) For the removal of doubts it is hereby declared that every licence issued under section 3 of the Act repealed under sub-section (1) and in force at the commencement of this Act shall, notwithstanding that the period specified therein has not expired, cease to be in force.

33. Amendment of Act 24 of 1958

In the Ancient Monuments and Archaeological Sites and Remains Act, 1958,—

(i) in section 1, for sub-section (2), the following sub-section shall be substituted, namely:

"(2). "It extends to the whole of India";

(ii) after section 2, the following section shall be inserted, namely:

2-A. *Construction of references to any law not in force in the State of Jammu and Kashmir.* — Any reference in this Act to any law which is not in force in the State of Jammu and Kashmir shall, in relation to that State, be construed as a reference to the corresponding law, if any, in force in that State";

(iii) in section 23,—

(a) in sub-sections (2) and (4), for the words "compulsory purchase", the words "compulsory acquisition" shall be substituted.

(b) in such-section (3), for the words "compulsory purchase of any such antiquities at their market value", the words "compulsory acquisition of any such antiquities" shall be substituted;

(iv) in section 26,—

(a) in sub-section (1), for the words "compulsory purchase of such antiquity at its market value", the words "compulsory acquisition of such antiquity" and for the words "to be purchased", the words "to be acquired" shall be substituted;

(b) in sub-sections (2) and (3), for the words "compulsory purchase", the words "compulsory acquisition" shall be substituted;

(v) in section 28, for sub-section (2), the following sub-section shall be substituted, namely:

"(2)For every antiquity in respect of which an order for compulsory acquisition has been made under sub-section (3) of section 23 or under sun-section (1) of section 26, there shall be paid compensation and the provisions of sections 20 and 22 of the Antiquities and Art Treasures Act, 1972 shall, so far as may be, apply in relation to the determination and payment of such compensation as they apply in relation to the determination and payment of compensation for any antiquity or art treasure compulsory acquired under section 19 of that Act."

NOTES AND REFERENCES

1. Ministry of Education and Social Welfare (Archaeological Survey of India), Notification No. 135, New Delhi, the 5th April, 1976.

   G.S.R. 279 (E)--In exercise of the powers conferred by sub-section (3) of section I of the Antiquities and Art Treasures Act, 1972 (52 of 1972), the Central Government hereby appoints the date of publication of this notification in the *Official Gazette* as the date on which the said Act shall come into force in the whole of India (except the State of Sikkim).

2. The Gazette of India, Extraordinary Part II – Section 3 – Sub-Section (i), Department of Culture (Archaeological Survey of India), Notification

   No. 391, New Delhi, the 1st December, 1976.

   G.S.R. 904 (E): In exercise of the powers conferred by clause (b) of sub-section (1) of the Section 2 of the Antiquities and Art Treasures Act, 1972 (52 of 1972), the Central Government hereby declares the following human works of art, not being antiquities, to be 'art treasures' for the purposes of the said Act, having regard to their artistic and aesthetic value, namely:-

Paintings (including drawings, sketches, diagrams and the like) and objects of plastic art by

1. Rabindranath Tagore;
2. Amrita Shergil;
3. Jamini Roy; and
4. Nandalal Bose.

The Gazette of India, Extraordinary, Part II - Section 3 - Sub-Section (i), Archaeological Survey of India (Department of Culture), Notification

No. 252, New Delhi, the 10th August, 1979

G.S.R. 477 (E)—In exercise of the powers conferred by clause (b) of sub-section (i) of section 2 of the Antiquities and Art Treasures Act, 1972 (52 of 1972), the Central Government hereby declares the following human works of art, not being antiquities, to be 'art treasures' for the purposes of the said Act having regard to their artistic and aesthetic value, namely:

Paintings (including drawing, sketches, diagrams and the like) and objects of plastic art by

1. Ravi Verma;
2. Gaganendra Nath Tagore;
3. Abanindra Nath Tagore;
4. Sailoz Mookerjee;
5. N. Roerich.

3. "As from the date of expiry of a period of six months from the commencement of this Act, no person shall, himself or by any other person on his behalf, carry on the business of selling or offering to sell any antiquity except under and in accordance with the terms and conditions of a licence granted under section 8.

4. Every application under sub-section (1) shall, in the case of such antiquities or class of antiquities as the Central Government may, by notification in the *Official Gazette*, specify, be accompanied by such photographs of the antiquity which is to be registered and by such number of copies, not exceeding six, as may be prescribed and shall be made in such form and shall contain such particulars as may be prescribed.

5. The Gazette of India, Extraordinary, Part II – Section 3 – Sub-section (i), Department of Culture (Archaeological Survey of India), Notification

   No. 104, New Delhi, the 1st April 1977.

   G.S.R. 152 (E) - In exercise of the powers conferred by section 18 of the Antiquities and Art Treasures Act, 1972 (52 of 1972), the Central Government hereby approves the following bodies for the purposes of the said section, namely:

(i) Every University within the meaning of clause (f) of section 2 of the University Grants Commission Act, 1956 (3 of 1956).

(ii) Every college affiliated to any university referred to in item (i).

(iii) Every private school or institution (other than a school or institution which primarily imparts music or dance) affiliated to a Board established by or under any law.

Note : For the purposes of this item, the expression "private school or institution" means a school or an institution which is not owned, controlled or managed by the Government or by any local authority.

(iv) Shri Hemchandracharya Ganana Mandira, Patna, Gujarat.

(v) Asiatic Society of Bengal, Calcutta.

(vi) Bhandarkar Oriental Research Institution, Poona.

(vii) Vrindaban Research Institute, Vrindaban.

(viii) Bharat Itihasa Samshodhak Mandal, Poona.

(ix) Asiatic Society of Bombay.

(x) The Gujarat Museum Society, Ahmedabad.

(xi) Heras Institute of Indian History and Culture, Bombay

(xii) Rao Madho Museum Trust, Kote.

(xiii) B.J. Institute of Learning and Research, Ahmedabad.

(xiv) L.D. Institute of Indology, Ahmedabad.

(xv) Maharaja Sawai Man Singh II Museum, Jaipur.

(xvi) Anand Bhawan, Allahabad.

(xvii) Birla Archaeological and Cultural Research Institute, Hyderabad.

(xviii) I.V.K. Rajwade Sansodhan Mandal, Dhulia.

(xix) Ahmednagar District Historical Museum, Ahmednagar.

(xx) Birla Academy of Art and Culture, Calcutta.

(xxi) Ananda Niketan Kirtishala, Bagnan, District Howrah.

(xxii) The Ramakrishna Mission Institute of Culture, Calcutta.

(xxiii) Ramakrishna Mission Vidyapity, District Purulia.

6. Owned, controlled or managed by the Government or by any local authority or by any such body as the Central Government may, for reasons to be recorded in writing, approve for the purpose of this section by general or special order.

9. The Antiquities and Art Treasures Rules, 1973*

G.S.R. 405(E)—In exercise of the powers conferred by section 31 of the Antiquities and Art Treasures Act, 1972 (52 of 1972), the Central Government hereby makes the following rules, namely :

1. Short title and commencement

(1) These rules may be called the Antiquities and Art Treasures Rules 1973.

(2) They shall come into force in a State on the date on which the Act comes into force in the State.

2. Definitions

(a) "Act" means the Antiquities and Art Treasures Act, 1972;

(b) "form" means a form appended to these rules;

(c) "licensee" means a holder of a licence granted under the Act;

(d) "section" means a section of the Act.

[1]2-A. Reference to committee of experts for report as to artistic and aesthetic value of any human work of art

Where having regard to the nature and other matters pertaining to any human work of art which the Central Government proposed to declare to be an art treasure under Cl. *(b)* of Sec. 2 of the Act is alive the Central Government considers it necessary so to do, it may, by notification in the Official Gazette, constitute a committee consisting of not less than three persons having expert knowledge as to like works of art to consider and submit a report on the artistic and aesthetic value of the work of art so proposed to be declared.

---

* (Archaeological Survey of India, New Delhi, the 31st August 1973)

2-B. Notice for ascertaining whether the author of a work of art is alive

(1) With a view to determining whether the author of any human work of art which the Central Government proposes to declare to be an art treasure under Cl. *(b)* of Sec. 2 of the Act is alive the Central Government may, by notification in the official Gazette, give notice of its intention to make such declaration and require—

(a) that in case the author thereof is alive, he shall, within two months from the date of publication of the notification in the *Official Gazette*, communicate the fact and his address to the Central Government;

(b) that any other person knowing such author to have been alive within thirty years, to make known to the Central Government [2][within two months from the date of the publication of the notification in the Official Gazette] the name of the author and the fact of the author being alive and his address or, as the case may be, the date on which the author was last seen alive, and the last known address of the author.

(2) A copy of a notice published under sub-rule (1) may also be published in any Indian or Foreign newspaper or journal.

3. Authority competent to issue permits under sub-section (2) of section 3

The Director-General shall be the authority competent to issue permit under section 3 for the export of any antiquity or art treasure.

Explanation—For the purposes of this rule, the expression "Director-General" means the Director-General, Archaeological Survey of India and includes an officer not below the rank of the Director, Archaeological Survey of India, [3][duly authorized in this behalf by the Director-General].

4. Form of application for licence to carry on business of selling antiquities

Every application for a licence to carry on the business of selling or offering to sell antiquities, shall be made in Form I and shall be accompanied with a challan of Rs. 100/- in token of having paid the fee for the licence applied for.

5. Grant of licence under sub-section (1) of section 8

(1) On receipt of an application for a licence to carry on the business of selling or offering to sell the antiquities, the licensing officer shall, in addition to considering the factors mentioned in clauses (a), (b) and (c) of sub-section (1) of section 8 consider the *bona fide* intention of the applicant and if satisfied about such intention, may grant a licence to the applicant in Form II.

[4](2) Every licence granted under sub-rule (1) shall be valid for two years from the date of issue. This period of two years may be extended by one year by the licensing officer, if application for such extension is received by him at least two months before the date of expiry and [5][the licensee *(i)* has been submitting all the prescribed returns; *(ii)* has satisfactorily maintained all the prescribed records; and *(iii)* continues to comply with all the conditions laid down for the grant of licence]:

[6][Provided that an application for extension under this sub-rule may be entertained by the licensing officer even up to one month before the date of expiry if he is satisfied that the delay in applying for extension was due to circumstances beyond the control of the applicant].

6. Conditions of licence under rule 5

Every licence granted under rule 5 shall be subject to the following conditions, namely :

(a) the licence shall not be transferrable:

Provided that where a licensee transfers his business to another person, the transferee may, on an application made in [5][Form I-A] be granted a fresh licence, without payment of a licence-fee, for the unexpired period of the licence of the transferor, by the licensing officer, having to the factors mentioned in rule 5;

[7][Provided further that in the case of the death of licensee when the licensee is an individual, a fresh licence for the unexpired period of the licence can be granted in Form II-A without payment of any fee, to the legal heir of the late licensee subject to the condition that an application in Form I-A is made by the heir to the licensing officer [8][within three months of the date of death of the licensee], and the licensing officer is satisfied with the factors mentioned in rule 5, in regard to the applicant].

Note—The grant of a fresh licence under the second proviso shall not be deemed to affect the rights of any other person over the business of business premises of the deceased licensee to which such other person may be lawfully entitled.

[9](b) No licensee shall enter into partnership, or if the licensee is already a partner ship firm, into further partnership, in regard to the business covered by the licence:

(c) Where a firm in respect of which a licence is granted is dissolved, every person who was a partner of that firm immediately before the dissolution shall, within ten days of such dissolution send a report thereof to the licensing officer.

(d) Where a licensee carries on his business at more than one place, he shall obtain a separate licence for each place.

[10](e) No licensee shall shift his business covered by the licence to new premises during the currency of the licence. However, if he wants to do so, he may apply in Form I-A to the licensing officer and if the licensing officer is satisfied with the fact mentioned in Sec. 8 (*b*) of the said Act, in regard to the proposed premises, he may modify the licence accordingly. The modified licence shall be valid in regard to the new premises only from the date of such modification.

(f) The licensee shall if so required by the licensing officer permit the licensing officer's photographer to take photographs of antiquities in the possession of the licensee.

(g) The licensee shall cause his licence to be prominently displayed at his licensed premises.

(h) The licensee shall submit to the licensing officer in Form III, a monthly return of sales and acquisition of antiquities, within fifteen days of the expiry of the month to which the return relates and shall also, on demand, within such time as the licensing officer may specify, produce such records.

(i) Where a licence is revoked or suspended under the Act, the licensee shall not be entitled to any compensation for such revocation or suspension nor shall he be entitled to claim refund of any sum paid in respect of his licence.

[11](j) In case of termination of a licence/through expiry/dissolution of partnership, the ex-holders of the licence shall be allowed to antiquities in his/her/their possession on the date of termination to a licensee or recognized museum in India within six months of the date of termination of the licence provided the ex-holder of the licence has/have properly declared his/her/their stock in Form V laid down in conditions (*k*) and (*m*).

(k) Tow months before the date of expiry of a licence, every licensee shall send to the licensing officer a declaration of stock in From V and another declaration of stock in Form VI immediately after six months from the date of expiry.

(l) In the case of revocation of a licence for non-compliance with any condition for the grant of a licence, an ex-licensee shall submit a declaration of stock in From V to licensing officer within fifteen days of revocation.

(m) In the case of dissolution of a partnership firm, which holds a licence, every partner in the firm shall immediately on dissolution jointly, or severally, send to the licensing officer a declaration of stock in From V and another, or severally, send to the licensing officer a declaration of stock in From V and another declaration of stock in Form VI immediately after six months from the date of dissolution.

(n) A licensee who wants to surrender his licence shall apply in From X to the licensing officer. The application shall be accompanied by a declaration of stock in Form V. If the licensing officer is satisfied that there has been compliance with all the conditions of the licence by the licensee, he may accept the surrender and the licence shall be deemed to have terminated from the date of such acceptance. This shall not entitle the licensee to any compensation by way of refund of licence fee in any form.

(o) The licensee who has surrender his licence shall be allowed to sell the antiquities declared to another licensee or recognized museum in India up to six months from the date of acceptance of the surrender of his licence provided that on the expiry of such six months, he shall send to the licensing officer a declaration of stock in From VI.

7. Renewal of licence under sub-section (1) of section 9

On an application made by the licensee for the renewal of the licence and on payment of a fee of rupees fifty, the licence may be renewed [12][for further period of two years at one time]:

[13][Provided that such application is received by the licensing officer at least two months before the date of expiry of the licence and is a accompanied by a declaration of stock in From VI.]

8. Maintenance of records, photographs and register by licensee

Every licensee shall maintain the following records, namely:

(a) A register of antiquities [14][* * *] in Form IV separately for each category of antiquity for which he has been authorised to carry on business of selling or offering to sell; and

(b) photo albums separately for each category of antiquities having clear photographs in at least post-card size, pasted in the album together with a loose photograph bearing the serial number of his register.

9. Form of [15][declaration under section 12 and rule 7] and period within which it shall be made

Every person whose licence has been revoked under section 11 shall make before the licensing officer—

(a) a declaration in Form V, within fifteen days from the revocation of his licence; and

(b) a declaration in Form VI, immediately after a period of six months from the date of revocation of his licence.

10. Amendment of licence

A licence may be waived or amended by the licensing officer *suo motu* or on an application made in that behalf by the licensee :

Provided that no amendment or variation shall be made *suo motu* by the licensing officer unless the licensee has been given a reasonable opportunity of being heard in the matter.

11. Application for certificate of registration under section 16

(1) Every application for a certificate of registration under section 16 shall be made in Form VII to the registering officer having jurisdiction over the area in which the applicant resides.

(2) Every such application shall be accompanied by [16][three copies of photographs in post or quarter size] in sharp focus, of each antiquity in the applicant's possession, and if so required by the registering officer, by an equal number of photographs of different sides, or facets of such antiquity.

12. Form of certificate of registration under section 16

The certificate of registration under section 16 shall be granted in Form VIII.

13. Transfer of ownership

When any person transfers the ownership, control or possession of a registered antiquity to any other person, the transfer shall be intimated in Form IX by the transferor within fifteen days of the date of transfer to the registering officer having jurisdiction over the area where the transferor resides and also to the registering officer having jurisdiction over the areas where the transferee resides.

14. Appeal against a decision of the licensing officer or registering officer

Any person aggrieved by a decision of a licensing officer under section 8 or section 9 or section 11 or by a decision of a registering officer under section 16 may, within thirty days from the date on which the decision is communicated, prefer an appeal to the Director-General, Archaeological Survey of India.

15. Director-General to sanction prosecution[17]

The Director-General shall be the officer competent in terms of sub-section (1) of Sec. 20 of the Act, to institute, or to sanction institution of, prosecution for offences under sub-section (1) of Sec. 25 of the Act.

[18]**Note**—The declaration in Form V and VI referred to in conditions *(j)* to *(o)* of rule 6 and sub-rule *(b)* of 9, shall be made either by registered post or in person.

NOTES AND REFERENCES

1. Ins. by G.S.R 683 (E), dated the 6th December, 1979.
2. Ins. by G.S.R. 815 (E), dated the 2nd November, 1983, published in the *Gazette of India, Extraordinary*, Pt. II, Sec. 3 (*i*), dated 2nd November, 1983.
3. Added by G.S.R. 546 (E), dated the 30th November, 1978.
4. Subs. by *ibid.*
5. Subs. by G.S.R. 56 (E), dated the 10th February, 1981.
6. Ins. by *ibid.*
7. Subs. by G.S.R. 564 (E), dated the 30th November, 1978.
8. Ins. by G.S.R 56 (E), dated the 10th February, 1981.
9. Subs. by G.S.R 564 (E), dated the 30th November, 1978.
10. *Ibid.*
11. Ins. by *ibid.*
12. Subs. by G.S.R 564 (E), dated the 30th November, 1978.
13. Ins. by *ibid.*
14. Deleted by *ibid.*
15. Sus. by *ibid.*
16. Subs. by G.S.R 564 (E), dated the 30th November, 1978.
17. Ins. by *ibid.*
18. *Ibid.*

The Antiquities and Art Treasures Rules, 1973

FORM I

Application for Licence to carry on Business of Selling or Offering to sell Antiquities

(See rule 4)

1. Name and address of applicant/s.
2. Name and address of firm including its branches or collaterals and other names (*aliases*) and addresses during the last 10 years.
3. Names and addresses of partners, if any, including adult members of the family having an interest in, or share in, the business.
4. Address of showroom/sale premises.
5. Address of all godowns and repositories including residential premises of the constituents.
6. The period for which the applicant has been in business giving the details of his experience.
7. Whether the applicant/firm (including all constituents individually and jointly) was convicted of any offence punishable under the Antiquities (Export Control) Act, 1947 or in any other case involving theft or smuggling of antiquities. If so, details thereof may be stated.
8. Whether the applicant/firm (including all constituents individually or jointly) is a subject of prosecution/investigation/inquiry regarding the infringement of the Antiquities (Export Control) Act, 1947 or the theft of antiquities or art treasures.
9. Whether all stock up to the date of application has been entered in the applicant's register.
10. The village, town or city, including District and State, where the applicant intends to carry on the business.
11. Nature, i.e. details of the varieties of antiquities in which the applicant wishes to deal in, such as, stone sculptures, metal works, wood works, coins, paintings, jewellery and the like.
12. Category-wise list of all objects on hand claimed by the applicants to be antiquities including those which have been registered with registering office.
13. Proof of deposition of licence fee, i.e. treasury challan of Rs. 100 payable into the Account No............ bearing No........... dated........... to be attached.

14. I declare that the above information is correct and complete to the best of my knowledge and belief. I/We also undertake to observe the provisions of the Antiquities and Art Treasures Act, 1972, and the rules made thereunder.

I also enclose an attested** copy of the Income Tax Certificate for the preceding year (19............ 19............) and the Registration No. of the business establishment. I also undertake to intimate any change of address or acquisition of new godown within a week*. I also undertake to maintain such records, photographs and registers and furnish at my expense periodical returns with such particulars and photographs as may be required under the rules. I also undertake to make available every record, photograph and register maintained in this connection for the inspection of the licensing officer, or any other gazetted officer of Government authorized in writing by the licensing officer in this behalf.

Name and signature of the applicant.

Seal of the organization

Place ________________________________ Date ____________

* Any change of address has to be promptly (within a week of shifting) intimated to the licensing officer.

** To be attested by a gazetted officer with seal of office.

FORM I-A

[See rule 6]

Application for grant of a fresh licence for carrying on business of selling or offering to sell antiquities in lieu of one, the holder of which has died, or the holder (s) of which has/have transferred his/their business to other (s) or the holder (s) of which propose (s) to enter into partnership/further partnership.

1. Name and address of applicant/s.
2. Name and address of firm including its branches or collaterals and other names (*aliases*) and addresses during the last 10 years.
3. Names and addresses of partners, if any, including adult members of the family having an interest in, or share in the business.

   Note—In case this application is in consequence of proposed entry into, or proposed enlargement of the existing partnership, the required details should be applied separately for the existing holders and the proposed partners.
4. Address of showroom/sale premises.
5. Address of all godowns and repositories including residential premises of the constituents.
6. The period for which the applicant has been in business giving the details of his experience.
7. Whether the applicant/firm (including all constituents individually and jointly) was convicted of any offence punishable under the Antiquities (Export Control) Act, 1947, or in any other case involving theft or smuggling of antiquities. If so details thereof may be stated.
8. Whether the applicant/firm (including all constituents individually or jointly) is a subject of prosecution/investigation/inquiry regarding the infringement of the Antiquities (Export Control) Act, 1947, or the theft of antiquities or art treasures.
9. Whether all stock up to the date of application has been entered in the applicant's register.
10. The village, town or city, including District and State, where the applicant intends to carry on the business.

11. Nature, i.e., details of the varieties of the business which applicant wishes to deal in, such as stone sculptures, metal works, wood works, coins, paintings, manuscripts, jewellery and the like.
12. Category-wise list of all objects on hand claimed by the applicants to be antiquities including those which have been registered with registering officer.
13. Particulars of the licence in lieu of which a fresh licence is needed.
    - (a) No.
    - (b) Date
    - (c) Name(s) of the licensee
    - (d) Period with dates for which issued/renewed.
14. The circumstance in consequence of which this application has been made. (Death of the licensee/transfer of business/entry into partnership enlargement of the existing partnership). Proof must be furnished.
15. I /We declare that the above information is correct and complete to the best of my/our knowledge and belief. I/We also undertake to observe the provisions of the Antiquities and Art Treasures Act, 1972, and the rules made thereunder. I/We also enclose an attested copy of the Income Certificate for the preceding year (19............ 19............) and the Registration Number of the business establishment. I/We also undertake to intimate any change of address or acquisition of new godown within a week. I/We also undertake to maintain such records, photographs and registers and furnish at my/our expense periodical returns with such particulars and photographs as may be required under the rules. I/We also undertake to make available every records, photographs and registers maintained in this connection for the inspection of the licensing officer, or any other gazetted officer of Government authorized in writing by the licensing officer in this behalf.

Name and signature of the applicant.

Seal of the organization

Place ____ Date____________

To be attested by a gazettted officer with seal of officer. Any change of address has to be promptly intimated to the licensing officer.

The Antiquities and Art Treasures Rules, 1973

FORM II

Licence No.

Date of issue

Licence for Carrying on the Business of Selling or Offering to sell Antiquities

[See rule 5(1)]

Not Transferable

Whereas...............(son of)............ of (address) has applied for a licence for carrying on the business of selling or offering to sell antiquities and has undertaken to observe the provisions of the Antiquities and Art Treasures Act, 1972 and the rules made thereunder and has further deposited the sum of Rs. 100 (Rupees one hundred) only as required by the rules.

I ...., licensing officer, do hereby grant this licence under sub-rule (1) of rule 5 of the Antiquities and Art Treasures Rules, 1973 .... for the period of .... years with effect from..............

The licence is granted subject to the provisions of the said Act, and rules and is further subject to the following conditions:-

(1) Accordingly licensee will deal only in the following categories of antiquities. The area where the business will be carried on will be......................

(1) (5)

(2) (6)

(3) (7)

(4) (8)

Seal of office | Signature

Place | Name

Date | Licensing Officer
(Designation)

The Antiquities and Art Treasures Rules, 1973

FORM II A

(See rule 6)

Licence No.

Date of Issue

Licence for carrying on the business of selling or offering to sell antiquities, in lieu of one the holder of which had died or the holder(s) of which has/have transferred his/their business to other(s) or the holder(s) which propose(s) to enter into partnership/further partnership.

Whereas the holder(s) of licence No.............. dated.......... valid from........... to .... has/have died/transferred his/her/their business to other/propose(s) to enter into partnership/further partnership.

And whereas the heir/transferee proposed partners whose particulars are given below, has/have applied for the issue of a fresh licence in lieu of the licence aforesaid for the unexpired period of the licence aforesaid.

Name ....

Father's Name ....

Address ....

And whereas the applicants aforesaid have undertaken to observe the provisions of the Antiquities and Art Treasures Act, 1972 and the rules made thereunder, as amended from time to time.

I, ... licensing officer do hereby grant this licence under sub-rule (1) of rule (5) of the Antiquities and Art Treasures Rules, 1973 .... for the period with effect from.

The licence is granted subject to the provisions of the said Act, and rules and is further subject to the following conditions:-

(1) The licensee will deal only in the following categories of antiquities. The area where the business will be carried on will be...........

(1) (5)
(2) (6)
(3) (7)
(4) (8)

Seal of Office — Signature
Place — Name
Date — Licensing Officer

The Antiquities and Art Treasures Rules, 1973

FORM III

Name of the firm (Licensee) ... .

Monthly Return of Sales or Acquisition of Antiquities

[see rule 6 (h)]

For the month of ....

1. Serial Number (in the register)
2. Description of object with a photograph

*3. Address of person to whom sold.

1. Serial number (in the register)
2. Description of object with photograph
3. Address of person from whom acquired

Seal of Organisation

Date

Place

** Signature of Licensee

---

* The nationality of foreigners to whom an antiquity is sold together with their address in India and at home and passport number should be recorded.

** In the case of a firm, the signature of the head of the organization.

The Antiquities and Art Treasures Rules, 1973

FORM IV

Register of antiquities

[See rule 8(a)]

Antiquities such as stone sculpture/terracottas/metal objects/objects of bone and ivory/jewellery/woodwork/seals/coins/paintings/manuscripts and textiles.

1	2	3	4	5
Serial No.	Identification of objects and description	Material	Size	Approximate Age

6	7	8
Date of acquisition	Source of acquisition including the Name of the person/firm from whom acquired with address	Mode of acquisition

9	10	11	12
Price paid for acquisition	Registration No.	Date of registration if registered	Date of sale, if any

13	14	15
Name and address of person or firm to whom sold	Place where object is kept	Reference to photo album No.

16	17
Photo No. and page	Photographs in 6 x 6 cm size (To be pasted in the register)

* In the case of a foreigner, his address in India and at home and passport number should also be recorded.

The Antiquities and Art Treasures Rules, 1973

FORM V

Declaration of Stock

[See conditions under rule 6 (j), (k), (l), (m), (n), rule 7 (ii) and rule 9 (a)]

Particulars of objects (Category-wise)

1 Serial No. in the register	2 Identification and description of the object (registered or unregistered)	3 Material Size

4 Approximate age	5 Date of registration, if registered	6 Registration No.

I/We declare our stock of antiquities as here above on the date of the declaration.

Seal of the organization	Signature of Licensee
Place	Name of Firm
Date	Licence No........................

The Antiquities and Art Treasures Rules, 1973

FORM VI

Declaration of stock

[See conditions under rule 6 (k), (m), (o) and rule 9 (b)]

Particulars of objects sold out of the stock declared on........

1 Serial No. in the register	2 Description of the objects with photograph	3 The name and address of the licensed firms/ licensee to whom sold	4 Date of Sale

5 Price at which sold	6 Approximate age	7 Balance with details (registration No. etc.) of the object in hand

I/We hereby declare the stock of antiquities as here above held by me/ us on the date of making this declaration.

Seal of the organization

Place

Date

Signature of Licensee

Name of Firm

Licence No.......................

The Antiquities and Art Treasures Rules, 1973

FORM VII

Application for Registration of Antiquities

(See rule 11)

1. Name of applicant (person or firm)
2. Address of applicant (person or firm)
3. Identification and description of object with [three copies of photographs in post-card or quarter size].
4. Material
5. Size
6. Approximate date
7. Source of acquisition
8. Where the applicant has come into ownership, control or possession of any antiquity which is already registered under the Act, registration number of such antiquity and the name of registering officer, who had registered it.
9. Date of acquisition
10. Mode of acquisition
11. Price paid, if any
12. (a) Present location and (b) Condition of preservation and security.
13. If the antiquity is already registered under the Act, whether its registration certificate has been attached.

I declare that the above information is correct and complete to the best of my knowledge and belief. I also undertake to observe the provisions of the Antiquities and Art Treasures Act, 1972, and the rules made thereunder.

Seal of the Organization Signature

Place Name of the applicant

Date

1. If the application is on behalf of an organization, the name thereof should be given.
2. If the application is on behalf of an organization, the signature should be that of the head of that organization.

---

1. Subs. by G.S.R. 564 (E), datd the 30th Novermer, 1978.

The Antiquities and Art Treasures Rules, 1973

FORM VIII

Certificate of Registration of Antiquities

(See rule 12)

Whereas .... resident of .... has applied for registration of the antiquity/antiquities mentioned below, and has undertaken to observe the provision of the Antiquities and Art Treasures Act, 1972, and the rules made thereunder.

I ...., registering officer .... (Place) do hereby grant this certificate under section 16 of the said Act to the said .... for the object described below with .... authenticated photographs.

(1) Name of object

(2) Material

(3) Size (height and width)

(4) Approximate date

(5) Location

The certificate is granted subject to the provisions of the said Act and the rules made thereunder and is further subject to the condition that in the event of change of location of the antiquity from area of registration to another or its sale, the fact must be communicated by the owner to the registering officer, with the name and address of the person/firm to whom/which it was sold or gifted.

Seal of office	Signature
Place	Name of registering officer
Date	Designation

The Antiquities and Art Treasures Rules, 1973

Form IX

Transfer of Ownership

(See rule 13)

N.B. 1. This form must be completed (in triplicate) simultaneously with the transfer of ownership.

2. One copy shall be sent to registering officer concerned and the other two to the Director-General, Archaeological Survey of India, New Delhi, by registered post so as to reach them within ten days of transfer.

3. In case the object is an unregistered antiquity, each copy of this form shall be accompanied by a photograph (in sharp focus) of the object in postcard or quarter-size. If the sides of the object are decorated differently than the front, the photographs, as stated above, shall be sent in respect of each such side also in addition to the front side.

4. The responsibility for completion of the above formalities rests with the seller/giver if the object has been sold, gifted or donated; otherwise with the new owner of the object.

Section A (to be completed by the seller/giver)

1. Name of owner
2. Address of owner
3. *Licence No.
4. Serial No. in Register
5. Serial No. in Album
6. Name/Subject of object
7. Nature (e.g. sculpture, painting, manuscript, coins, etc.)
8. Whether it is registered?

If so—

(i) Name and Station of registering officer

(ii) Registration No.

9. Material

10. Size

Price offered	Signature of Owner
Place	Name (In block letter)
Date	as signed and Seal.

---

* Applicable in the case ofdealers only.

Section B (To be completed by the new owner)

1. Name
2. Complete Address (i) Present
   (ii) Permanent
3. Mode of acquisition
   (e.g. purchase, gift, inheritance, donation etc.)
4. Present location of object
5. Safeguards for preservation and security of the object
6. Nationality*
7. Passport No.*
8. Duration of stay in India*
9. Purpose of visit*

I hereby declare that the information given above by me is correct and complete to the best of my knowledge and belief. I undertake to observe the provisions of the Antiquities and Art Treasures Act, 1972, and the rules made thereunder as in force from time to time.

I am aware that the object now acquired by me is an antiquity, that it cannot be taken or sent out of the territorial limits of India except on the authority or a permit issued by Director General, Archaeological Survey of India and that any attempt to take or send out of India without such a valid permit is punishable under the law.

Station
Date

Signature
Name (in capital letters)
as signed.

---

* Applicable in the case of foreigners only.

The Antiquities and Art Treasures Rules, 1973

FORM X

Application for surrender of a licence for carrying on the business of selling or offering to sell antiquities.

[See rule 6 (n)]

1. Name of the applicant
2. Present address of the applicant
3. Particulars of the licence to be surrendered:
   (a) Number
   (b) Date
   (c) Name of the holder
   (d) Period with dates of validity
4. Reason for surrendering the licence.

I/We hereby declare my/our intention of surrendering the licence aforesaid, of which I/We/am/are holder(s) and am/are aware that on the acceptance of this surrender, I/We will not be entitled to any compensation by way of refund of licence fee or in any other form.

I/We hereby attach a declaration on Form V of the stock of antiquities held by me/us on the date of this declaration and hereby undertake to submit another declaration on Form VI immediately six months after the date of acceptance of this surrender.

Place — Signature and name of the applicant

Date — No. of licence

Seal of the firm

10. How's and Why's of Antiquities' Registration. Some Questions Answered*

1.Q. What's the object of the Act?

A. The object of the Act is threefold: to regulate the export trade in antiquities and art treasures; to provide for the prevention of smuggling of, and fraudulent dealing in antiquities; and to provide for the compulsory acquisition of antiquities and art treasures for preservation in public places. Besides, the Act also provides the Government power to take any other steps which are necessary for the country. One of the objects of the Act through the registration and licensing of dealers of antiquities is to prepare a National Register of Antiquities.

2.Q. What's the meaning of antiquity under the Act?

A. Under the Act any coin, sculpture, painting, epigraph or other work of art or craftsmanship, any article, object or thing detached from building or cave; any article, object or thing illustrative of science, art, crafts, literature, religion, customs, morals or politics in bygone ages; any article, object or thing declared by the Central Government, by notification in the *Official Gazette* to be an antiquity for the purpose of this Act, which has been in existence for not less than one hundred years, come under the category of antiquities. Apart from these, any manuscript, record or other document which is of scientific, historical, literary or aesthetic value and which has been in existence for not less than seventy-five years, is an antiquity.

3.Q. What is an art-treasure?

A. Any human work of art not being an antiquity, declared by the Central Government by notification in the *Official Gazette* to be an art-treasure for the purposes of this Act, provided the author of such work of art is not alive.

---

* A.S.I (Govt. of India) Press Information Bureau, New Delhi, Bhadra 12,1889, September 3, 1976.

4.Q. Does the Act ban private export of antiquities or art-treasures altogether?

A. Yes. No person other than the Central Government or any authority or agency authorised by the Central Government can export any antiquity or art treasure.

5.Q. What are the new export arrangements?

A. No arrangements have yet been formulated.

6.Q. What are the essential requirements of the Act in regard to registration and licensing?

A. For registration of antiquities every person who owns, controls or is in possession of any antiquity specified in the notification published in the Gazette of India, Extraordinary, or will be specified in the notification in the Gazette of India, Extraordinary, from time to time has to apply in a prescribed form (Form VII) along with three copies of photographs in quarter size (10 x 7.5 cm) of the object. In case of small antiquities, like terracottas, miniature metal-sculptures (maximum height and width may not exceed 15 cm and 7 cm respectively) three objects could be combined in one quarter size (10 x 7.5 cm) or six in one full size (16.5 x 21.6 cm) photograph. Normally, for each object, a separate application may be given. The applications are to be addressed to the Registering Officer of the area where the person resides. For obtaining licence any person who intends to carry on the business of selling or offering to sell antiquities may make an application for the grant of a licence to the Licensing Officer in whose area of jurisdiction the applicant who intends to carry on the business resides. The application is to be given in the prescribed form (Form I) and should be accompanied with a challan of Rs. 100/- (Budget-head in which the amount is to be paid is 078 Art & Culture: Other Receipts) in token of having paid the licensing fee and attested copy of the income-tax certificate for the preceding year. Besides, the dealer in antiquities will have to maintain a register of antiquities in the prescribed form (Form IV) for each category of antiquities for which he has been authorised and maintain photo albums separately for each category of antiquity having clear photographs at least in quarter size (10 x 7.5 cm) pasted in the album together with a loose photograph bearing the serial number of his register. The licensee shall also have to submit to the Licensing Officer in Form III a monthly return of sale and acquisition of antiquities within 15 days of the expiry of the month to which the return relates. It is also necessary that the antiquities specified for the purpose of registration should be registered with the Registering Officer of the area in the prescribed form.

7.Q. How many of these officers have been appointed and where are they based?

A. For registration purpose there are 104 posts of Registering Officers all over the country and for licensing 11 Licensing Officers have been appointed.

8.Q. Does the Government provide experts to help collectors or owners to determine whether or not what they held is an antiquity or art-treasure?

A. Government does not provide experts in determining whether an object is an antiquity or a non-antiquity. The owner may, however, informally seek the advice of the various experts committees that have been formed in States attached to the State Director of Archaeology & Museums, or the Experts Advisory Committees for the Export of Non-Antiquities at Bombay, Bangalore, Calcutta, Trivandrum, New Delhi, Patna, Madras and Srinagar.

9.Q. What's the procedure to procure such help?

A. The person may contact the Director of Archaeology & Museums of his State or the Convenors of the Expert Advisory Committees for the Export of Non-Antiquities at Bombay, New Delhi, Calcutta, Patna, Madras, Trivandrum, Bangalore and Srinagar for opinion.

10.Q. To whom should a person, possessing information about antiquities or art-treasures, report?

A. The information may be given to the Registering Officer of the area, the Superintendent Archaeologist of the Archaeological Survey of India or the Director-General of the Archaeological Survey of India, New Delhi, or the Directors of various State Departments of Archaeology and Museums.

11.Q. Will photographers be provided at all district and teshil headquarters?

A. No.

12.Q. Where can the forms to be filled in and copies of the Act be had in States and Union Territories?

A. Copies of the form for registration of antiquities can be obtained from the Registering Officer of the area or from the Director of Archaeology & Museums of the State where the owner of the antiquity resides. The copies of the Act are available with the booksellers authorised to sell Government publications. These forms are published in the Antiquities & Art Treasures Rules, 1973.

13.Q. What are the items of antiquities and art-treasures covered by the latest notification?

A. According to the latest notification in the Gazette of India the following antiquities which are more than one hundred years old are to be registered: (i) sculptures in stone, terracotta, metals, ivory and bone; (ii) paintings (including miniatures and tankas) in all media, that is to say, paper, wood, cloth, skin, silk and the like; (iii) manuscripts where such manuscripts contain paintings, illustrations or illuminations (that is adornment with coloured lettering or illustrations). So far no work of art has been declared as art-treasure.

14.Q. What's the deadline as of date for filling applications for private owners and the deadline for obtaining licence for traders?

A. The last date for registration of antiquities for the items included in the latest notification is October 1, 1976 and the last date for applying for licence to carry on the business of selling or offering to sell antiquities is October 4, 1976.

15.Q. Could you outline the entire procedure from ascertaining the antiquity of a piece to filling in the forms?

A. The owner of an object if he is in doubt about its age so as to determine whether it is an antiquity or not may consult the Registering Officer or the expert committee formed in most of the States to assist the Registering Officers or the Experts Advisory Committee for the Export of Non-Antiquities at Bangalore, Bombay, Calcutta, New Delhi, Patna, Srinagar, Madras and Trivandrum. In the form, simple mention of more than one hundred years or more than seventy-five years, as the case may be, will suffice, if the approximate or precise age of the object is not known.

16.Q. Is the Government proposing to categorize the antiquities and art-treasures so that some of them could be freely exported?

A. There is no proposal to categorise the antiquities or art-treasures. But repetitive types may be allowed to be exported through authorised agencies at some later stage.

17.Q. What's the provision for compulsory acquisition?

A. Compulsory acquisition of objects of national importance can be made only by paying just compensation to be arrived at by an agreement. Where no such agreement can be reached, the Central Government shall appoint an arbitrator. The power of compulsory acquisition will not be extended to any object used for *bon afide* religious observances.

18.Q. Is there any provision for payment of compensation?

A. Yes.

19.Q. Will the Act with its amendments be available in all regional languages?

A. English and Hindi editions of the Act are available.

20.Q. What's the position in regard to art-treasures? Are they subject to registration?

A. Art-treasures are not subject to registration.

21.Q. Now, about some points made by critics. Firstly, why insist on photographs and why four of them?

A. Photographs are the only authentic documents for the identification of an antiquity. No amount of description can be a substitute for a photograph. In the case of theft or smuggling, the only acceptable document is a photograph. Under a new order only three photographs in quarter size (10 x 7.5 cm) — one to be returned to the owner, one to be retained with the Registering Officer and the third copy for the Archaeological Survey of India for the National Register of Antiquities - are required.

22.Q. Has the Archaeological Survey of India been able to arrange for photographic documentation of its own sculptures and paintings? What's been the magnitude of the work involved?

A. The documentation of about 5,000 Centrally Protected Monuments and 31 Archaeological Museums under the control of the Archaeological Survey of India has already been taken up to build up the Central Registry of Antiquities. This involves complete photographic documentation and recording of data relating to sculptures, architectural fragments, whether loose or on a monument, excavated and explored antiquities from sites and the objects displayed or stored in the Archaeological Museums under the control of the Archaeological Survey of India.

23.Q. Has the Archaeological Survey of India any arrangement for checking the export of antiquities at airports and ports?

A. Yes, an archaeologist has been posted at all important international exit-points in Delhi, Calcutta, Bombay, Madras and Cochin to assist the Customs officials.

24.Q. In case of doubt, how's the antiquity of an article determined?

A. The antiquity of an article is determined in case of doubt by a committee consisting of experts specialised in the respective branches of art and archaeology.

25.Q. While preventing surreptitious export of antiquities, has the Archaeological Survey of India any plan to popularise abroad our cultural heritage?

A. Yes, there are already programmes for exchange of antiquities with different countries. Exhibitions of Indian art-objects have also been organised and are going to be organised in foreign countries. Documentaries on Indian art have been prepared and more will be prepared for this purpose. Books written by Indian authors and published in foreign countries help considerably in popularising our cultural heritage.

26.Q. What's been the public response to the Act, as of date, in terms of filing returns?

A. Nearly six thousand antiquities till July 1976 have been registered. We are aware that those with large collections are taking steps to register their antiquities. From the number of enquiries made it is expected that a large number of antiquities will be registered. Besides, there is still some time left for registration and as the last date will be approaching a large number of antiquities are expected to be registered.

27.Q. On the basis of the information in your possession, which are the first these one towns and cities in the order of their antiquitarian wealth?

A. Bombay, Delhi, Calcutta, Madras, Agra, Jaipur, Kottayam, Ahmedabad, Allahabad, Gaya and Visakhapatnam.

28.Q. Does the Act also provide for possible nationalisation of the trade in antiquities?

A. Yes.

29.Q. Are there any exemptions provided under the Act?

A. Museums, offices, archives, or educational or cultural institutions owned, controlled or managed by the Government or any other institution to be approved by the Central Government for the purpose are exempted from registering their antiquities.

30.Q. What are the penalties prescribed under the Act for non-compliance with the provisions?

A. If any person attempts to export any antiquity or art-treasure in contravention of the provisions of the Act he shall, without prejudice to any confiscation or penalty to which he may be liable under the provisions of the Customs Act 1962, be punishable with imprisonment for a term which shall not be less than six months but which may extend to three years and with fine.

If any person contravenes the provisions of registration or licensing, he shall be punishable with imprisonment for a term which may extend to six months or with fine or with both and the antiquity in respect of which the offence has been committed shall be liable to confiscation.

PART II
INTERNATIONAL CONVENTIONS

11. UNESCO Convention for the Protection of Cultural Property in the Event of Armed Conflict (The Hague, 1954)

The High Contracting Parties

Recognizing that cultural property has suffered grave damage during recent armed conflicts and that, by reason of the developments in the technique of warfare, it is in increasing danger of destruction;

Being convinced that damage to cultural property belonging to any people whatsoever means damage to the cultural heritage of all mankind, since each people makes its contribution to the culture of the world;

Considering that the preservation of the cultural heritage is of great importance for all peoples of the world and that it is important that this heritage should receive international protection;

Guided by the principles concerning the protection of cultural property during armed conflict, as established in the Conventions of The Hague of 1899 and of 1907 and in the Washington Pact of 15 April, 1935;

Being of the opinion that such protection cannot be effective unless both national and international measures have been taken to organize it in time of peace;

Being determined to take all possible steps to protect cultural property;

Have agreed upon the following provisions:

CHAPTER I

GENERAL PROVISIONS REGARDING PROTECTION

Article 1. Definition of cultural property

For the purposes of the present Convention, the term 'cultural property' shall cover, irrespective of origin or ownership :

(a) movable or immovable property of great importance to the cultural heritage of every people, such as monuments of architecture, art or history, whether religious or secular; archaeological sites; groups of buildings which, as a whole, are of historical or artistic interest; works of art; manuscripts, books and other objects of artistic, historical or archaeological interest; as well as scientific collections and important collections of books or archives or of reproductions of the property defined above;

(b) buildings whose main and effective purpose is to preserve and exhibit the movable cultural property defined in sub-paragraph (a) such as museums, large libraries and depositaries of archives, and refuges intended to shelter, in the event of armed conflict, the movable cultural property defined in sub-paragraph (a);

(c) centres containing a large amount of cultural property as defined in sub-paragraphs (a) and (b), to be known as 'centres containing monuments'.

Article 2. Protection of cultural property

For the purposes of the present Convention, the protection of cultural property shall comprise the safeguarding of and respect for such property.

Article 3. Safeguarding of cultural property

The High Contracting Parties undertake to prepare in time of peace for the safeguarding of cultural property situated within their own territory against the foreseeable effects of an armed conflict, by taking such measures as they consider appropriate.

Article 4. Respect for cultural property

1. The High Contracting Parties undertake to respect cultural property situated within their own territory as well as within the territory of other High Contracting Parties by refraining from any use of the property and its immediate surroundings or of the appliances in use for its protection for purposes which are likely to expose it to destruction or damage in the event of armed conflict; and by refraining from any act of hostility directed against such property.

2. The obligations mentioned in paragraph 1 of the present Article may be waived only in cases where military necessity imperatively requires such a waiver.

3. The High Contracting Parties further undertake to prohibit, prevent

and, if necessary, put a stop to any form of theft, pillage or misappropriation of, and any acts of vandalism directed against, cultural property. They shall refrain from requisitioning movable cultural property situated in the territory of another High Contracting Party.

4. They shall refrain from any act directed by way of reprisals against cultural property.

5. No High Contracting Party may evade the obligations incumbent upon it under the present Article, in respect of another High Contracting Party, by reason of the fact that the latter has not applied the measures of safeguard referred to in Article 3.

Article 5. Occupation

1. Any High Contracting Party in occupation of the whole or part of the territory of another High Contracting Party shall as far as possible support the competent national authorities of the occupied country in safeguarding and preserving its cultural property.

2. Should it prove necessary to take measures to preserve cultural property situated in occupied territory and damaged by military operations, and should the competent national authorities be unable to take such measures, the Occupying Power shall, as far as possible, and in close co-operation with such authorities, take the most necessary measures of preservation.

3. Any High Contracting Party whose government is considered their legitimate government by members of a resistance movement, shall, if possible, draw their attention to the obligation to comply with those provisions of the Convention dealing with respect for cultural property.

Article 6. Distinctive marking of cultural property

In accordance with the provisions of Article 16, cultural property may bear a distinctive emblem so as to facilitate its recognition.

Article 7. Military measures

1. The High Contracting Parties undertake to introduce in time of peace into their military regulations or instructions such provisions as may ensure observance of the present Convention, and to foster in the members of their armed forces a spirit of respect for the culture and cultural property of all peoples.

2. The High Contracting Parties undertake to plan or establish in peace-

time, within their armed forces, services or specialist personnel whose purpose will be to secure respect for cultural property and to co-operate with the civilian authorities responsible for safeguarding it.

CHAPTER II

SPECIAL PROTECTION

Article 8. Granting of special protection

1. There may be placed under special protection a limited number of refuges intended to shelter movable cultural property in the event of armed conflict, of centres containing monuments and other immovable cultural property of very great importance, provided that they:

(a) are situated at an adequate distance from any large industrial centre or from any important military objective constituting a vulnerable point, such as, for example, an aerodrome, broadcasting station, establishment engaged upon work of national defence, a port or railway station of relative importance or a main line of communication;

(b) are not used for military purposes.

2. A refuge for movable cultural property may also be placed under special protection, whatever its location, if it is so constructed that, in all probability, it will not be damaged by bombs.

3. A centre containing monuments shall be deemed to be used for military purposes whenever it is used for the movement of military personnel or material, even in transit. The same shall apply whenever activities directly connected with military operations, the stationing of military personnel, or the production of war material are carried on within the centre.

4. The guarding of cultural property mentioned in paragraph 1 above by armed custodians specially empowered to do so, or the presence, in the vicinity of such cultural property, of police forces normally responsible for the maintenance of public order shall not be deemed to be use for military purposes.

5. If any cultural property mentioned in paragraph 1 of the present Article is situated near an important military objective as defined in the said paragraph, it may nevertheless be placed under special protection if the High Contracting Party asking for that protection undertakes, in the event of armed conflict, to make no use of the objective and particularly, in the case of a

port, railway station or aerodrome, to divert all traffic therefrom. In that event, such diversion shall be prepared in time of peace.

6. Special protection is granted to cultural property by its entry in the 'International Register of Cultural Property under Special Protection'. This entry shall only be made, in accordance with the provisions of the present Convention and under the conditions provided for the Regulations for the execution of the Convention.

Article 9. Immunity of cultural property under special protection

The High Contracting Parties undertake to ensure the immunity of cultural property under special protection by refraining, from the time of entry in the International Register, from any act of hostility directed against such property and, except for the cases provided for in paragraph 5 of Article 8, from any use of such property or its surroundings for military purposes.

Article 10. Identification and control

During an armed conflict, cultural property under special protection shall be marked with the distinctive emblem described in Article 16, and shall be open to international control as provided for in the Regulations for the execution of the Convention.

Article 11. Withdrawal of immunity

1. If one of the High Contracting Parties commits, in respect of any item of cultural property under special protection, a violation of the obligations under Article 9, the opposing Party shall, so long as this violation persists, be released from the obligation to ensure the immunity of the property concerned. Nevertheless, whenever possible, the latter Party shall first request the cessation of such violation within a reasonable time.

2. Apart from the case provided for in paragraph 1 of the present Article, immunity shall be withdrawn from cultural property special protection only in exceptional cases of unavoidable military necessity, and only for such time as that necessity continues. Such necessity can be established only by the officer commanding a force the equivalent of a division in size or larger. Whenever circumstances permit, the opposing Party shall be notified, a reasonable time in advance, of the decision to withdraw immunity.

3. The Party withdrawing immunity shall, as soon as possible, so inform

the Commissioner-General for Cultural Property provided for in the Regulations for the execution of the Convention, in writing, stating the reasons.

CHAPTER III

TRANSPORT OF CULTURAL PROPERTY

Article 12. Transport under special protection

1. Transport exclusively engaged in the transfer of cultural property, whether within a territory or to another territory, may, at the request of the High Contracting Party concerned, take place under special protection in accordance with the conditions specified in the Regulations for the execution of the Convention.

2. Transport under special protection shall take place under the international supervision provided for in the aforesaid Regulations and shall display the distinctive emblem described in Article 16.

3. The High Contracting Parties shall refrain from any act of hostility directed against transport under special protection.

Article 13. Transport in urgent cases

1. If a High Contracting Party considers that the safety of certain cultural property requires its transfer and that the matter is of such urgency that the procedure laid down in Article 12 cannot be followed, especially at the beginning of an armed conflict, the transport may display the distinctive emblem described in Article 16, provided that an application for immunity referred to in Article 12 has not already been made and refused. As far as possible, notification of transfer should be made to the opposing Parties. Nevertheless, transport conveying cultural property to the territory of another country may not display the distinctive emblem unless immunity has been expressly granted to it.

2. The High Contracting Parties shall take, so far as possible, the necessary precautions to avid acts of hostility directed against the transport described in paragraph 1 of the present Article and displaying the distinctive emblem.

Article 14. Immunity from seizure, capture and prize

1. Immunity from seizure, placing in prize, or capture shall be granted to:

(a) cultural property enjoying the protection provided for in Article 12 or that provided for in Article 13;

(b) the means of transport exclusively engaged in the transfer of such cultural property.

2. Nothing in the present Articles shall limit the right of visit and search.

CHAPTER IV

PERSONNEL

Article 15. Personnel

As far as is consistent with the interests of security, personnel engaged in the protection of cultural property shall, in the interests of such property, be respected and, if they fall into the hands of the opposing Party, shall be allowed to continue to carry out their duties whenever the cultural property for which they are responsible has also fallen into the hands of the opposing Party.

CHAPTER V

THE DISTINCTIVE EMBLEM

Article 16. Emblem of the Convention

1. The distinctive emblem of the Convention shall take the form of a shield, pointed below, per saltire blue and white (a shield consisting of a royal-blue triangle above the square, the space on either side being taken up by a white triangle).

2. The emblem shall be used alone, or repeated three times in a triangular formation (one shield below), under the conditions provided for in Article 17.

Article 17. Use of the emblem

1. The distinctive emblem repeated three times may be used only as a means of identification of:

(a) immovable cultural property under special protection;

(b) the transport of cultural property under the conditions provided for in Articles 12 and 13;

(c) improvised refuges, under the conditions provided for in the Regulations for the execution of the Convention.

2. The distinctive emblem may be used alone only as a means of identification of :

(a) cultural property not under special protection;

(b) the persons responsible for the duties of control in accordance with the Regulations for the execution of the Convention;

(c) the personnel engaged in the protection of cultural property;

(d) the identity cards mentioned in the Regulations for the execution of the Convention.

3. During an armed conflict, the use of the distinctive emblem in any other cases than those mentioned in the preceding paragraphs of the present Article, and the use for any purpose whatever of a sign resembling the distinctive emblem, shall be forbidden.

4. The distinctive emblem may not be placed on any immovable cultural property unless at the same time there is displayed an authorization duly dated and signed by the competent authority of the High Contracting Party.

CHAPTER VI

SCOPE OF APPLICATION OF THE CONVENTION

Article 18. Application of the Convention

1. Apart from the provisions which shall take effect in time of peace, the present Convention shall apply in the event of declared war or of any other armed conflict which may arise between two or more of the High Contracting Parties, even if the state of war is not recognized by one or more of them.

2. The Convention shall also apply to all cases of partial or total occupation of the territory of a High Contracting Party, even if the said occupation meets with no armed resistance.

3. If one of the Powers in conflict is not a Party to the present Convention, the Powers which are Parties thereto shall nevertheless remain bound by it in their mutual relations. They shall furthermore be bound by the Convention, in relation to the said Power, if the latter has declared that it accepts the provisions thereof and so long as it applies to them.

Article 19. Conflicts not of an international character

1. In the event of an armed conflict not of an international character occurring within the territory of one of the High Contracting Parties, each party to the conflict shall be bound to apply, as a minimum, the provisions of the present Convention which relate to respect for cultural property.

2. The parties to the conflict shall endeavour to bring into force, by means of special agreements, all or part of the other provisions of the present Convention.

3. The United Nations Educational, Scientific and Cultural Organization may offer its services to the parties to the conflict.

4. The application of the preceding provisions shall not affect the legal status of the parties to the conflict.

CHAPTER VII

EXECUTION OF THE CONVENTION

Article 20. Regulations for the execution of the Convention

The procedure by which the present Convention is to be applied is defined in the Regulations for its execution, which constitute an integral part thereof.

Article 21. Protecting Powers

The present Convention and the Regulations for its execution shall be applied with the co-operation of the Protecting Powers responsible for safeguarding the interests of the Parties to the conflict.

Article 22. Conciliation procedure

1. The Protecting Powers shall lend their good offices in all cases where they may deem it useful in the interests of cultural property, particularly if there is disagreement between the Parties to the conflict as to the application or interpretation of the provisions of the present Convention or the Regulations for its execution.

2. For this purpose, each of the Protecting Powers may, either at the invitation of one Party, of the Director-General of the United Nations Educational, Scientific and Cultural Organization, or on its own initiative, propose to the parties to the conflict a meeting of their representatives, and

in particular of the authorities responsible for the protection of cultural property, if considered appropriate on suitable chosen neutral territory. The Parties to the conflict shall be bound to give effect to the proposals for meeting made to them. The Protecting Powers shall propose for approval by the Parties to the conflict a person belonging to a neutral Power or a person presented by the Director-General of the United Nations Educational, Scientific and Cultural Organization, which person shall be invited to take part in such a meeting in the capacity of Chairman.

Article 23. Assistance of Unesco

1. The High Contracting Parties may call upon the United Nations Educational, Scientific and Cultural Organization for technical assistance in organizing the protection of their cultural property, or in connexion with any other problem arising out of the application of the present Convention or the Regulations for its execution. The Organization shall accord such assistance within the limits fixed by its programme and by its resources.

2. The Organization is authorized to make, on its own initiative, proposals on this matter to the High Contracting Parties.

Article 24. Special agreements

1. The High Contracting Parties may conclude special agreements for all matters concerning which they deem it suitable to make separate provision.

2. No special agreement may be concluded which would diminish the protection afforded by the present Convention to cultural property and to the personnel engaged in its protection.

Article 25. Dissemination of the Convention

The High Contracting Parties undertake, in time of peace as in time of armed conflict, to disseminate the text of the present Convention and the Regulations for its execution as widely as possible in their respective countries. They undertake, in particular, to include the study thereof in their programmes of military and, if possible, civilian training, so that its principles are made known to the whole population, especially the armed forces and personnel engaged in the protection of cultural property.

Article 26. Translations, reports

1. The High Contracting Parties shall communicate to one another,

through the Director-General of the United Nations Educational, Scientific and Cultural Organization, the official translations of the present Convention and of the Regulations for its execution.

2. Furthermore, at least once every four years, they shall forward to the Director-General a report giving whatever information they think suitable concerning any measures being taken, prepared or contemplated by their respective administrations in fulfilment of the present Convention and of the Regulations for its execution.

Article 27. Meetings

1. The Director-General of the United Nations Educational, Scientific and Cultural Organization may, with the approval of the Executive Board, convene meetings of representatives of the High Contracting Parties. He must convene such a meeting if at least one-fifth of the High Contracting Parties so request.

2. Without prejudice to any other functions which have been conferred on it by the present Convention or the Regulations for its execution, the purpose of the meeting will be to study problems concerning the application of the Convention and of the Regulations for its execution, and to formulate recommendations in respect thereof.

3. The meeting may further undertake a revision of the Convention or the Regulations for its execution if the majority of the High Contracting Parties are represented, and in accordance with the provisions of Article 39.

Article 28. Sanctions

The High Contracting Parties undertake to take, within the framework of their ordinary criminal jurisdiction, all necessary steps to prosecute and impose penal or disciplinary sanctions upon those persons, of whatever nationality, who commit or order to be committed a breach of the present Convention.

FINAL PROVISIONS

Article 29. Languages

1. The present Convention is drawn up in English, French, Russian and Spanish, the four texts being equally authoritative.

2. The United Nations Educational, Scientific and Cultural Organization shall arrange for translations of the Convention into the other official languages of its General Conference.

Article 30. Signature

The present Convention shall bear the date of 14 May 1954 and, until the date of 31 December 1954, shall remain open for signature by all states invited to the Conference which met at The Hague from 21 April 1954 to 14 May 1954.

Article 31. Ratification

1. The present Convention shall be subject to ratification by signatory States in accordance with their respective constitutional procedures.

2. The instruments of ratification shall be deposited with the Director-General of the United Nations Educational, Scientific and Cultural Organization.

Article 32. Accession

From the date of its entry into force, the present Convention shall be open for accession by all States mentioned in Article 30 which have not signed it, as well as any other State invited to accede by the Executive Board of the United Nations Educational, Scientific and Cultural Organization.

Article 33. Entry into force

1. The present Convention shall enter into force three months after five instruments of ratification have been deposited.

2. Thereafter, it shall enter into force, for each High Contracting Party, three months after the deposit of its instrument of ratification or accession.

3. The situations referred to in Articles 18 and 19 shall give immediate effect to ratification or accessions deposited by the Parties to the conflict either before or after the beginning of hostilities or occupation. In such cases the Director-General of the United Nations Educational, Scientific and Cultural Organization shall transmit the communications referred to in Article 38 by the speediest method.

Article 34. Effective application

1. Each State Party to the Convention on the date of its entry into force shall take all necessary measures to ensure its effective application within a period of six months after such entry into force.

2. This period shall be six months from the date of deposit of the instruments of ratification or accession for any State which deposits its

instrument of ratification or accession after the date of the entry into force of the Convention.

Article 35. Territorial extension of the Convention

The High Contracting Parties may, at the time of ratification or accession, or at any time thereafter, declare by notification addressed to the Director-General of the United Nations Educational, Scientific and Cultural Organization, that the present Convention shall extend to all or any of the territories for whose international relations it is responsible. The said notification shall take effect three months after the date of its receipt.

Article 36. Relation to previous Conventions

1. In the relations between Powers which are bound by the Conventions of The Hague concerning the Laws and Customs of War on Land (IV) and concerning Naval Bombardment in Time of War (IX), whether those of 29 July 1899 or those of 18 October 1907, and which are Parties to the present Convention, this last convention shall be supplementary to the aforementioned Convention (IX) and to the Regulations annexed to the aforementioned Convention (IV) and shall substitute for the emblem described in Article 5 of the aforementioned Convention (IX) the emblem described in Article 16 of the present Convention, in case in which the present Convention and the Regulations for its execution provide for the use of this distinctive emblem.

2. In the relation between Powers which are bound by the Washington Pact of 15 April 1935 for the Protection of Artistic and Scientific Institutions and of Historic Monuments (Roerich Pact) and which are Parties to the present Convention, the latter Convention shall be supplementary to the Roerich Pact and shall substitute for the distinguishing flag described in Article III of the Pact the emblem defined in Article 16 of the present Convention, in cases in which the present Convention and the Regulations for its execution provide for the use of this distinctive emblem.

Article 37. Denunciation

1. A High Contracting Party may denounce the present Convention, on its own behalf, or on behalf of any territory for whose international relations it is responsible.

2. The denunciation shall be notified by an instrument in writing, deposited with the Director-General of the United Nations Educational,

Scientific and Cultural Organization.

3. The denunciation shall take effect one year after the receipt of the instrument of denunciation. However, if, on the expiry of this period, the denouncing Party is involved in an armed conflict, the denunciation shall not take effect until the end of hostilities, or until the operations of repatriating cultural property are completed, whichever is the later.

Article 38. Notifications

The Director-General of the United Nations Educational, Scientific and Cultural Organization shall inform the States referred to in Articles 30 and 32, as well as the United Nations, of the deposit of all the instruments of ratification, accession or acceptance provided for in Articles 31, 32 and 39 and of the notifications and denunciations provided for respectively in Articles 35, 37 and 39.

Article 39, Revision of the Convention and of the Regulations for its Execution

1. Any High Contracting Party may propose amendments to the present Convention or the Regulations for its execution. The text of any proposed amendment shall be communicated to the Director-General of the United Nations Educational, Scientific and Cultural Organization who shall transmit it to each High Contracting Party with the request that such Party reply within four months stating whether it:

(a) desires that a conference be convened to consider the proposed amendment;

(b) favours the acceptance of the proposed amendment without a conference; or

(c) favours the rejection of the proposed amendment without a conference.

2. The Director-General shall transmit the replies, received under paragraph 1 of the present Article, to all High Contracting Parties.

3. If all the High Contracting Parties which have, within the prescribed time-limit, stated their views to the Director-General of the United Nations Educational, Scientific and Cultural Organization, pursuant to paragraph 1 (b) of this Article, inform him that they favour acceptance of the amendment without a conference, notification of their decision shall be made by the Director-General in accordance with Article 38. The amendment shall become

effective for all the High Contracting Parties on the expiry of ninety days from the date of such notification.

4. The Director-General shall convene a conference of the High Contracting Parties to consider the proposed amendment if requested to do so by more than one-third of the High Contracting Parties.

5. Amendments to the Convention or to the Regulations for its execution, dealt with under the provisions of the preceding paragraph, shall enter into force only after they have been unanimously adopted by the High Contracting Parties represented at the Conference and accepted by each of the High Contracting Parties.

6. Acceptance by the High Contracting Parties of amendments to the Convention or to the Regulations for its execution, which have been adopted by the Conference mentioned in paragraphs 4 and 5, shall be effected by the deposit of a formal instrument with the Director-General of the United Nations Educational, Scientific and Cultural Organization.

7. After the entry into force of amendments to the present Convention or to the Regulations for its execution, only the text of the Convention or of the Regulations for its execution thus amended shall remain open for ratification or accession.

12. Review of the Convention for the Protection of Cultural Property in the Event of Armed Conflict (The Hague Convention of 1954): Extract—Patrick J. Boylan, 1993*

EXECUTIVE SUMMARY AND RECOMMENDATIONS

A. TO UNESCO, OTHER INTER-GOVERNMENTAL INTERNATIONAL ORGANISATIONS, ALL STATES PARTY TO THE 1954 HAGUE CONVENTION, NON-SIGNATORY COUNTRIES, AND INTERESTED NON-GOVERNMENTAL ORGANISATIONS

A.1. There have been many negative cases in more than one hundred wars and other armed conflicts that have occurred in different parts of the world since the adoption of the *Convention on the Protection of Cultural Property in the Event of Armed Conflict* and its supporting *Protocol* at The Hague in 1954, most recently in many parts of ex-Yugoslavia. In many of these wars and conflicts there have been serious losses of important cultural property and hence of the patrimony of all peoples. These losses have been due in most cases to the failure of parties in the various international and internal armed conflicts to comply with international law, and to both respect and positively safeguard physical evidence of the local, regional, national and international heritage.

A.2. Nevertheless, despite these apparent failures over the past forty years, the *Convention, Regulations and Protocol on the Protection of Cultural Property in the Event of Armed Conflict,* The Hague, 1954, are still entirely valid and realistic as international law, and remain fully applicable and relevant to present circumstances. The problem is essentially one of failure

---

* Report by City University, London, for UNESCO and the Government of the Netherlands, p. 248

in the application of the *Convention* and *Protocol* rather than of inherent defects in the international instruments themselves.

A.3. The 1954 *Convention* is so well established that it is now regarded as an integral part of Customary International Law,[1] and as falling within the category of International Humanitarian Law,[2] because of the intimate, and ever-closer, relationship between the physical evidence of the culture of a people and its national, culture, ethnic and spiritual identity.

A.4. Technical improvements to the detailed provisions of the *Convention* and *Protocol*, may perhaps be desirable in the long term. However, these are a far lower priority at this time than the overriding priority of achieving greater recognition, acceptance and application of their provisions. This is extremely urgent in view of the many cases, some highly-publicised, in which cultural property has been destroyed, damaged or looted in flagrant contravention of international law in both international and internal armed conflicts in recent years. Consequently, formal amendments to the *Convention* and *Protocol* are not recommended at the present time, though some points for possible future clarifications and improvements are identified in section G of these Recommendations.

A.5. No reasonable interpretation of the 1954 *Convention*, which deals specifically and exclusively with *cultural* heritage property of importance to humanity, would permit its extension to include natural heritage property of similar importance, even though both are covered by the UNESCO World Heritage Convention of 1972 (*Convention concerning the Protection of the World Cultural and Natural Heritage*). Incorporating the natural heritage in the provisions would require fundamental amendments to its basic objectives or, more likely, a completely new treaty.

A.6. As a first step in achieving greater recognition and more effective implementation of the 1954 *Convention*, it is essential that the number of States Party to it be greatly increased, since the effectiveness of any international law ultimately depends on the principle of universal acceptance.[3]

A.7. However, some of the most important provisions of the 1954 *Convention*—those relating to the concept of the pre-registered and internationally notified 'special protection' of localities of pre-eminent world cultural importance—have clearly not been effective because of the almost total failure of High Contracting Parties to submit proposals for 'special protection'. High priority must be given to making progress in this area, particularly (though by no means exclusively) by urging High Contracting Parties to the 1954 *Convention* to submit potentially eligible World Heritage Convention cultural sites for 'special protection' designation as 'centres containing monuments and other immovable cultural property of great importance'.[4]

A.8. In armed conflicts, whether international, inter-community or otherwise internal to a single sovereign state, in addition to unlawful action against protected cultural property there are all too often large numbers of civilian casualties or other cases of abuse of other aspects of international law and civilised values. It is inevitable that in such cases the human tragedies will usually attract greater international and media attention than the loss or damage of the physical patrimony. However, it is important that all parties recognise that in many recent cases the destruction of the physical evidence of the existence of national, ethnic and/or religious community under attack has been an integral part of the various types and levels of humanitarian abuse of the civilian peoples, through to the level of alleged genocide, as legally defined.[5] Consequently it is most important that all parties take urgent action to increase understanding of, and respect for, the culture, symbols and values of all peoples, especially of minority peoples.

B. TO UNESCO

B.1. The current policy of the Director-General of urging newly admitted Member States to adopt without delay (*inter alia*) the 1954 *Hague Convention* and *Protocol* is welcomed, and should be continued. In addition the Executive Board should immediately request Director-General to approach again every other non-signatory sovereign State recognised by the United Nations and/or UNESCO, whether or not they are UNESCO members, in accordance with Articles 31 and 32 of the *Convention*, urging them to adopt the *Convention*.

B.2. In addition to taking action in times of armed conflict either through the appointment of Commissioners-General or Special Representatives of the Director-General, UNESCO should appoint or nominate experts to serve as liaison and advisory officers in the field to commanders of United Nations Peace-keeping Forces in support of UN peace-keeping and peacemaking operations.

B.3. It is probably inevitable that in times of actual or threatened armed conflict international public opinion will focus attention on particularly famous and important sites: Angkor Wat in Cambodia, Dubrovnik in Crotia, Tyre in Lebanon. While World Heritage and other famous sites should certainly never be neglected, UNESCO and other international organisations, when under such pressure, should not restrict their actions and practical measures to such sites at the expense of more broadly based support for the wider cultural patrimony suffering serious damage or under threat in the region concerned.

B.4. There is a considerable body of practical information and experience, dating from at least the period of the Spanish Civil War and the Second World War onwards, on practical measures for the protection of monuments, museums, libraries, archive repositories, etc. in the face of the prospect of armed conflict. For example, the International Museums Office prepared for the International Institute of Intellectual Cooperation (in many respects UNESCO's predecessor under the League of Nations system), a very substantial practical handbook in the autumn of 1939, and especially UNESCO's own substantial Museums and Monuments Series Handbook by A. Noblecourt published in 1954 (French edition) and 1958 (English edition).[6] UNESCO should commission and publish up-to-date research and advice on practical protection measures, integrating this advice with recommendations on necessary practical measures for the prevention and mitigation of natural and civil disasters.

B.5. UNESCO should work closely with all relevant non-governmental international organisations, including all of the NGOs associated with UNESCO working in the field of material culture,[7] and with the International Committee of the Red Cross, in both developing and actively promoting such professional and technical advice.

B.6. One of the highest priorities for all international and national bodies in relation to both immovable and movable cultural property, and especially for UNESCO, must be to develop greater understanding of, and respect for, the great many different cultures and traditions of the different peoples of the world. Work towards this should include additional programmes of education and information for peoples of all ages, and especially within multi-ethnic and multicultural societies. Some of the greatest losses in recent armed conflicts have been the result of deliberate damage and destruction of the cultural evidence of the existence of enemy, or indeed just different, peoples.

B.7. In times of war and other armed conflict UNESCO should put additional resources into attempting to counter by all practicable means the prevailing negative cultural propaganda, particularly through the presentation of unbiased radio and television programmes both from ground stations and satellite stations.[8]

B.8. Pending any future revision or updating of the provisions of the 1954 *Convention* and *Protocol*, it is strongly recommended that the next General Conference of UNESCO should be asked to consider and adopt a substantial composite Resolution incorporating a series of practical Recommendations in relation to the Protection of Cultural Property in the Event of Armed Conflict, and in particular aimed at greatly improving the effectiveness and practical application of the 1954 *Convention* including:

1. a Recommendation urging all non-signatory Sovereign States of the world to adopt and implement in terms of national legislation and administrative procedures both the *Convention for the Protection of Cultural Property in the Event of Armed Conflict, The Hague, 1954*, and its *Protocol* without delay;
2. a Resolution urging that in view of the alarming scale or loss of movable cultural property from monuments, museums, libraries, archives and other depositaries of cultural property in times of both international and internal armed conflict, all High Contracting Parties to the 1954 Convention be urged to adopt both the 1954 *Hague Protocol* and the 1970 UNESCO *Convention on the Means of Prohibiting and Preventing the Illicit Import, Export and Transfer of Ownership of Cultural Property*, and to institute effective national and international measures to prevent trafficking in cultural material from war zones;
3. a Resolution establishing a UNESCO Intergovernmental Advisory Committee on the Protection of Cultural Property in the Event of Armed Conflict, constituted under Category II (Articles 18 - 20) of the UNESCO *Regulations for the general classification of the various categories of meetings convened by UNESCO*.[9] The Committee should follow in general terms the model of the World Heritage Committee,[10] though it would not have executive powers. The main purpose would be keep under review the effectiveness and implementation of the 1954 *Convention* and *Protocol*, to advise the Director-General, the General Conference, States Party to the Convention, as well as non-signatory sovereign states, on appropriate practice in relation to all aspects of the implementation of the *Convention* and more

generally on the Protection of Cultural Property in terms of Armed Conflict. The Intergovernmental Advisory Committee would in particular receive, review and formally publish the periodic reports of High Contracting Parties specified in Article 26(2) of the 1954 Convention, and would assist the Director General in relation to the training and education programmes referred to below. Draft terms of reference and outline rules of procedure for the proposed Advisory Committee are proposed in Appendix X of this Report;

4. authorization of plans for UNESCO to establish a programme of regional intergovernmental information/training seminars for both High Contracting Parties and non-signatory States in different parts of the world (perhaps one per year for five or six years), as it is clear that many of the non-signatory Member States of UNESCO and some High Contracting Parties are uncertain about what adopting and implementing 1954 *Convention* would mean in practical terms. This is particularly true of the large number of States in the Americas which in 1954 were already parties to the 1935 'Roerich Pact',[11] and of the many Member States in Africa, Asia and the Caribbean which became independent during the period of de-colonisation during the third quarter of the century;
5. a Resolution reminding all High Contracting Parties to the 1954 *Convention* of the importance of their obligation under Article 26 of the *Convention* to forward four-yearly reports to the Director-General on the 'measures being taken, prepared or contemplated... in fulfilment of ...' the *Convention* and Regulations.
6. a Recommendation proposing urgent new programmes of action to improve public understanding and tolerance in relation to the values of cultural property and cultural diversity, at both the international level through both UNESCO and relevant Non-Governmental Organisations, and at national, regional and local levels, through Member States, National Commissions for UNESCO, and educational and non-governmental organisations;
7. proposals for additions to UNESCO's Third Medium Term Plan, especially Programmes III.3 (Preservation and enhancement of the cultural heritage), VII.1 (Peace in the minds of men) and VII.2 (Human rights),[12] to provide additional staff and financial resources for necessary urgent action to enable UNESCO to respond more effectively to current crises, and to establish the proposed

programmes of regional intergovernmental information/training seminars and of public information and education;

8. authorization for UNESCO support of United Nations peacemaking and peace-keeping operations in areas of cultural importance through the appointment or nomination of appropriate experts to liaise with United Nations Force commanders in the field;
9. a Resolution calling on the United Nations to take appropriate action through the General Assembly, Security Council, Military Staff Committee and Secretary-General respectively to adopt the policies and role proposed for the United Nations in Section C of these Recommendations.

C. TO THE UNITED NATIONS

C.1. Historically, and even in recent times, disputes over issues relating to the physical evidence of the national, cultural and especially religious identities of peoples have been significant factors in the development and escalation of international disputes, and have even on occasion provided the final *casus belli* for international and civil wars. The United Nations should recognise that even in less extreme cases such issues can be potent factors in escalating conflicts, and in the promotion and spread of international and inter-community fear and hatred. They can, therefore, be a significant threat to the maintenance of peace and of both peacemaking and peace-keeping. Consequently, the implications of the possible threat to peace of such matters is an entirely proper consideration for the Security Council under its responsibilities relating to the 'Pacific Settlement of Disputes' and 'Threats to Peace' under Chapters VI and VII of the United Nations Charter (see also the current Secretary-General's 1992 *An Agenda for Peace*).[13]

C.2. In accordance with these principles, the United Nations should continue to support the efforts of UNESCO and the High Contracting Parties to the 1994 Convention in relation to promoting the understanding and recognition of the cultural dimension in international relations and in both international and internal armed conflicts;

C.3. In future, the United Nations should, as a matter of routine, seek expert advice through UNESCO on the cultural protection implications of proposals for action under Chapters VI and VII of the *Charter* in relation to threats to international peace, armed conflicts and peace-keeping.

C.4. In relation to the issue of possible 'cultural' war crimes in the former Yugoslavia, the Secretary-General of the United Nations should accept the offer of the Director-General of UNESCO to assist in this investigation of possible war crimes. In particular it is most desirable that the United Nations' team of experts investigating the complaints and allegations in respect of Yugoslavia should be augmented by the appointment of at least one expert in relevant cultural property issues.

C.5. The United Nations is urged to develop and present to the proposed International War Crimes Tribunal on cases relating to ex-Yugoslavia[14] some test cases in relation to war crimes against cultural property in violation of the provisions of the 1954 *Convention*, in order to determine the extent of the application and effectiveness of international law in such matters, and to establish precedents and examples in this respect.

C.6. The assistance of the United Nations in providing assistance to UNESCO official representatives undertaking duties in relation to the provisions of the 1954 *Convention* in some past peace-keeping (including Observer Mission) operations has been of great importance. The United Nations should in future provide such necessary facilities and logical support for UNESCO-appointed or-nominated experts on a regular basis. In addition to undertaking their functions on behalf of UNESCO and in relation to the 1954 *Convention*, where appropriate, such experts should also act as liaison and advisory officers in the field to commanders of United Nations Peace-keeping Forces, on the line successfully pioneered in the later stages of the Second World War in western and central Europe.

C.7. It is recognised that the training and other preparations for their missions of peace-keeping etc. forces allocated to the United Nations is primarily the responsibility of the military systems of the Member States providing the forces. However, it is most important that both officers and the ordinary troops engaged on peace-keeping missions should have adequate training in relevant international and national military and civilian law relating to cultural protection (and indeed in respect of the cultural, ethnic and religious values of the peoples of the country of the operation in question). The United Nations should develop standard minimum requirements in terms of training, briefing and/or the applicable national military operations manual, including issues relating to the protection of cultural property. Participating Member States should then be requested to ensure that forces allocated to United Nations operations are adequately trained and briefed in such matters, and that appropriate military discipline is maintained in relation to both the respecting of monuments and other cultural property, and the enforcement of relevant cultural property export laws and codes.

C.8. Because important cultural monuments and collections are frequently seen as amongst the clearest expressions of the identity and values of peoples, the United Nations should recognise as a form of humanitarian aid measures to provide emergency practical assistance, including the services of international experts and of essential measures such as the supply of specialised conservation materials and equipment required for the preservation of cultural property of international, national or other cultural importance damaged or threatened by armed conflict. Such essential assistance should not be subjected to undue restriction or delay under any United Nations sanctions regime.

C.9. In the context of the *Universal Declaration of Human Rights* (1948) and the 1992 *Declaration* of the United Nations in relation to the rights (including cultural rights) of minority peoples, and especially Articles 1, 4(2), and 4(4),[15] the United Nations should drawn up programmes of public information and education about cultural and ethnic diversity and respect for the cultures of all peoples, especially within multi-ethnic, multi-religious and multicultural societies.

D. TO ALL HIGH CONTRACTING PARTIES TO THE 1954 CONVENTION

D.1. Most High Contracting Parties to the 1954 *Convention* still have very much to do at the practical level to implement the solemn pledges they have given to the world community, and indeed to their own citizens, in their ratification of, or accession to, this important Treaty. Far more needs to be done at the practical level to meet the obligations that States Parties to the *Convention* have entered into in their acceptance of it. There are however some notable exceptions to this generalisation, though they number perhaps four or five at the most, for example, Austria, Switzerland and The Netherlands (and indeed in some respects the former Yugoslavia). These examples of serious and successful application of the practical provisions of the *Convention* show that the task is not a very onerous one in terms of either money or resources. Information on the practical measures taken needs to be shared more widely, for example through the proposed new UNESCO training/information seminar and publications programmes.

D.2. Particularly high priorities are the implementing of effective provisions within national military and civilian criminal law for the investigation and punishing of alleged 'cultural' war crimes and other offences by nationals and other residents of the State, and of active programmes of military and public education and information intended to increase knowledge and understanding of, and respect for, the protection of the cultural property and cultural values of all peoples.

D.3. In view of the grave losses of movable cultural property from areas affected by international wars and internal armed conflicts such as civil wars and inter-communal conflicts, high priority needs to be given to effective national administrative and criminal law measures to stop the international trafficking in stolen or otherwise illicitly acquired and transported cultural property from such war zones, in accordance with the spirit of the 1954 *Protocol* and the 1970 UNESCO *Convention on the Means of Prohibiting and Preventing the Illicit Import, Export and Transfer of Ownership of Cultural Property.*

D.4. All High Contracting Parties should review their arrangements for the training of military personnel of all levels in relation to their obligations under the *Convention* and other relevant aspects of international law. Member States participating in United Nations operations should ensure that the forces allocated to particular operations are adequately and specifically re-trained and briefed in such matters, and that appropriate military discipline is maintained in relation to the respect of monuments and other cultural property, and relevant cultural property export laws and codes.

D.5. All High Contracting Parties which are also parties to the 1972 *World Heritage Convention* should review each of the cultural localities within the State which are inscribed on the World Heritage List and consider whether they are eligible for the granting of 'Special Protection' as 'centres containing monuments' under Article 2(c) of the 1954 *Convention.*

D.6. All High Contracting Parties should note that in the absence of specific provisions for the resolution or enforcement of inter-governmental disputes or complaints concerning the interpretation and application of the 1954 *Convention* and *Protocol,* such matters may be referred to the International Court of Justice under Chapter XIV of the *Charter of the United Nations,* and specifically under Chapter II of the Statutes of the International Court of Justice annexed to the United Nations *Charter.*[16]

D.7. All High Contracting Parties should establish a national advisory committee to assist with the practical implementation of the 1954 *Convention* and *Protocol,* in accordance with Recommendation II of the

1954 Inter-governmental Conference.

E. TO ALL STATES WHICH ARE NOT YET PARTIES TO THE 1954 CONVENTION

E.1. All States which previously decided not to ratify or accede to the 1954 *Convention* and *Protocol*, or which have so far not considered accession to it should review their position in relation to the *Convention* as a matter of urgency, since such international instruments ultimately derive their authority from their universal acceptance by the world community.

E.2. The principles of the 1954 *Convention* should, nevertheless, be respected as Customary International Law, and as the successor and supplementary provisions and clarification of the principles established in earlier International Instruments, particularly the 1899 and 1907 *Hague Conventions* and the 1935 *Washington Treaty ('Roerich' Pact)*, and also as the applicable law in many parts of the world where their armed forces may be in action, e.g., as part of a United Nations peace-keeping operation.

E.3. Whether or not such States decide to ratify or accede to the 1954 *Convention*, they should take all necessary action to implement effective provisions within national military and civilian criminal law for the investigation and punishing of alleged 'cultural' war crimes and other offences by nationals and other residents of the State. They should also establish active programmes of military and public education and information intended to increase knowledge and understanding of, and respect for, the protection of the cultural property and cultural values of all peoples.

E.4. In particular, Member States participating in United Nations operations should ensure that the forces allocated to particular operations are adequately and specifically trained and briefed in their obligations under Customary International Law and in the 1954 *Hague Convention* (since this could very well be applicable law in the theatre of operations), and that appropriate military discipline is maintained in relation to the respect of monuments and other cultural property, and relevant cultural property export laws and codes.

F. TO NON-GOVERNMENTAL ORGANISATIONS

F.1. All non-governmental organisations and especially international NGOs in relationship with UNESCO operating in the tangible culture sector, and relevant regional organisations, should recognise the important role they can play in developing both practical advice and training procedures in relation to the protection of monuments and collections etc., within their respective fields of interest in the face of the risk of both natural and civilian disasters as well as armed conflicts. They should work closely with UNESCO in both developing and actively promoting at the professional level the measures that it has recommended to undertake under Recommendations B.3 to B.7 above.

F.2. The relevant international, regional and national non-governmental organisations, together with National Commissions of UNESCO, should take an active role in promoting knowledge and acceptance of the 1954 *Convention* and *Protocol* among their members and their governments, urging both the adoption and active implementation of their provisions, especially in countries which have not yet adopted the *Convention* and/or which have not yet taken the necessary legal and administrative measures required for its effective implementation.

F.3. Non-governmental organisations have the potential to play a most important role in providing direct assistance in terms of professional and technical labour, specialised equipment and materials for protection and emergency conservation, and for assisting with the temporary evacuation of important movable cultural property in times of actual or threatened armed conflict. The role of the voluntary sector could be especially crucial in those cases where international and governmental organisations are unable to offer such assistance because of the (unavoidable) political consequences, e.g., where the country is under a *de facto* government or administration which is not recognised as legitimate by the United Nations or other international organisations.

G. POSSIBLE FUTURE AMENDMENTS OF THE 1954 CONVENTION

G.1. As indicated above, although technical improvements to the detailed provisions of the *Convention* and *Protocol,* are certainly desirable in the long term, these are less urgent at this time than the overriding priority of achieving greater recognition, acceptance and application of their provisions in the face of current and continuing breaches on the one hand, and the comparatively low level of ratification on the other. Nevertheless, in the course of this study significant issues have been raised, which ought to be incorporated into the provisions of the 1954 Hague Instruments as soon as circumstances permit, probably by means of an *Additional Protocol,* rather than by a revision of the *Convention* itself, though that may be desirable in the future.

G.2. The present definition of 'cultural property' in the 1954 *Convention* is rather out-of-date and very imprecise. Subsequent UNESCO international instruments, particularly the 1970 and 1972 *Conventions*, and various UNESCO *Recommendations* have adopted more comprehensive and explicit definitions (though these others are not at all consistent in their wording)[17] In relation to future Instruments and policy statements it would be desirable for UNESCO to adopt a more consistent approach to definitions, subject of course to the special needs of the particular case. It would be desirable for UNESCO to adopt a more consistent approach to the question of definitions in future international instruments and policy statements. Also, in view of the growing importance of non-traditional catalogue and other record systems for both movable and immovable cultural property, in any future revision of, or *Additional Protocol* to, the 1954 *Convention*, the definition of 'cultural property' in Article 1 (a) the phrase 'or of reproductions of the property defined above' be replaced by *'or of paper, microform or electronic catalogues, documentation, or copies of the property defined above'.*

G.3. In the 1954 Convention, legal enforcement and action in respect of e.g. alleged 'cultural' war crimes, rest almost entirely with national governments and national legal systems. Further, there is no explicit provision in the *Convention* for the resolution of inter-governmental disputes about its application and interpretation,[18] and it would be desirable to establish some appropriate, relatively simple and quick, means of arbitrating on inter-governmental disputes relating to the application of the 1954 *Convention.*[19]

G.4. Bearing in mind the precedents of the 1949 *Geneva Conventions* the inclusion of the 'military necessity' exemption was already inappropriate by the time of the 1954 Intergovernmental Conference. It is strongly recommended that in any revision of the primary text of the 1954 Convention or in any new Additional Protocol to it, High Contracting Parties should renounce the provisions of Article 3(2) allowing the waiving of the provisions of the *Convention* in the case of military necessity.

G.5. It seems clear that the concept of 'Special Protection' in the *Convention* was devised primarily in order to protect a strictly limited number of permanent and temporary shelters and other 'refuges', though it is also possible for High Contracting Parties to propose for 'Special Protection' what are defined as 'centres containing monuments and other *immovable* cultural property of very great importance'. However, neither definition covers even the most important museums, libraries, archive repositories, etc., and 'Special Protection' for these can only be applied as well. Any future updating should revert to the precedents of the 1907 *Hague Convention* and the 1935 *Washington ('Roerich') Pact* and offer the possibility of 'ordinary' protection for important cultural institutions such as museums, important reference libraries, archives, etc., and also provide for the granting of 'Special Protection' to the world's greatest museums and similar institutions on the basis of the pre-eminent importance of their collections (providing, of course, it is possible in the case of either category to meet the other requirements for 'Special Protection' - particularly the demilitarising of the surrounding area).

G.6. The proposal that natural sites should be brought within a treaty which is explicitly defined (even within its title) as dealing only with 'cultural' sites raises very important issues. There are also major differences in the size and nature of the territory that might e.g., be brought under 'Special Protection': the examples of the two categories on the World Heritage List show that on average the geographical areas of territory involved are often of a quite different order of magnitude in many cases raising the very real possibility of serious military objections, which might in turn weaken the existing protection afforded by the 1954 *Convention*. It would seem more fruitful to try to reach agreement on a separate Convention for the protection of natural sites, with more appropriate provisions to meet the specialist requirements of natural sites.

G.7. There are currently serious problems in relation to the procedures for the appointment of Commissioners-General for Cultural Property in times of armed conflict, both in general and particularly in relation to situations where there are no nominated Protecting Powers. Changes in this area are needed, with the aim of making the Commissioner-General provisions enforceable on both parties to an armed conflict. However, achieving this would require solutions to difficult problems of international law, and the matter therefore needs to be considered by appropriate legal experts.

G.8. In order to improve the understanding and application of the *Hague Convention* there is a need for it to be supported by an Intergovernmental Advisory Committee on the Protection of Cultural Property in the Event of Armed Conflict, modelled on the World Heritage Committee. The proposed terms of reference and composition are outlined in Appendix X of this Report.

G.9. In terms of the mechanism for making such changes, the first five of these issues relating to the definitions in the *Convention*, to enforcement measures and the extension of the concept of 'Special Protection', and the establishment of the proposed Advisory Committee could probably be dealt with by means of the adoption of an *Additional Protocol*. However, the sixth, the suggested extension of the 1954 *Convention* to cover the natural heritage as well as the cultural heritage, would involve a fundamental change in its underlying purpose, and would probably require a completely new international instrument.

NOTES AND REFERENCES

1. See for example the views of the United States Department of Defence in its submission to Congress of 19 January 1993—Appendix VIII of this Report.
2. Although the relevant Nuremberg War Crimes trials, particularly that of Rosenberg, appeared on the surface to focus on issues of ownership, and hence might be regarded as relating to property law or private international law, the fact that the actions were brought as war crimes under customary law as expressed in, for example, the *Hague Conventions* placed the issue beyond doubt. Most recently this position has been re-affirmed by the United Nations Commission of Experts investigating alleged war crimes in ex-Yugoslavia (U.N. Doc. S/25274 dated 26 January 1993, p. 13) and senior United Nations officials in interviews on 24 February 1993. Report by City University, London, for UNESCO and the Government of the Netherlands, pp. 248.
3. Though there are now grounds for regarding the 1954 *Convention* as so well established that it can now be regarded as Customary International Law (see for example the views of the United States of America Department of Defence in its submission to Congress, 19 January 1993 - Appendix VIII of this report), formal ratification or accession and legislative implementation at the national level are clearly desirable, if only for the avoidance of doubt on its applicability.
4. The only major cultural complex currently on the list of five sites granted 'Special Protection' under chapter II of the 1954 *Convention* is the Vatican City: the others are all temporary refuges or war-time evacuation shelters. It must be recognised that many World Heritage List cultural sites may not be eligible for 'Special protectiong' because the Contracting Party concerned finds it impossible or impracticable to meet the conditions of the *Convention* because of their proximity to actual or potential legitimate military targets.
5. *Convention on the Prevention and Punishment of the Crime of Genocide, 1948.*
6. Noblecourt, 1954 & 1958: see also paras. 5.6 - 5.9 of this Report.

7. A non-exhaustive list of organisations which should be involved is given in the suggested composition of the proposed UNESCO Intergovernmental Advisory Committee on the Protection of Cultural Property in the Event of Armed Conflict—see Appendix X.

8. The UNESCO Radio tape service programme giving information on the 1991-92 bombardment of the World Heritage list city of Dubrovnik was an excellent example of what could be done in this respect.

9. Regulations adopted at the 14th, 18th and 25th sessions of the UNESCO General Conference (UNESCO *Basic Texts,* 1992, pp. 120-22).

10. UNESCO, 1972, *Convention concerning the Protection of the World Cultural and Natural Heritage,* Chapter III, Articles 8 - 10.

11. Washington Pact of 15 April 1935 for the *Protection of Artistic and Scientific Institutions and of Historic Monuments* (Roerich Pact).

12. UNESCO 1990. *Third Medium-Term Plan (1990-1995)* [25 C/4 Approved] [UNESCO, Paris].

13. United Nations, 1990 : particularly Articles 34 and 39 respectively; Boutros-Ghali, 1992, pp. 13-22.

14. Under Security Council Resolution 808 of February 1993.

15. United Nations *Declaration on the Rights of Persons Belonging to National or Ethnic, Religious or Linguistic Minorities* (General Assembly Resolution 47/135, dated 18 December 1992).

16. United Nations, 1990 (Doc. DPI/511).

17. See the comparison of definitions used in various UNESCO and other texts in Appendix VI.

18. Though there is of course always the possibility of recourse to the International Court of Justice in accordance with Chapter XIV of the United Nations *Charter.*

19. In the case of disputes between States Parties to the Convention whichw are also parties to the 1977 Geneva Protocols there is also the possibility of organising mediation through the International Committee of the Red Cross.

13. Recommendation for the Protection of Movable Cultural Property, 1978

The General Conference of the United Nations Educational, Scientific and Cultural Organisation meeting in Paris from 24 October to 28 November 1978, at its twentieth session,

Noting the great interest in cultural property now finding expression throughout the world in the creation of numerous museums and similar institutions, the growing number of exhibitions, the constantly increasing flow of visitors to collections, monuments and archaeological sites, and the intensification of cultural exchanges,

Considering that this is a very positive development which should be encouraged, in particular by applying the measures advocated in the Recommendation concerning the International Exchange of Cultural Property adopted by the General Conference at its nineteenth session in 1976,

Considering that the growing desire of the public to know and appreciate the wealth of the cultural heritage, of whatever origin, has nevertheless led to an increase in all the dangers to which cultural property is exposed as a result of particularly easy access or inadequate protection, the risks inherent in transport, and recrudescence, in some countries, of clandestine excavations, thefts, illicit and traffic acts of vandalism,

Noting that because of this aggravation of the risks, but also as a consequence of the increase in the market value of cultural items, the cost of comprehensive insurance in countries where there is no adequate system of governmental guarantees is beyond the means of most museums and is a definite impediment to the CV of international exhibitions and other exchanges between different countries,

Considering that movable cultural property representing the different cultures forms part of the common heritage of mankind and that every state is therefore morally responsible to the international community as a whole for its safeguarding,

Considering that States should accordingly intensify and give general effect to such measures for the prevention and management of risks as will ensure the effective protection of movable cultural property and, at the same time, reduce the cost of covering the risks incurred,

Wishing to supplement and extend the scope of the norms and principles laid down in this respect by the General Conference, in particular in the Convention for the Protection of Cultural Property in the Event of Armed Conflict (1954), the Recommendation on International Principles Applicable to Archaeological Excavations (1956), the Recommendation on the Most Effective Means of Rendering Museums Accessible to Everyone (1960), the Recommendation on the Means of Prohibiting and Preventing the Illicit Export, Import and Transfer of Ownership of Cultural Property (1964), the Convention on the Means of Prohibiting and Preventing the Illicit Import, Export and Transfer of Ownership of Cultural Property (1970), the Recommendation concerning the Protection, at National Level, of the Cultural and Natural Heritage (1972), the Convention concerning the Protection of the World Cultural and Natural Heritage (1972) and the Recommendation concerning the International Exchange of Cultural Property (1975),

Having before it proposals concerning the protection of movable cultural property,

Having decided, at its nineteenth session, that this question should take the form of a recommendation to Member States,

Adopts, this twenty-eighth day of November 1978, the present Recommendation.

The General Conference recommends that Member States apply the following provisions by taking whatever legislative or other steps may be required, in conformity with the constitutional system or practice of each State, to give effect within their respective territories to the principles and norms formulated in this Recommendation.

The General Conference recommends that Member States submit to it, by dates and in the form to be decided upon by the Conference, reports concerning the action taken by them in pursuant of this Recommendation.

1. DEFINITIONS

1. For the purposes of this Recommendation:

(a) "movable cultural property" shall be taken to mean all movable objects which are expression and testimony of human creation or of the evolution of nature and which are of archaeological, historical, artistic, scientific or technical value and interest, including items in the following categories :

(i) products of archaeological exploration and excavations conducted on land and under water;

(ii) antiquities such as tools, pottery, inscriptions, coins, seals, jewellery, weapons and funerary remains, including mummies;

(iii) items resulting from the dismemberment of historical monuments;

(iv) material of anthropological and ethnological interest;

(v) items relating to history, including the history of science and technology and military and social history, to the life of peoples and national leaders, thinkers, scientists and artists and to events of national importance;

(vi) items of artistic interest, such as,

paintings and drawings, produced entirely by hand on any support and in any material (excluding industrial designs and manufactured articles decorated by hand);

original prints, and posters and photographs, as the media for original creativity;

original artistic assemblages and montages in any material;

works of statuary art and sculpture in any material;

works of applied art in such materials as glass, ceramics, metal, wood etc.;

(vii) manuscripts and incunabula, codices, books, documents or publications of special interest;

(viii) items of numismatic (medals and coins) and philatelic interest;

(ix) archives, including textual records, maps and other cartographic materials, photographs, cinematographic films, sound recordings and machine-readable records;

(x) items of furniture, tapestries, carpets, dress and musical instruments;

(xi) zoological, botanical and geological specimens.

(b) "protection" shall be taken to mean the prevention and coverage of risks as defined below :

(i) "prevention of risks" means all the measures required, within a comprehensive protection system, to safeguard movable cultural property from every risk to which such property may be exposed, including those resulting from armed conflict, riots or other public disorders;

(ii) "risk coverage" means the guarantee of indemnification in the case of damage to, deterioration, alteration or loss of movable cultural property resulting from any risk whatsoever, including risks incurred as a result of armed conflict, riots or other public disorders whether such coverage is effected through a system of governmental guarantees and indemnities, through the partial assumption of the risks by the State under a deductible or excess loss arrangement, through commercial or national insurance or through mutual insurance arrangement.

2. Each Member State should adopt whatever criteria it deems most suitable for defining the items of movable cultural property within its territory which should be given the protection envisaged in this Recommendation by reason of their archaeological, historical, artistic, scientific or technical value.

II. GENERAL PRINCIPLES

3. The movable cultural property thus defined includes objects belonging either to the State or public bodies or to private bodies or individuals. Since all this property constitutes an important element of the cultural heritage of the nations concerned, the prevention and coverage of the various risks, such as damage, deterioration and loss, should be considered as a whole, even though the solutions adopted may vary from case to case.

4. The growing perils which threaten the movable cultural heritage should incite all those responsible for protecting it, in whatever capacity, to play their parts staff of national and local administrations in charge of safeguarding cultural property, administrators and curators of museums and similar institutions, private owners and those responsible for religious buildings, art and antique dealers, security experts, services responsible for the suppression of crime, customs officials and the other public authorities involved.

5. The co-operation of the public is essential for truly effective protection. The public and private bodies responsible for information and teaching should strive to instil general awareness of the importance of cultural property, the dangers to which it is exposed, and the need to safeguard it.

6. Cultural property is liable to deterioration as a result of poor conditions of storage, exhibition, transport and environment (unfavourable lighting, temperature or humidity, atmospheric pollution), which in the long run may have more serious effects than accidental damage or occasional vandalism. Suitable environmental conditions should consequently be maintained in order to ensure the material security of cultural property. The responsible specialists should include in the inventories data on the physical state of the objects and recommendations concerning the requisite environmental conditions.

7. The prevention of risks also calls for the development of conservation techniques and restoration workshops and the installation of effective protection systems in museums and other institutions possessing collections of movable cultural property. Each Member State should endeavour to ensure that the most suitable measures are taken in accordance with local circumstances.

8. Offences concerning works of art and other cultural property are increasing in some countries, most frequently being linked to fraudulent transfers across frontiers. Thefts and plunder are organized systematically and on a large scale. Acts of vandalism are also increasing. To combat these forms of criminal activity, be they of an organized nature or the action of individuals, strict control measures are necessary. Since fakes can be used for theft or the fraudulent transformation of authentic objects, measures must also be taken to prevent their circulation.

9. Protection and the prevention of risks are much more important than compensation in the event of damage or loss, since the essential purpose is to preserve the cultural heritage, not to replace by sums of money objects which are irreplaceable.

10. Because of the considerable increase in the risks resulting during transport and temporary exhibition, from environmental changes, inept handling, faulty packaging or other unfavourable conditions, adequate coverage against damage or loss is essential. The cost of risk coverage should be reduced through the rational management by museums and similar institutions of insurance contracts or by means of full or partial governmental guarantees.

III. MEASURES RECOMMENDED

11. In accordance with the principles and norms set out above Member States should take all necessary steps, in conformity with their legislation and constitutional system, to protect movable cultural property effectively and, in the case of transport in particular, should ensure the application of the necessary measures of care and conservation and the coverage of the risks incurred.

Measures for the prevention of risks: Museums and other similar institutions

12. Member States should take all necessary steps to ensure adequate protection for cultural property in museums and similar institutions. In particular, they should :

(a) encourage the systematic inventorying and cataloguing of cultural property, with the fullest possible details and in accordance with methods specially developed for the purpose (standardized fiches, photographs - and also, if possible, colour photographs - and, as appropriate, microfilms). Such an inventory is useful when it is desired to determine damage or deterioration to cultural property. With such documentation the necessary information can be given, with all due precautions, to the national and international authorities responsible for combating thefts, illicit trading and the circulation of fakes;

(b) encourage, as appropriate, the standardized identifications of movable cultural property using unobtrusive means offered by contemporary technology;

(c) urge the museums and similar institutions to reinforce the preventions of risks by a comprehensive system of practical security measures and technical installations and to ensure that all cultural property is kept, exhibited and transported in such a way as to protect it from all elements likely to damage or destroy it, including in particular heat, light, humidity, pollution, the various chemical and biological agents, vibration and shock;

(d) provide the museums and similar institutions for which they are responsible with the necessary funds for implementing the measures set out in subparagraph (c) above;

(e) take the necessary steps to ensure that all the tasks associated with the conservation of movable cultural property are carried out in accordance with the traditional techniques best suited to the particular cultural property and the most advanced scientific methods and technology; for the purpose, a suitable system for training and the vetting of professional qualifications should be established, in order to ensure that all those involved possess the required level of competence. The facilities for this should be strengthened or, if necessary, established. If appropriate, for the sake of economy, the establishment of regional conservation and restoration centres is recommended;

(f) provide suitable training for supporting staff (including security staff) and draw up guidelines for such staff, laying down standard for the performance of their duties;

(g) encourage regular training for protection, conservation and security staff;

(h) ensure that the staff of museums and similar institutions also receive the necessary training to enable them, in the event of disasters, to co-operate effectively in the rescue operations carried out by the competent public services;

(i) encourage the publication and dissemination to those responsible, if necessary in confidential form, of the latest technical and scientific information on all aspects of the protection, conservation and security of movable cultural property;

(j) issue performance standards for all security equipment for museums and public and private collections and encourage their application.

13. No effort should be spared to avoid giving in to ransom demands, so as to discourage the theft or illegal appropriation of movable cultural property carried out for that purpose. The persons or institutions concerned should consider ways and means of making this policy known.

Private Collections

14. Member States should also in conformity with their legislation and constitutional system, facilitate the protection of collections belonging to private bodies or individuals by:

(a) inviting the owners to make inventions of their collections, to communicate the inventories to the official services responsible for the protection of the cultural heritage and, if the situation requires, to grant access to the competent official curators and technicians in order to study and advice on safeguarding measures;

(b) if appropriate, providing for incentives to the owners, such as assistance for the conservation of items listed in the inventories or appropriate fiscal measures;

(c) studying the possibility of granting fiscal benefits to those who donate or bequeath cultural property to museums or similar institutions;

(d) entrusting an official body (the department responsible for museums or the police) with the organization of an advisory service for private owners on security installations and other protective measures, including fire protection.

Movable cultural property situated in religious buildings and archaeological sites

15. To ensure that movable cultural property situated in religious buildings and archaeological sites is suitably preserved and protected against theft and plunder, Member States should encourage the construction of installations for storing it and the application of special security measures. Such measures should be in proportion to the value of the property and the extent of the risks to which it is exposed. If appropriate, governments should provide technical and financial assistance for this purpose. In view of the special significance of movable cultural property situated in religious buildings, Member States and the competent authorities should endeavour to provide for the proper protection and presentation of such property where it is located.

International exchanges

16. Since movable cultural property is particularly exposed, during transport and temporary exhibition, to risks of damage which can arise from inept handling, faulty packaging, poor conditions during temporary storage or climate changes, as well as inadequate reception arrangements, special measures of protection are required. In the case of international exchanges Member States should:

(a) take the necessary measures to ensure that appropriate conditions of protection and care during transport and exhibition as well as adequate coverage of risks are specified and agreed on between the parties concerned. Governments through whose territory the cultural property will transit should provide assistance, if so requested;

(b) encourage the institutions concerned to s:

(i) ensure that cultural property is transported, packed and handled in accordance with the highest standards. The measures to be taken to this effect could include the determination of experts of the most appropriate form of packaging, as well as the type and timing of transport; it is recommended that, where appropriate, the responsible curator of the lending museum accompany the property during transport and certify its conditions; the institutions responsible for the shipping and packing of the objects should attach a list describing their physical appearance, and the receiving institutions should check the objects against those lists;

(ii) take appropriate measures to prevent any direct or indirect damage which might arise from the temporary or permanent overcrowding of the exhibition premises;

(iii) agree, where necessary, on the methods to be used for measuring, recording and regulating the degree of humidity in order to maintain the relative humidity within definite limits, and on the measures to be taken to protect light-sensitive objects (exposure to daylight, type of lamp to be used, maximum level of illumination in lux, methods used to measure and control this level);

(c) simplify the administrative formalities relating to the lawful movement of cultural property and arrange for appropriate identification of crates and other forms of packaging containing cultural property;

(d) take steps to protect cultural property in transit or temporarily imported for the purpose of cultural exchanges, and in particular facilitate rapid customs clearance in suitable premises, which should be situated close to, and if possible on, the premises of the institution concerned, and ensure that clearance is effected with all the desirable precautions; and

(e) whenever necessary, give instructions to their diplomatic and consular representatives to enable them to take effective action to accelerate customs procedures and ensure the protection of cultural property during transport.

Education and information

17. To ensure that the population as a whole becomes aware of the value of cultural property and of the need to protect it, particularly with a view to the preservation of their cultural identity, Member States should encourage the competent authorities at national, regional or local level to:

(a) provide children, young people and adults with the means of acquiring knowledge and respect for movable cultural property, using all available educational and information resources for that purpose;

(b) draw the attention of the public at large by every possible means to :

(i) the significance and importance of cultural property, but without stressing the purely commercial value of that property;

(ii) the opportunities available to them for participating in the activities undertaken by the competent authorities in order to protect such property.

Control measures

18. To combat thefts, illegal excavations, vandalism and the use of fakes, Member States should, where the situation demands, establish or strengthen services specifically responsible for the prevention and suppression of these offences.

19. Member States should, where the situation calls for it, take the necessary measures to :

(a) provide for sanctions or any appropriate measures, whether under the penal or civil or administrative or other measures, in the case of the theft, pillage, receiving or illegal appropriation of movable cultural property, and of damage intentionally caused to such property; these sanctions or measures should take into account the gravity of the offence;

(b) ensure better co-ordination between all services and sectors working for the prevention of offences concerning movable cultural property and organize a system of rapid dissemination of information on such offences, including information on fakes, among official bodies and the various sectors concerned, such as museum curators and art and antique dealers;

(c) ensure proper conditions for the safeguarding of movable cultural property by taking steps to counter the neglect and abandon to which it is very often exposed and which is conducive to its deterioration.

20. Member States should also encourage private collectors and art and antique dealers to transmit all information concerning fakes to the official bodies mentioned in paragraph 19(b).

Measures to improve the financing risk coverage: Governmental guarantees

21. Member States should:

(a) give special attention to the problem of covering adequately the risks to which movable cultural property is exposed during transport and temporary exhibition;

(b) in particular, consider instituting in any legislative, statutory or other form, a system of governmental guarantees such as those which exist in certain countries, or a system of partial assumption of the risks by the State or any community concerned with a view to covering an insurance franchise deductible or an excess of loss;

(c) within the framework of such systems and in the forms mentioned above, provide for compensation to lenders in the event of damage to, or the deterioration, alteration or loss of cultural objects loaned for the purpose of exhibition in museums or similar institutions. The provisions instituting these systems should specify the conditions and procedures governing the payment of such compensation.

22. The provisions concerning governmental guarantees should not apply to cultural property which is the object of transactions for commercial purposes.

Measures at the level of museums and similar institutions

23. Member States should also urge museums and other similar institutions to apply the principles of risks management, comprising the determination, classification, assessment, control and financing of risks of all kinds.

24. The risk management programme of all institutions which have taken out insurance should include the internal drafting of a procedures manual, periodic surveys on types of risks and the probable maximum loss, analysis of contracts and rates, market studies and a competitive bidding procedure. A person or body should be specifically entrusted with risk management.

IV. INTERNATIONAL CO-OPERATION

25. Member States should :

(a) collaborate with intergovernmental and non-governmental organizations competent in regard to the prevention and coverage of risks;

(b) strengthen at international level co-operation between official bodies responsible for the suppression of thefts and illicit trading in cultural property and for the discovery of fakes, and, in particular, urge these bodies to circulate rapidly among themselves, through machinery provided for this purpose, all useful information on illegal activities;

(c) if necessary conclude international agreements for co-operation in regard to legal aid and the prevention of offences;

(d) take part in the organisation of international training course in the conservation and restoration of movable cultural property, and in risk management, and ensure that they are regularly attended by their specialized staff;

(e) establish, in collaboration with the specialized international organizations, ethical and technical standards in the fields covered by the present recommendation and encourage the exchange of scientific and technical information, particularly on innovations relating to the protection and conservation of movable cultural property.

14. Final Act of the Diplomatic Conference for the Adoption of the Draft Unidroit Convention on the International Return of Stolen or Illegally Exported Cultural Objects

1. The Diplomatic Conference for the adoption of the draft Unidroit Convention on the International Return of Stolen or Illegally Exported Cultural Objects was held in Rome, Italy from 7 to 24 June 1995.

2. Representatives of 70 States participated in the Conference, namely representatives of:

the Republic of Albania; the People's Democratic Republic of Algeria; the Republic of Angola; the Argentine Republic; Australia; the Republic of Austria; the Republic of Belarus; the Kingdom of Belgium; the Republic of Bolivia; the Federative Republic of Brazil; the Republic of Bulgaria; Burkina Faso; the Kingdom of Cambodia; the Republic of Cameroon; Canada; the People's Republic of China; the Republic of Colombia; the Republic of Cote d'lvoire; the Republic of Croatia; the Republic of Cyprus; the Czech Republic; the Kingdom of Denmark; the Republic of Ecuador; the Arab Republic of Egypt; the Republic of Finland; the French Republic; the Republic of Georgia; the Federal Republic of Germany; the Republic of Guinea; the Hellenic Republic; the Holy See; the Republic of Hungary; the Republic of India; the Islamic Republic of Iran; Ireland; the State of Israel; the Italian Republic; Japan; the State of Kuwait; the Socialist People's Libyan Arab Jamahiriya; the Republic of Lithuania; the Grand Duchy of Luxembourg; the Republic of Malta; the United Mexican States; the Kingdom of Morocco; the Union of Myanmar; the Kingdom of the Netherlands; the Federal Republic of Nigeria; the Kingdom of Norway; the Islamic Republic of Pakistan; the Republic of Paraguay; the Republic of Peru; the Republic of Poland; the Portuguese

Republic; the Republic of Korea; Romania; the Russian Federation; the Republic of Slovenia; the Republic of South Africa; the Kingdom of Spain; the Kingdom of Sweden; the Swiss Confederation; the Kingdom of Thailand; the Republic of Tunisia; the Republic of Turkey; Ukraine; the United Kingdom of Great Britain and Northern Ireland; the United States of America; the Republic of Yemen; the Republic of Zambia.

3. Eight States sent observers to the Conference, namely:

the Republic of Bosnia-Herzegovina; the Republic of Ghana; the Republic of Guatemala; the Republic of Honduras; the Heshemite Kingdom of Jordan; the Kingdom of Saudi Arabia; the Syrian Arab Republic; the Republic of Venezuela.

4. The following intergovernmental Organisations were represented by observers at the Conference:

the Commission of the European Communities

the Council of Europe

the Council of the European Union

The Hague Conference on Private International Law

the International Centre for the Study of the Preservation and the Restoration of Cultural Property

the International Criminal Police Organization

the United Nations Educational, Scientific and Cultural Organisation.

5. The following international non-governmental Organisations were represented by observers at the Conference:

the International Association of Lawyers

the International Bar Association

the International Council on Archives

the International Law Association

the International Union of Latin Notariat.

6. The following international professional association was represented by observers at the Conference:

the International Association of Dealers in Ancient Art.

7. The Sovereign Military Order of Malta was represented by an observer at the Conference.

8. The Conference elected Mr. Walter Gardini (Italy) as President.

9. The Conference elected as Vice-Presidents the following representatives :

Mr. M. Ghomrasni (Tunisia)

Mr. A.G. Khodakov (Russian Federation)

Mr. M. Kima Tabong (Cameroon)

Mr. J. Sánchez Cordero Dávila (Mexico)

Mr. A. Wichiencharoen (Thailand).

10. The following committees were set up by the Conference:

Steering Committee

Chair : The President of the Conference

Members : The President and the Vice-Presidents of the Conference and the Chair of the Committee of the Whole

In addition the Secretary-General of the Conference participated in the work of the Steering Committee, at the invitation of the Chair

Committee of the Whole

Chair : Mr. P. Lalive (Switzerland)

First Vice-Chair : Ms. V. Hughes (Canada)

Second Vice-Chair: Mr. A. Beksta (Lithuania)

Final Clauses Committee

Chair : Mr. V. Marotta Rangel (Brazil)

Vice-Chair : Mr. I. Zimba Chabala (Zambia)

Drafting Committee

Chair : Ms. R. Balkin (Australia)

Members : Australia; China; Egypt; Finland; France; Nigeria; Portugal; Turkey; United States of America.

Credentials Committee

Chair : Mr. N. Peri (Argentina)

Members : Argentina; Czech Republic; France; Guinea; Pakistan

11. The Secretary-General of the Conference was Mr. M. Evans, Secretary-General of Unidroit.

12. The basic working materials used by the Conference and its organs were the draft Unidroit Convention on the international return of stolen or illegally exported cultural objects as adopted by a Unidroit committee of governmental experts on 8 October 1993 with an explanatory report prepared by the Unidroit Secretariat (CONF. 8/3) and the draft final provisions capable of embodiment in the draft Unidroit Convention on the international return of stolen or illegally exported cultural objects with explanatory notes drawn up by the Unidroit Secretariat (CONF. 8/4). The Conference and its organs also considered proposals and comments by Governments and international Organisations on the draft Unidroit Convention on the international return of stolen or illegally exported cultural objects (CONF. 8/5 and Addenda, CONF.8/6 and Addenda, CONF.8/W.P. 1-7 and CONF.8/C.1/W.P. 1-82) and on the draft final provisions capable of embodiment in the draft Unidroit Convention on the international return of stolen or illegally exported cultural objects (CONF.8/C.2/W.P.1-25).

13. The Conference assigned to the Committee of the Whole the first and second readings of the draft Unidroit Convention on the international return of stolen or illegally exported cultural objects, Articles C and F of the draft final provisions capable of embodiment in the aforementioned draft Convention and the title of the said draft Convention. The Conference assigned to the Final Clauses Committee the first and second readings of all but Articles C and F of the draft final provisions capable of embodiment in the aforementioned draft Convention.

14. On the basis of the deliberations recorded in the summary records of the Conference (CONF.8/S.R. 1-7), the summary records of the Committee of the Whole (CONF.8/C.1/S.R. 1-19) and its report (CONF.8/C.1/Doc.1) and the report of the Final Clauses Committee (CONF.8/C.2/Doc.1), the Conference drew up THE UNIDROIT CONVENTION ON STOLEN OR ILLEGALLY EXPORTED CULTURAL OBJECTS.

15. The Unidroit Convention on Stolen or Illegally Exported Cultural Objects, the text of which is set out in an appendix to this Final Act, was adopted

by the Conference on 23 June 1995 and opened for signature at the closing session of the Conference on 24 June 1995. The Convention will remain open for signature in Rome, Italy until 30 June 1996. It was also opened for accession on 24 June 1995.

16. The Convention is deposited with the Government of Italy.

IN WITNESS WHEREOF the representatives

GRATEFUL, to the Government of Italy for having invited the Conference to Italy and for its generous hospitality

HAVE SIGNED this Final Act.

DONE at Rome, this twenty-fourth day of June, one thousand nine hundred and ninety-five, in a single copy in the English and French languages, each text being equally authentic.

The Vice-President

The Secretary-General

APPENDIX

Unidroit Convention on Stolen or Illegally Exported Cultural Objects

THE STATES PARTIES TO THIS CONVENTION

ASSEMBLED in Rome at the invitation of the Government of the Italian Republic from 7 to 24 June 1995 for a Diplomatic Conference for the adoption of the draft Unidroit Convention on the International Return of Stolen or Illegally Exported Cultural Objects,

CONVINCED of the fundamental importance of the protection of cultural heritage and of cultural exchanges for promoting understanding between peoples, and the dissemination of culture for the well-being of humanity and the progress of civilisation,

DEEPLY CONCERNED by the illicit trade in cultural objects and the irreparable damage frequently caused by it, both to these objects themselves and to the cultural heritage of national, tribal, indigenous or other communities, and also to the heritage of all peoples, and in particular by the pillage of archaeological sites and the resulting loss of irreplaceable archaeological, historical and scientific information,

DETERMINED to contribute effectively to the fight against illicit trade in cultural objects by taking the important step of establishing common, minimal legal rules for the restitution and return of cultural objects between Contracting States, with the objects of improving the preservation and protection of the cultural heritage in the interest of all,

EMPHASISING that this Convention is intended to facilitate the restitution and return of cultural objects, and that the provision of any remedies, such as compensation needed to effect restitution and return in some States, does not imply that such remedies should be adopted in other States,

AFFIRMING that the adoption of the provisions of this Convention for the future in no way confers any approval or legitimacy upon illegal transactions of whatever kind which may have taken place before the entry into force of the Convention,

CONSCIOUS that this Convention will not by itself provide a solution to the problems raised by illicit trade, but that it initiates a process that will enhance international cultural co-operation and maintain a proper role for legal trading and inter-State agreements for cultural exchanges,

ACKNOWLEDGING that implementation of this Convention should be accompanied by other effective measures for protecting cultural objects, such as the development and use of registers, the physical protection of archaeological sites and technical co-operation,

RECOGNISING the work of various bodies to protect cultural property, particularly the 1970 UNESCO Convention on illicit traffic and development of codes of conduct in the private sector,

HAVE AGREED as follows :

CHAPTER I

SCOPE OF APPLICATION AND DEFINITION

Article 1

This Convention applies to claims of an international character for :

(a) the restitution of stolen cultural objects;

(b) the return of cultural objects removed from the territory of a Contracting State contrary to its law regulating the export of cultural objects for the purpose of protecting its cultural heritage (hereinafter "illegally exported cultural objects").

Article 2

For the purposes of this Convention cultural objects are those which, on religious or secular grounds, are of importance for archaeology, prehistory, history, literature, art or science and belong to one of the categories listed in the Annex to this Convention.

CHAPTER II

RESTITUTION OF STOLEN CULTURAL OBJECTS

Article 3

(1) The possessor of a cultural object which has been stolen shall return it.

(2) For the purposes of this Convention, a cultural object which has been unlawfully excavated or lawfully excavated but unlawfully retained shall be considered stolen, when consistent with the law of the State where the excavation took place.

(3) Any claim for restitution shall be brought within a period of three years from the time when the claimant knew the location of the cultural object and the identity of its possessor, and in any case within a period of fifty years from the time of the theft.

(4) However, a claim for restitution of a cultural object forming an integral part of an identified monument or archaeological site, or belonging to a public collection, shall not be subject to time limitations other than a period of three years from the time when the claimant knew the location of the cultural object and the identity of its possessor.

(5) Not with standing the provisions of the preceding paragraph, any Contracting State may declare that a claim is subject to a time limitation of 75 years or such longer period as is provided in its law. A claim made in another Contracting State for restitution of a cultural object displaced from a monument, archaeological site or public collection in a Contracting State making such a declaration shall also be subject to that time limitation.

(6) A declaration referred to in the preceding paragraph shall be made at the time of signature, ratification, acceptance, approval or accession.

(7) For the purposes of this Convention, a "public collection" consists of a group of inventoried or otherwise identified cultural objects owned by:

(a) a Contracting State

(b) a regional or local authority of a Contracting State;

(c) a religious institution in a Contracting State; or

(d) an institution that is established for an essentially cultural, educational or scientific purpose in a Contracting State and is recognised in that State as serving the public interest.

(8) In addition, a claim for restitution of a sacred communally important cultural object belonging to and used by a tribal or indigenous community in a Contracting State as part of that community's traditional or ritual use, shall be subject to the time limitation applicable to public collection.

Article 4

(1) The possessor of a stolen cultural object required to return it shall be entitled, at the time of its restitution, to payment of fair and reasonable compensation provided that the possessor neither knew nor ought reasonably to have known that the object was stolen and can prove that it exercised due diligence when acquiring the object.

(2) Without prejudice to the right of the possessor to compensation referred to in the preceding paragraph, reasonable efforts shall be made to have the person who transferred the cultural objects to the possessor, or any prior transferor, pay the compensation where to do so would be consistent with the law of the State in which the claim is brought.

(3) Payment of compensation to the possessor by the claimant, when this is required, shall be without prejudice to the right of the claimant to recover it from any other person.

(4) In determining whether the possessor exercised due diligence, regard shall be had to all the circumstances of the acquisition, including the character of the parties, the price paid, whether the possessor consulted any reasonably accessible register of stolen cultural objects, and any other relevant information and documentation which it could reasonably have obtained, and whether the possessor consulted accessible agencies or took any other step that a reasonable person would have taken in the circumstances.

(5) The possessor shall not be in a more favourable than the person from whom it acquired the cultural objects by inheritance or otherwise gratuitously.

CHAPTER III

RETURN OF ILLEGALLY EXPORTED CULTURAL OBJECTS

Article 5

(1) A Contracting State may request the court or other competent authority of another Contracting State to order the return of a cultural object illegally

exported from the territory of the requesting State.

(2) A cultural object which has been temporarily exported from the territory of the requesting State, for purposes such as exhibition, research or restoration, under a permit issued according to its law regulating its export for the purpose of protecting its cultural heritage and not returned in accordance with the terms of that permit shall be deemed to have been illegally exported.

(3) The court or other competent authority of the State addressed shall order the return of an illegally exported cultural object if the requesting State establishes that the removal of the object from its territory significantly impairs one or more of the following interests:

(a) the physical preservation of the objects or of its context;

(b) the integrity of a complex object;

(c) the preservation of information of, for example, a scientific or historical character;

(d) the traditional or ritual use of the object by a tribal or indigenous community;

or establishes that the object is of significant cultural importance for the requesting State.

(4) Any request made under paragraph 1 of this article shall contain or be accompanied by such information of a factual or legal nature as may assist the court or other competent authority of the State addressed in determining whether the requirements of paragraphs 1 to 3 have been met.

(5) Any request for return shall be brought within a period of three years from the time when the requesting State knew the location of the cultural object and the identity of its possessor, and in any case within a period of fifty years from the date of the export or from the date on which the object should have been returned under a permit referred to in paragraph 2 of this article.

Article 6

(1) The possessor of a cultural object who acquired the object after it was illegally exported shall be entitled, at the time of its return, to payment by the requesting State of fair and reasonable compensation, provided that the possessor neither knew nor ought reasonably to have known at the time of acquisition that the object had been illegally exported.

(2) In determining whether the possessor knew or ought reasonably to have known that the cultural object had been illegally exported, regard shall be had to the circumstances of the acquisition, including the absence of an export certificate required under the law of the requesting State.

(3) Instead of compensation, and in agreement with the requesting State, the possessor required to return the cultural object to that State, may decide :

(a) to recall ownership of the object, or

(b) to transfer ownership against payment or gratuitously to a person of its choice residing in the requesting States who provides the necessary guarantees.

(4) The cost of returning the cultural object in accordance with this article shall be borne by the requesting State, without prejudice to the right of that State to recover costs from any other person.

(5) The possessor shall not be in a more favourable position than the person from whom it acquired the cultural object by inheritance or otherwise gratuitously.

Article 7

(1) The provisions of this Chapter shall not apply where :

(a) the export of a cultural object is no longer illegal at the time at which the return is requested; or

(b) the object was exported during the lifetime of the person who created it or within a period of fifty years following the death of that person.

(2) Notwithstanding the provisions of sub-paragraph (b) of the preceding paragraph, the provisions of this Chapter shall apply where a cultural object was made by a member or members of a tribal or indigenous community for traditional or ritual use by that community and the object will be returned to that community.

CHAPTER IV

GENERAL PROVISIONS

Article 8

(1) A claim under Chapter II and a request under Chapter III may be brought

before the courts or other competent authorities of the Contracting State where the cultural object is located, in addition to the courts or other competent authorities otherwise having jurisdiction under the rules in force in Contracting States.

(2) The parties may agree to submit the dispute to any court or other competent authority or to arbitration.

(3) Resort may be had to the provisional, including protective, measures available under the law of the Contracting State where the object is located even when the claim for restitution or request for return of the object is brought before the courts or other competent authorities of another Contracting State.

Article 9

(1) Nothing in this Convention shall prevent a Contracting State from applying any rules more favourable to the restitution or the return of stolen or illegally exported cultural objects than provided for by this Convention.

(2) This article shall not be interpreted as creating an obligation to recognise or enforce a decision of a court or other competent authority of another Contracting State that departs from the provisions of this Convention.

Article 10

(1) The provisions of Chapter II shall apply only in respect of a cultural object that is stolen after this Convention enters into force in respect of the State where the claim is brought, provided that:

> (a) the object was stolen from the territory of a Contracting State after the entry into force of this Convention for that State; or
>
> (b) the object is located in a Contracting State after the entry into force of the Convention for that State.

(2) The provisions of Chapter III shall apply only in respect of a cultural object that is illegally exported after this Convention enters into force for the requesting State as well as the State where the request is brought.

(3) This Convention does not in any way legitimise any illegal transaction of whatever nature which has taken place before the entry into force of this Convention or which is excluded under paragraphs (1) or (2) of this article, nor limit any right of a State or other person to make a claim under remedies available outside the framework of this Convention for the restitution or return

of a cultural object stolen or illegally exported before the entry into force of this Convention.

CHAPTER V

FINAL PROVISIONS

Article 11

(1) This Convention is open for signature at the concluding meeting of the Diplomatic Conference for the adoption of the draft Unidroit Convention on the International Return of Stolen or Illegally Exported Cultural Objects and will remain open for signature by all States at Rome until 30th June 1996.

(2) This Convention is subject to ratification, acceptance or approval by States which have signed it.

(3) This Convention is open for accession by all States which are not signatory States as from the date it is open for signature.

(4) Ratification, acceptance, approval or accession is subject to the deposit of a formal instrument to that effect with the depositary.

Article 12

(1) This Convention shall enter into force on the first day of the sixth month following the date of deposit of the fifth instrument of ratification, acceptance, approval or accession.

(2) For each State that ratifies, accepts, approves or accedes to this Convention after the deposit of the fifth instrument of ratification, acceptance, approval or accession, this Convention shall enter into force in respect of that State on the first day of the sixth month following the date of deposit of its instrument of ratification, acceptance, approval or accession.

Article 13

(1) This Convention does not affect any international instrument by which any Contracting State is legally bound and which contains provisions on matters governed by this Convention, unless a contrary declaration is made by the States bound by such instrument.

(2) Any Contracting State may enter into agreements with one or more Contracting States, with a view to improving the application of this

Convention in their mutual relations. The States which have concluded such an agreement shall transmit a copy to the depositary.

(3) In their relations with each other, Contracting States which are Members of organisations of economic integration or regional bodies may declare that they will apply the internal rules of these organisations or bodies and will not therefore apply as between these States the provisions of this Convention the scope of applications of which coincides with that of those rules.

Article 14

(1) If a Contracting State has two or more territorial units, whether or not possessing different systems of law applicable in relation to the matters dealt with in this Convention, it may, at the time of signature or of the deposit of its instrument of ratification, acceptance, approval or accession, declare that this Convention is to extend to all its territorial units or only to one or more of them, and may substitute for its declaration another declaration at any time.

(2) These declarations are to be notified to the depositary and are to state expressly the territorial units to which the Convention extends.

(3) If, by virtue of a declaration under this article, this Convention extends to one or more but not all of the territorial units of a Contracting State, the reference to :

(a) the territory of a Contracting State in Article I shall be construed as referring to the territory of a territorial unit of that State;

(b) a court or other competent authority of the Contracting State or of the State addressed shall be construed as referring to the court or other competent authority of a territorial unit of that State;

(c) the Contracting State where the cultural object is located in Article 8(1) shall be construed as referring to the territorial unit of that State where the object is located;

(d) the law of the Contracting State where the object is located in Article 8(3) shall be construed as referring to the law of the territorial unit of that State where the object is located; and

(e) a Contracting State in Article 9 shall be construed as referring to a territorial unit of that State.

(4) If a Contracting State makes no declaration under paragraph 1 of this article, this Convention is to extend to all territorial units of that State.

Article 15

(1) Declarations made under this Convention at the time of signature are subject to confirmation upon ratification, acceptance or approval.

(2) Declarations and confirmations of declarations are to be in writing and to be formally notified to the depositary.

(3) A declaration shall take effect simultaneously with the entry into force of this Convention in respect of the State concerned. However, a declaration of which the depository receives formal notification after such entry into force shall take effect on the first day of the sixth month following the date of its deposit with the depositary.

(4) Any State which makes a declaration under this Convention may withdraw it at any time by a formal notification in writing addressed to the depositary. Such withdrawal shall take effect on the first day of the sixth month following the date of the notification.

Article 16

(1) Each Contracting State shall at the time of signature, ratification, acceptance, approval or accession, declare that for the restitution, or requests for the return, of cultural objects brought by a State under Article 8 may be submitted to it under one or more of the following procedures:

(a) directly to the courts or other competent authorities of the declaring State;

(b) through an authority or authorities designated by that State to receive such claims or requests and to forward them to the courts or other competent authorities of that State;

(c) through diplomatic or consular channels.

(2) Each Contracting State may also designate the courts or other authorities competent to order the restitution or return of cultural objects under the provisions of Chapters II and III.

(3) Declarations made under paragraphs 1 and 2 of this article may be modified at any time by a new declaration.

(4) The provisions of paragraphs 1 to 3 of this article do not affect bilateral or multilateral agreements on judicial assistance in respect of civil and commercial matters that may exist between Contracting States.

Article 17

Each Contracting State shall, not later than six months following the date of deposit of its instrument of ratification, acceptance, approval or accession, provide the depositary with written information in one of the official languages of the Convention concerning the legislation regulating the export of its cultural objects. This information shall be updated from time to time as appropriate.

Article 18

No reservations are permitted except those expressly authorised in this Convention.

Article 19

(1) This Convention may be denounced by any State Party, at any time after the date on which it enters into force for that State, by the deposit of an instrument to that effect with the depositary.

(2) A denunciation shall take effect on the first day of the sixth month following the deposit of the instrument of denunciation with the depositary. Where a longer period for the denunciation to take effect is specified in the instrument of denunciation it shall take effect upon the expiration of such longer period after its deposit with the depositary.

(3) Notwithstanding such a denunciation, this Convention shall nevertheless apply to a claim for restitution or a request for return of a cultural object submitted prior to the date on which the denunciation takes effect.

Article 20

The President of the International Institute for the Unification of Private Law (Unidroit) may at regular intervals, or at any time at the request of five Contracting States, convene a special committee in order to review the practical operation of this Convention.

Article 21

(1) This Convention shall be deposited with the Government of the Italian Republic.

(2) The Government of the Italian Republic shall:

(a) inform all States which have signed or acceded to this Convention and the President of the International Institute for the Unification of Private Law (Unidroit) of:

(i) each. new signature or deposit of an instrument of ratification, acceptance, approval or accession, together with the date thereof;

(ii) each declaration made in accordance with this Convention;

(iii) the withdrawal of any declaration;

(iv) the date of entry into force of this Convention;

(v) the agreements referred to in Article 13;

(vi) the deposit of an instrument of denunciation of this Convention together with the date of its deposit and the date on which it takes effect;

(b) transmit certified true copies of this Convention to all signatory States, to all States acceding to the Convention and to the President of the International Institute for the Unification of Private Law (Unidroit);

(c) perform such other functions customary for depositaries.

IN WITNESS WHEREOF the undersigned plenipotentiaries, being duly authorised, have signed this Convention.

DONE at Rome, this twenty-fourth day of June, one thousand nine hundred and ninety-five, in a single original, in the English and French languages, both texts being equally authentic.

Annex

(a) Rare collections and specimens of fauna, flora, minerals and anatomy, and objects of palaeontological interest;

(b) property relating to history, including the history of science and technology and military and social history, to the life of national leaders, thinkers, scientists and artists and to events of national importance;

(c) products of archaeological excavations (including regular and clandestine) or of archaeological discoveries;

(d) elements of artistic or historical monuments or archaeological sites which have been dismembered;

(e) antiquities more than one hundred years old, such as inscriptions, coins and engraved seals:

(f) objects of ethnological interest;

(g) property of artistic interest, such as:

(i) pictures, paintings and drawings produced entirely by hand on any support and in any material (excluding industrial designs and manufactured articles decorated by hand);

(ii) original works of statuary art and sculpture in any material;

(iii) original engravings, prints and lithographs;

(iv) original artistic assemblages and montages in any material;

(h) rare manuscripts and incunabula, old books, documents and publications of special interest (historical, artistic, scientific, literary, etc.) singly or in collections;

(i) postage, revenue and similar stamps, singly or in collections;

(j) archives, including sound, photographic and cinematographic archives;

(k) articles of furniture more than one hundred years old and old musical instruments.

States which Signed the Unidroit Convention on Stolen or Illegally Exported Cultural Objects

Burkina Faso	24.VI.1995
Cambodia	24.VI.1995
Côte d'Ivoire	24.VI.1995
Croatia	24.VI.1995
France (*ad referendum*)	24.VI.1995
Guinea	24.VI.1995
Hungary	24.VI.1995
Italy	24.VI.1995
Lithuania	24.VI.1995
Zambia	24.VI.1995
Georgia	27.VI.1995
Finland	1.XIII.1995
Portugal	23.IV.1996
Paraguay	13.VI.1996
Switzerland	26.VI.1996
Romania	27.VI.1996
Pakistan	27.VI.1996
The Netherlands (with declarations)	28.VI.1996
Peru	28.VI.1996
Bolivia	29.VI.1996
Senegal	29.VI.1996
Russia	29.VI.1996

15. Standard Form Concerning Requests for Return or Restitution

USE OF THIS STANDARD FORM

This form must not be used:

1. *If bilateral negotiations have not yet taken place between the country/museum holding a cultural object and the country/museum requesting its return;*
2. *If the object in question is the subject of legal proceedings already under way.*

This form may be used:

When bilateral negotiations not involving legal proceedings have broken down or come to a halt.

The present form has been established by the Intergovernmental Committee in order to facilitate bilateral negotiations concerning the return or restitution of cultural property. It is intended to provide a means of recording information relating to objects whose return may be requested and is designed therefore to contain the data and observations supplied by the competent authorities in both the requesting country and the country in which they are now held. Please type entries in the space available. If necessary, *additional information may be provided on separate sheets attached to the form*. The Intergovernmental Committee will retain all supporting documentation (publications, photographs, drawings, etc.).

The form completed in English or French should be sent in three copies to:

The Secretariat
Intergovernmental Committee for Promoting the Return of Cultural Property to its Country of Origin or its Restitution in Case of Illicit Appropriation,
Division of Cultural Heritage,
UNESCO, 7, place de Fontenony
75700 - Paris (France)

UTILISATION DE CE FORMULAIRE TYPE

Ne pas utiliser ce formulaire:

1. *S'il n'y a pas encore eu de négociations bilatérales entre le pays ou le musée qui détient un object culturel et le pays ou le musée qui demande son retour;*
2. *Si une action en justice est déjà engagée en ce qui concerne l'objet en question.*

Le présent formulaire peut être utilisé:

Lorsque les négociations bilatérales ont échoué ou sont au point mort, étant entendu qu'aucune action en justice n'a été engagée.

Le présent formulaire a été établi par le Comité intergouvernmental afin de faciliter les négociations bilatérales concernant le retour ou la restitution de biens culturels. Il a pour object de permettre de recueillir des renseignements relatifs aux objects dont le retour peut être demandé, et il est donc conçu pour qu'y figurent les données et les observations communiquées par les autorités compétentes du pays demandeur comme du pays ùu les objects sont actuellement détenus. Veuillez dactylographier les réponses dans l'espace prévu à cet effet. Le cas échéant, d'autres informations peuvent être fournies sur des feuilles séparées jointes au formulaire. Le Comité conservera toute documentation complémentaire (publications, photographies, dessins, etc.).

Le formulaire, rempli en anglais ou en français, devra être envoyé en trois exemplaires à l'adresse suivante:

Secrétariat
Comité intergouvernmental pour la promotion du retour de biens culturels à leur pays d'origine ou de leur restitution en cas d'appropriation illégale
Division du patrimoine culturel
Unesco
7, place de Fountenoy
75700 Paris (France)

NOTES ON COMPLETING THE FORM

General

1. The present form has been established by the Intergovernmental Committee as a mechanism to enable it to promote bilateral negotiations concerning the return or restitution of cultural property. The form is to be used therefore only in cases where negotiations already initiated have made unsatisfactory progress. It is intended to be a comprehensive yet flexible framework, which allows Member State to provide information as completely as possible.

2. The requesting country should use the form to submit its request to the Secretariat of the Committee which will transmit the document to the holding country concerned. The holding country should in turn use the form to provide its reply to the request and return it to the Secretariat of the Committee within a period of one year from the date of receipt.

3. Please note that the use of the form is limited to one object per form. It is not practicable to deal with information on more than one distinct object at a time. In the case of a request for an entire collection of objects it is understood that the collection, for the purposes of the present form, would be treated as an entry i.e. 'an object'.

INDICATIONS POUR REMPLIR LE FORMULAIRE

Généralités

1. Le présent formulaire a été établi par le Comité intergouvernemental pour lui permettre de promouvoir les négociations bilatérales concernant le retour ou la restitution de biens culturels. Il ne doit donc être utilisé que dans les can où les négociations déjà engagées ne progressent pas de manière satisfaisante. Il a été conçu comme un cadre global mais souple, qui permet aux Etats members de fournir des renseignements aussi complets que possible.

2. Le pays demandeur doit utiliser le formulaire pour adresser sa demande au Secrétariat du Comité, qui transmettra le document au pays détenteur concerné. Le pays détenteur doit utiliser le formulaire pour répondre à la demande et le renvoyer au Secrétariat dans un délai d'un an à compter de la date de réception.

3. Veuillez noter que chaque formulaire ne peut servir que pour un seul object. Il n'est guére possible sur le plan pratique de traiter des informations concernant plus d'un objet distir à la fois. En cas de demande relative à une collection entiére d'objets, il est entendu qu'aux fins du présent formulaire, la collection sera considérée comme une entité, c'est-à-dire comme "un objet".

Name of the requesting country/Nom du pays demandeur

Name of the requesting institution or service/Nom de l'institution ou du service demandeur

A. DOCUMENTARY DATA ON THE OBJECT

A.1. Description of the object

Information should be provided if possible with respect to :

(a) **Type of object** : painting, sculpture, manuscript, ceramics, textiles, archaeological finds, buildings or monuments, etc.

(b) **Characteristics** : material of which made (wood, stone, metal, parchment, etc.), dimensions, weight, form, period, authorship (if applicable, special distinctive features).

RENSEIGNEMENTS CONCERNANT L'OBJET

A.1. Description de l'objet

Dans la mesure du possible on donnera des renseignements sur :

(a) Le type d'objet : peinture, sculpture, manuscrit, céramique, textile, objets de fouilles, constructions, éléments de constructions ou de monuments, etc.

(b) Ses caractéristiques: matériau (bois, pierre, métal, parchemin, etc.), dimensions, poids, forme, péroide, auteur (s'il y a lieu), caractéres distinctifs particuliers.

Requesting country/Pays demandeur

Holding country/Pays détenteur

A.2. Location of the object

The place where the object is currently displayed or held in the holding country should be specified, e.g., a museum gallery or reserve collection. If not known, the holding country may wish to state the presumed location, according to the latest information available.

A.2. Lieu où se trouve l'objet

Le lieu où l'objet est actuellement exposé ou détenu dans le pays détenteur doit être précisé (par exemple. les salles d'exposition ou les réserves d'un musée). Si ce lieu n'est pas connu, le pays détenteur voudra peut-êtra indiquer l'emplacement présumé de l'objet d'aprés les informations les plus récentes.

Requesting country/Pays demandeur

Holding country/Pays détenteur

Requesting country/Pays demandeur

Holding country/Pays détenteur

A.3. Ownership

It should be made clear whether the object was/is the property of a public or private organization or of a private individual.

A.3. Propriété

Il conviendra de préciser si l'objet êtait/est la propriété d'un organisme public ou privé ou d'un particulier.

Requesting country/Pays demandeur	Holding country/Pays détenteur

A.4. Date of acquisition

A.4. Date d'acquisition

A.5. Legal status

Is the object part of the national heritage; is it part of the collection of a public or private museum; is it held on short- or long-term loan, deposit, etc.?

Requesting country/Pays demandeur

A.5. Statut juridique

L'objet fait-il partie du partimoine national ? Fait-il partie des collections d'un musée public ou privé ? Est-il détenu au tiare d'un prêt à court ou à long term, en dépôt, etc. ?

Holding country/Pays détenteur

A.6. State of conservation

Here details may be given concerning the decay of constituent materials, deterioration noted, international or accidental mutilations, if any, restoration carried out.

Requesting country/Pays demandeur

A.6. Etat de conservation

On pourra donner ici des renseignements sur l'altération des matériaux, les détériorations constatées, les dégradations intentionnelles ou accidentelles et, le cas échéant, les restaurations effectuées.

Holding country/Pays détenteur

A.7. Conservation requirements for the object

Information should be provided as to the environmental conditions required, possible conservation treatment indicated, etc.

A.7. Conditions requises pour la conservation de l'objet

Des informations seront fournies en ce qui concerne l'environnment dont a besoin l'objet, le traitment éventuellement nécessaire pour assurer sa conservation, etc.

Requesting country/Pays demandeur/

Holding country/Pays détenteur

A.8. References and documentation

Bibliographic or other references concerning the object should be provided. Other documentation such as labels, catalogue cards, information about the archaeological site from which the object originated, etc. should also be included whenever possible. Such material may be attached to the present form.

A.8. Références et documentation

Les références bibliographiques ou autres concernant l'objet devront être fournies. Tous les autres éléments de documentation tels qu'étiquettes, fiches de catalogue, renseignements, sur le site archéologique dont provient l'objet, etc., devront aussi être produits chaque fois que cela sera possible. Ces documents pourront être joints au présent formulaire.

Requesting country/Pays demandeur

Holding country/Pays détenteur

A.9. Circumstances in which the object left country of origin

Information should be provided if possible with respect to the means by which the object left its country of origin, e.g. trade, illicit appropriation, colonial or foreign occupation, exchange, gift, loan for repair and/or reproduction, temporary export licence for scientific purpose including conservation or exhibition.

A.9. Circonstances dans lesquelles l'objet a quitté son pays d'origine

Des renseignements seront fournis, dans la mesure du possible, sur la façon dont l'objet a quitté son pays d'origine: transaction commerciale, appropriation illicite, occupation coloniale ou étrangère, échange, don, prêt pour réparation et/ou reproduction, autorisation temporaire d'exportation à des fins scientifiques (y compris conservation ou exposition).

Requesting country/Pays demandeur	Holding country/Pays détenteur

A.10. Mode of acquisition by institution in holding country

The mode of acquisition should be specified, e.g. purchase, gift, exchange, loan, archaeological excavation, temporary import for scientific purposes, illicit acquisition, colonial or foreign occupation etc.

Requesting country/Pays demandeur

A.10. Mode d'acquisition par l'institution du pays détenteur

Il conviendra de spécifier le mode d'acquisition de l'objet, par exemple : achat, don échange, prêt, fouille archéologique, importation temporaire à des fins scientifiques, acquisition illicite, occupation coloniale ou étrangère, etc.

Holding country/Pays détenteur

A.11. Particular significance for the requiring country

This may be historical cultural, religious or scientific in nature or a combination of several of these. The object may be a 'missing link' in a given cultural tradition and/or in the country's national collections.

Requesting country/Pays demandeur

A.11. Signification particuliére pour le pays demdandeur

Cette signification peut être de nature historique, culturelle, religieuse ou scientifique, ou encore associer plusieurs de ces éléments. L'objet peut être un "chaînon manquant" d'une tradition culturelle déterminée et/ou des collections nationales du pays demandeur.

A.12. Details of similar objects known to exist in country of origin or elsewhere

Information may be provided concerning objects of the same period provenance or type, or (where applicable) by the same author; objects whose significance is similar to that described under A.11 above may also be mentioned.

A.12. Renseignements sur les objets similaires dont l'existence dans le pays d'origine ou ailleurs est connue

Des renseignments sur les objets de la même période, de la même provenance ou du même type, ou encore (s'il y a lieu) du même auteur peuvent être fournis ; les objets dont la signification est similaire à celle qui a été décrite à la rubrique A.11 peuvent également être mentionnés.

Requesting country/Pays demandeur

Holding country/Pays détenteur

A.13. Significance of the object for the holding country

Requesting country/Pays demandeur

A.13. Signification de l'objet pour le pays détenteur

Holding country/Pays détenteur

B. REFERENCES TO LEGISLATION AND REGULATION TO PREVENT ILLICIT TRAFFIC IN CULTURAL PROPERTY

RÉFÉRENCES CONCERNANT LES DISPOSITIONS LÉGISLATIVES ET RÉGLEMENTAIRES VISANT A EMPECHER LE TRAFIC ILLICITE DE BEINS CULTURELS

Full reference to the relevant articles of national legislation or regulation concerning illicit traffic should be provided, both with respect to export of cultural property and its import from other countries. The texts of such legislation or regulation may be attached to the present form if necessary.

Des références complétes aux dispositions pertinentes de la législation ou de la réglementation nationale concerning le trafic illicite devront êtra fournies, tant en ce qui concerne l'exportation de biens culturels que leur importation d'autres pays. Les textes législatifs et réglementaires en question pourront, s'il y a lieu, être joints au présent formulaire.

Requesting country/Pays demandeur	Holding country/Pays détenteur

C.SUGGESTED ACTION
MESURES SUGGÉRÉES

C.1. Previous negotiations

Give full details of negotiations carried out so far. What progress has been achieved? Please indicate reasons for lack of progress with respect to these negotiations.

Requesting country/Pays demandeur

C.1. Négociations antérieures

Donner des renseignements détaillés sur les négociations menées jusqu'ici. Quels résultats ont été obtenus? Veuillez indiquer les raisons pour lesquelles ces négociations piétinent.

Holding country/Pays détenteur

C.2. Proposals of requesting country

Proposals with respect to further steps necessary or new forms of co-operation or negotiation to be initiated may be outlined here.

Requesting country/Pays demandeur

C.2. Propositions du pays demandeur

Les propositions concernant les nouvelles initiatives jugées nécessaires ou les nouvelles modalités de coopération ou de négociation à envisager pourront être brièvement exposées ici.

C.3. Legal status object would have in requesting country

Information should be provided as to whether the object would become part of the national heritage or of the collection of a public or private museum or other institution.

C.3. Statut juridique qu'aurait l'objet dans le pays demandeur

Il conviendra d'indiquer si l'objet deviendrait un élément du patrimoine national ou s'il entrerait dans les collections d'un musée public ou privé ou d'une autre institution.

Requesting country/Pays demandeur

C.4. Place of display in requesting country

Information should be provided as to whether the object will be displayed in a state museum or other institution; in a private museum or institution; in a place of worship, etc.

C.4. Lieu d'exposition dans le pays demandeur

Il conviendra d'indiquer si l'objet sera exposé dans un musée ou une autre institution d'Etat, dans un musée ou une autre institution privée, dans un lieu de culte, etc.

Requesting country/Pays demandeur

C.5. Facilities available

Information should be provided concerning the curatorial, managerial and conservation facilities available to the museum or other institution which will receive the object.

C.5. Moyens disponibles

Des informations devront être fournies sur les moyens de conservation, de gestion et d'administration dont dispose le musée ou l'institution qui recevra l'objet.

Requesting country/Pays demandeur

C.6. Response by holding country

C.6. Réponse du pays détenteur

Holding country/Pays détenteur

C.7. Institutions or persons responsible for negotiations

C.7. Institutions ou personnes chargées des négociations

Requesting country/Pays demandeur

Holding country/Pays détenteur

D.OTHER OBSERVATIONS/AUTRES OBSERVATIONS

Requesting country/pays demandeur	Holding country/Pays détenteur

Requesting country/Pays demandeur	Holding country/Pays détenteur
Signed/Signature	Signed/Signature
Full Name/Nom	Full Name/Nom
Title/Titre	Title/Titre
Date	Date

Reserved for Unesco Secretariat	Reserve pour le Secretariat de l'Unesco

16. Convention on the Means of Prohibiting and Preventing the Illicit Import, Export and Transfer of Ownership of Cultural Property (Paris, 1970)*

Recalling the importance of the provisions contained in the Declaration of the Principles of International Cultural Co-operation, adopted by the General Conference at its fourteenth session,

Considering that the interchange of cultural property among nations of scientific, cultural and educational purposes increases the knowledge of the civilization of Man, enriches the cultural life of all peoples and inspires mutual respect and appreciation among nations,

Considering that cultural property constitutes one of the basic elements of civilization and national culture, and that its true value can be appreciated only in relation to the fullest possible information regarding its origin, history and traditional setting,

Considering that it is incumbent upon every State to protect the cultural property existing within its territory against the danger of theft, clandestine excavation, and illicit export,

Considering that, to avert these dangers, it is essential for every State to become increasingly alive to the moral obligations to respect its own cultural heritage and that of all nations,

Considering that, as cultural institutions, museums, libraries and archives should ensure that their collections are built up in accordance with universally recognised moral principles,

---

* Adopted by the General Conference of the United Nations Educational, Scientific and Cultural Organisation at its sixteenth session, Paris, 14 November 1970.

Considering that illicit import, export and transfer of ownership of cultural property is an obstacle to that understanding between nations which it is part of Unesco's mission to promote by recommending to interested State's international conventions to this end,

Considering that the protection of cultural heritage can be effective only if organised both nationally and internationally among States working in close cooperation,

Considering that the Unesco General Conference adopted a Recommendation to this effect in 1964,

Having before it further proposals on the means of prohibiting and preventing the illicit import, export and transfer of ownership property, a question which is on the agenda for the session as item 19,

Having decided, at its fifteenth session, that this question should be made the subject of an international convention,

Adopts this Convention on the fourteenth day of November 1970.

Article 1

For the purposes of this Convention, the term "cultural property" means property which, on religious or secular grounds, is specifically designated by each State as being of importance for archaeology, prehistory, history, literature, art or science and which belongs to the following categories:

(a) rare collections and specimens of flora, fauna, minerals and objects of palaeontological interest;

(b) property relating to history, including the history of science and technology and military and social history, to the life of national leaders, thinkers, scientist and to events of national importance;

(c) products of archaeological excavations (including regular and clandestine) or of archaeological discoveries;

(d) elements of artistic or historical monuments or archaeological sites which have been dismembered;

(e) antiquities more than one hundred years old, such as inscriptions, coins and engraved seals;

(f) objects of ethnological interests;

(g) property of artistic interests, such as,

(i) pictures, paintings and drawings produced entirely by hand on any support and in any material (excluding industrial designs and manufactured articles decorated by hand);

(ii) original works of statuary art and sculpture in any material;

(iii) original engravings, prints and lithographs;

(iv) original artistic assemblages and montages in any material;

(h) rare manuscripts and incunabula, old books, documents and publications of special interest (historical, artistic, scientific, literary, etc.) singly or in collections;

(i) postage, revenue, and similar stamps, singly or in collections;

(j) archives, including sound, photographic and cinematographic archives;

(k) articles of furniture more than one hundred years old and old musical instruments.

Article 2

1. The States Parties to this Convention recognise that the illicit import, export and transfer of ownership of cultural property is one of the main causes of the impoverishment of the cultural heritage of the countries of origin of such property and the international co-operation constitutes one of the most efficient means of protecting each country's cultural property against all the dangers resulting therefrom.

2. To this end, the States Parties undertake to oppose such practices with the means at their disposal, and particularly by removing their causes, putting a stop to current practices, and by helping to make the necessary reparations.

Article 3

The import, export or transfer of ownership of cultural property effected contrary to the provisions adopted under this Convention by the States Parties thereto, shall be illicit.

Article 4

The State Parties to this Convention recognise that for the purpose of the Convention property which belongs to the following categories forms part of the cultural heritage of each State:

(a) cultural property created by the individual or collective genius of nationals of the State concerned, and cultural of importance to the State concerned created within the territory of the State by foreign nationals or stateless persons resident within such territory;

(b) cultural property found within the national territory;

(c) cultural property acquired by archaeological, ethnological or natural science missions, with the consent of the competent authorities of the country of origin of such property;

(d) cultural property which has been the subject of a freely agreed exchanges;

(e) cultural property received as a gift or purchased legally with the consent of the competent authorities of the country of origin of such property.

Article 5

To ensure the protection of their cultural property against illicit import, export and transfer of ownership, the States Parties to this Convention undertake, as appropriate for each country, to set up within their territories one or more national services, where such services do not already exist, for the protection of the cultural heritage, with qualified staff sufficient in number for the effective carrying out of the following functions:

(a) Contributing to the formation of draft laws and regulations designed to secure the protection of the cultural heritage and particularly prevention of the illicit import, export and transfer of ownership of important cultural property;

(b) establishing and keeping up to date, on the basis of national inventory of protected property, a list of important public and private cultural property whose export would constitute an appreciable impoverishment of the national cultural heritage;

(c) promoting the development or the establishment of scientific and technical institutions (museums, libraries, archives, laboratories, workshops) required to ensure the preservation and presentation of cultural property;

(d) organising the supervision of archaeological excavations, ensuring the preservation "in situ" of certain cultural property, and protecting certain areas reserved for future archaeological research;

(e) establishing, for the benefit of those concerned (curators, collectors, antique dealers, etc.) rules in conformity with the ethical principles set forth in this Convention; and taking steps to ensure the observance of those rules;

(f) taking educational measures to stimulate and develop respect for the cultural heritage of all States, and spreading knowledge of the provisions of this Convention;

(g) seeing that appropriate publicity is given to the disappearance of any items of cultural property.

Article 6

The States Parties to this Convention undertake :

(a) To introduce an appropriate certificate in which the exporting State would specify that the export of the cultural property in question is authorised. The certificate should accompany all items of cultural property exported in accordance with the regulations;

(b) to prohibit the exportation of cultural property from their territory unless accompanied by the above-mentioned export certificate;

(c) to publicize this prohibition by appropriate means, particularly among persons likely to export or import cultural property.

Article 7

The States Parties to this Convention undertake :

(a) To take the necessary measures, consistent with national legislation, to prevent museums and similar institutions within their territories from acquiring cultural property originating from another State Party which has illegally exported after entry into force of this Convention, in the States concerned. Whenever possible, to inform a State of origin party to this Convention of an offer of such cultural property illegally removed from that State after the entry into force of this Convention into both States;

(b) (i) to prohibit the import of cultural property stolen from a museum or a religious or secular public monument or similar institution in another State Party to this Convention after the entry into force of this Convention for the States concerned, provided that such property is documented as appertaining to the inventory of that institution;

(ii) at the request of the State Party of origin, to take appropriate steps to recover and return any such cultural property imported after the entry into force of this Convention in both States concerned, provided, however, that the requesting State shall pay just compensation to an innocent purchaser or to a person who has valid title to that property. Requests for recovery and return shall be made through diplomatic offices. The requesting parties shall furnish, at its expense, the documentation and other evidence necessary to establish its claim for recovery and return. The parties shall impose no customs duties or other charges upon cultural property returned pursuant to this Article. All expenses incidental to the return and delivery of the cultural property shall be borne by the requesting Party.

Article 8

The States Parties to this Convention undertake to impose penalties or administrative sanctions on any person responsible for infringing the prohibitions referred to under Articles 6(b) and 7 (b) above.

Article 9

Any State Party to this Convention whose cultural patrimony is in jeopardy from pillage of archaeological or ethnological materials may call upon other States Parties who are affected. The States Parties to this Convention undertake, in these circumstances, to participate in a concerted international effort to determine and to carry out the necessary concrete measures, including the control of exports and imports and international commerce in the specific materials concerned. Pending agreement each State concerned shall take provisional measures to the extent feasible to prevent irremediable injury to the cultural heritage of the requesting State.

Article 10

The States Parties to this Convention undertake:

(a) To restrict by education, information and vigilance, movement of cultural property illegally removed from any State Party to this Convention and, as appropriate for each country, oblige antique dealers, subject to penal or administrative sanctions, to maintain a register recording the origin of each item of cultural property, names and addresses of the supplier, description and price of each item sold and to inform the purchaser of the cultural property of the export prohibition to which such property may be subject;

(b) to endeavour by educational means to create and develop in the public mind a realisation of the value of cultural property and the threat to the cultural heritage created by theft, clandestine excavations and illicit exports.

Article 11

The export and transfer of ownership of cultural property under compulsion arising directly or indirectly from the occupation of a country by a foreign power shall be regarded as illicit.

Article 12

The States Parties to this Convention shall respect the cultural heritage within the territories for the international relations of which they are responsible, and shall take all appropriate measures to prohibit and prevent illicit import, export and transfer of ownership of cultural property in such territories.

Article 13

The States Parties to this Convention also undertake, consistent with the laws of each State:

(a) To prevent by all appropriate means transfer of ownership of cultural property likely to promote the illicit import or export of such property;

(b) to ensure that their competent services co-operate in facilitating the earliest possible restitution of illicitly exported cultural property to its rightful owner;

(c) to admit actions for recovery of lost or stolen items of cultural property brought by or on behalf of the rightful owners;

(d) to recognise the indefeasible right of each State Party to this Convention to classify and declare certain cultural property as inalienable which should therefore *ipso facto* not be exported, and to facilitate recovery of such property by the State concerned in cases where it has been exported.

Article 14

In order to prevent illicit export and to meet the obligations arising from the implementation of this Convention, each State Party to the Convention should, as far as it is able, provide the national services responsible for the protection of its cultural heritage with an adequate budget and, if necessary, should set up a fund for this purpose.

Article 15

Nothing in this Convention shall prevent States Parties thereto from concluding special agreements among themselves or from continuing to implement agreements already concluded regarding the restitution of cultural property removed, whatever the reason, from its territory of origin, before the entry into force of this Convention for the States concerned.

Article 16

The States Parties to this Convention shall in their periodic reports submitted to the General Conference of the United Nations Educational, Scientific and Cultural Organisation on dates and in a manner to be determined by it, give information on the legislative and administrative provisions which they have adopted and other actions which they have taken for the application of this Convention, together with details of the experience acquired in this field.

Article 17

1. The States Parties to this Convention may call on the technical assistance of the United Nations Educational, Scientific and Cultural Organisation, particularly as regards :

(a) information and education;

(b) consultation and expert advices;

(c) co-ordination and good offices.

2. The United Nations Educational, Scientific and Cultural Organisation may on its own initiative conduct research and publish studies on matters relevant to the illicit movement of cultural property.

3. To this end, the United Nations Educational, Scientific and Cultural Organisation may also call on the co-operation of any competent non-governmental organisation.

4. The United Nations Educational, Scientific and Cultural Organisation may, on its own initiative, make proposals to this Convention for its implementation.

5. At the request of at least two States Parties to this Convention which are engaged in a dispute over its implementation, Unesco may extend its good offices to reach a settlement between them.

Article 18

The Convention is drawn up in English, French, Russian and Spanish, the four texts being equally authoritative.

Article 19

1. This Convention shall be subject to ratification or acceptance by States members of the United Nations Educational, Scientific and Cultural Organisation in accordance with their respective constitutional procedures.

2. The instruments of ratification or acceptance shall be deposited with the Director-General of the United Nations Educational, Scientific and Cultural Organisation.

Article 20

1. This Convention shall be open to accession by all states not members of the United Nations Educational, Scientific and Cultural Organisation which are invited to accede to it by the Executive Board of the organisation.

2. Accession shall be effected by the deposit of an instrument of accession with the Director-General of the United Nations Educational, Scientific and Cultural Organisation.

Article 21

The Convention shall enter into force three months after the date of the deposit of the third instrument of ratification, acceptance or accession, but only with respect to those States which have deposited their respective instrument on or before the date. It shall enter into force with respect to any other State three months after the deposit of its instrument of ratification, acceptance or accession.

Article 22

The States Parties to this Convention recognise that the Convention is applicable not only to their metropolitan territories but also to all territories for the international relations of which they are responsible; they undertake to consult, if necessary, the governments or other competent authorities of these territories on or before ratification, acceptance or accession with a view to securing the application of the Convention to those territories, and to notify the Director-General of the United Nations Educational, Scientific and Cultural Organisation of the territories to which it is applied, the notification to take effect three months after the date of its receipt.

Article 23

1. Each State Party to this Convention may denounce the Convention on its own behalf or on behalf of any territory for whose international relations it is responsible.

2. The denunciation shall be notified by an instrument in writing, deposited with the Director-General of the United Nations Educational, Scientific and Cultural Organisation.

3. The denunciation shall take effect twelve months after the receipt of the instrument of denunciation.

Article 24

The Director-General of the United Nations Educational, Scientific and Cultural Organisation shall inform the States members of the Organisation, the States not members of the Organisation which are referred to in Article 20, as well as the United Nations, of the deposit of all the instruments of ratification, acceptance and accession provided for in Articles 19 and 20, and of the notifications and denunciations provided for in Articles 22 and 23 respectively.

Article 25

1. This Convention may be revised by the General Conference of the United Nations Educational, Scientific and Cultural Organisation. Any such revision shall, however, bind only the States which shall become Parties to the revising Convention.

2. If the General Conference should adopt a new convention revising this Convention in whole or in part, then, unless the new convention otherwise provides, this Convention shall cease to be open to ratification, acceptance or accession, as from the date on which the new revising convention enters into force.

Article 26

In conformity with Article 102 of the Charter of the United Nations, this Convention shall be registered with the Secretariat of the United Nations at the request of the Director-General of the United Nations Educational, Scientific and Cultural Organisation.

Done in Paris in the seventeenth day of November 1970, in two authentic copies bearing the signature of the President of the sixteenth session of the General Conference and the Director-General of the United Nations Educational, Scientific and Cultural Organisation, which shall be deposited in the archives of the United Nations Educational, Scientific and Cultural Organisation, and certified true copies of which shall be delivered to all the States referred to in Articles 19 and 20 as to the United Nations.

The foregoing is the authentic text of the Convention duly adopted by the General Conference of the United Nations Educational, Scientific and Cultural Organisation during its sixteenth session, which was held in Paris and declared closed on the fourteenth day of November 1970.

IN FAITH WHEREOF we have appended our signatures this seventeenth day of November, 1970.

The President of the General Conference
Atilio Dell' Oro Maini
The Director-General
Rene Maheu
Director, Office of International
Standards and Legal Affairs,
United Nations Educational,
Scientific and Cultural Organisation
Certified copy

17. List of States having Deposited an Instrument of Ratification, Acceptance, Accession or Succession as of July, 1995

14 November 1970, Paris

Total Number : 85

States	Date of Deposit Ratification (R) Acceptance (Ac) Accession (A) Succession (S) (Day, Month, Year)	Date of Entry into Force (Day, Month, Year)
Algeria	24.6.1974 (R)	24.9.1974
Angola	7.11.1991 (R)	7.2.1992
Argentina	11.1.1973 (R)	11.4.1973
Armenia (Republic of)	5.09.1993 (S)	See Note 1
Australia	30.10.1989 (Ac)	30.1.1990
Bangladesh	9.12.1987 (R)	9.3.1988
Belarus	28.4.1988 (R)	28.7.1988
Belize	26.1.1990 (R)	26.4.1990
Bolivia	4.10.1976 (R)	4.1.1977
Bosnia-Herzegovina (Republic of)	12.07.1993 (R)	See Note 2
Brazil	16.2.1973 (R)	16.5.1973
Bulgaria	15.9.1971 (R)	24.4.1972

States	Date of Deposit Ratification (R) Acceptance (Ac) Accession (A) Succession (S) (Day, Month, Year)	Date of Entry into Force (Day, Month, Year)
Burkina Faso	7.4.1987 (R)	7.7.1987
Cambodia	26.9.1972 (R)	26.12.1972
Cameroon	24.5.1972 (R)	24.8.1972
Canada	28.3.1978 (Ac)	28.06.1978
Central African Republic	1.2.1972 (R)	1.5.1972
China (People's Republic of)	28.11.1989 (Ac)	28.2.1990
Colombia	24.5.1988 (Ac)	24.8.1988
Cote d'Ivoire	30.10.1990 (R)	30.1.1991
Croatia (Republic of)	6.7.1992 (S)	See Note 2
Cuba	30.1.1980 (R)	30.4.1980
Cyprus	19.10.1979 (R)	19.1.1980
Czech Republic	26.3.1993 (S)	See Note 4
Dominican Republic	7.3.1973 (R)	7.6.1973
France	takes effect in April 1997	Jaunuary 7th
Ecuador	24.3.1971 (Ac)	24.4.1972
Egypt	5.4.1973 (Ac)	5.7.1973
El Salvador	20.2.1978 (R)	20.5.1978
Georgia (Republic of)	4.11.1992 (S)	See Note 1
Greece	5.6.1981 (R)	5.9.1981
Grenada	10.9.1992 (Ac)	10.12.1992
Guatemala	14.1.1985 (R)	14.4.1985
Guinea	18.3.1979 (R)	18.6.1979

States	Date of Deposit Ratification (R) Acceptance (Ac) Accession (A) Succession (S) (Day, Month, Year)	Date of Entry into Force (Day, Month, Year)
Honduras	19.3.1979 (R)	19.6.1979
Hungary	23.10.1978 (R)	23.1.1979
India	24.1.1977 (R)	24.4.1977
Iran (Islamic Republic of)	27.1.1975 (Ac)	27.4.1975
Iraq	12.2.1973 (R)	12.5.1973
Italy	2.10.1978 (R)	2.1.1979
Jordan	15.3.1974 (R)	15.6.1974
Korea (Democratic People's Republic of)	13.5.1983 (R)	13.8.1983
Korea, Republic of	14.2.1983 (R	14.5.1983
Kuwait	22.6.1972 (R)	22.9.1972
Lebanon	25.8.1992 (R)	25.11.1992
Libya	9.1.1973 (R)	9.4.1973
Madagascar	21.6.1989 (R)	21.9.1989
Mali	6.4.1987 (R)	6.7.1987
Mauritania	27.4.1977 (R)	27.7.1977
Mauritius	27.2.1978 (Ac)	27.5.1978
Mexico	4.10.1972 (Ac)	4.1.1973
Mongolia	23.6.1991 (Ac)	23.8.1991
Nepal	23.6.1976 (R)	23.9.1976
Nicaragua	19.4.1977 (R)	19.7.1977
Niger	16.10.1972 (R)	16.1.1973

States	Date of Deposit Ratification (R) Acceptance (Ac) Accession (A) Succession (S) (Day, Month, Year)	Date of Entry into Force (Day, Month, Year)
Nigeria	24.1.1972 (R)	24.4.1972
Oman	2.6.1978 (R)	2.9.1978
Pakistan	30.4.1978 (R)	30.7.1981
Panama	13.8.1973 (R)	13.11.1973
Peru	24.10.1979 (R)	24.1.1980
Poland	31.1.1974 (R)	30.4.1974
Portugal	9.12.1985 (R)	9.3.1986
Qatar	20.4.1977 (R)	20.7.1977
Romania	06.12.1993 (R)	06.03.1994
Russian Federation	28.4.1988 (R)	See Note 3
Saudi Arabia	8.9.1976 (Ac)	8.12.1976
Senegal	9.12.1984 (R)	9.3.1985
Slovak Republic	31.3.1993 (S)	See Note 4
Slovenia (Republic of)	10.10.1992 (S)	See Note 2
Spain	10.1.1986 (R)	10.4.1986
Sri Lanka	7.4.1981 (Ac)	7.7.1981
Syria	21.2.1975 (Ac)	21.5.1975
Tadjikistan (Republic of)	11.8.1992 (S)	See Note 1
Tanzania	2.8.1977 (R)	2.11.1977
Tunisia	10.3.1975 (R)	10.6.1975
Turkey	21.4.1981 (R)	21.7.1981
Ukraine	28.4.1988 (R)	28.7.1988

States	Date of Deposit Ratification (R) Acceptance (Ac) Accession (A) Succession (S) (Day, Month, Year)	Date of Entry into Force (Day, Month, Year)
United States of America	2.9.1983 (Ac)	2.12.1983
Uruguay	9.8.1977 (R)	9.11.1977
Yugoslavia	3.10.1972 (R)	3.1.1973
Zaire	23.9.1974 (R)	23.12.1974
Zambia	21.6.1985 (R)	21.9.1985

REFERENCES AND NOTES

1. The Republic of Armenia, the Republic of Georgia, and the Republic of Tadjikistan each deposited notification of succession in which each declared itself bound by the Convention as ratified by the USSR on 28 April 1988 and which entered into force on 28 July 1988.
2. Bosnia-Herzegovina, Croatia, and the Republic of Slovenia each deposited notification of succession in which each declared itself bound by the Convention as ratified by Yugoslavia on 3 October 1972 and entered into force on 3 January 1973.
3. The Government of Russian Federation informed the Director-General of UNESCO that the Russian Federation continues without interruption the participation of the former USSR in all UNESCO Conventions. The instrument of ratification was deposited by the former USSR on 28 April 1988 and entered into force on 28 July 1988.
4. The Czech Republic and the Slovak Republic each deposited a notification of succession in which each declared itself bound by the Convention as accepted by Czechoslovakia on 14 February 1977 and which entered into force on 14 May 1977.

18. Regulation for the Execution of the Convention for the Protection of Cultural Property in the Event of Armed Conflict

Article 40. Registration

In accordance with Article 102 of the Charter of the United Nations, the present convention shall be registered with the Secretariat of the United Nations at the request of the Director-General of the United Nations Educational, Scientific and Cultural Organization.

In faith whereof the undersigned, duly authorized, have signed the present convention.

Done at The Hague, this fourteenth day of May, 1954, in a single copy which shall be deposited in the archives of the United Nations Educational, Scientific and Cultural Organization, and certified true copies of which shall be delivered to all the States referred to in Articles 30 and 32 as well as to the United Nations.

CHAPTER I

CONTROL

Article 1. International list of persons

On the entry into force of the Convention, the Director-General of the United Nations Educational, Scientific and Cultural Organization shall compile an international list consisting of all persons nominated by the High Contracting Parties as qualified to carry out the functions of Commissioner-General for Cultural Property. On the initiative of the Director-General of the United Nations Educational, Scientific and Cultural Organization, this list shall be periodically revised on the basis of requests formulated by the High Contracting Parties.

Article 2. Organization of control

As soon as any High Contracting Party is engaged in an armed conflict to which Article 18 of the Convention applies :

(a) it shall appoint a representative for cultural property situated in its territory; if it is in occupation of another territory, it shall appoint a special representative for cultural property situated in that territory;

(b) the Protecting Power acting for each of the Parties in conflict with such High Contracting Party shall appoint delegates accredited to the latter in conformity with Article 3 below;

(c) a Commissioner-General for Cultural Property shall be appointed to such High Contracting Party in accordance with Article 4.

Article 3. Appointment of delegates of Protecting Power

The Protecting Power shall appoint its delegates from among the members of its diplomatic or consular staff or, with the approval of the Party to which they will be accredited, from among other persons.

Article 4. Appointment of Commissioner-General

1. The Commissioner-General for Cultural Property shall be chosen from the international list of persons by joint agreement between the Party to which he will be accredited and the Protecting Powers acting on behalf of the opposing Parties.

2. Should the Parties fail to reach agreement within three weeks from the beginning of their discussions on this point, they shall request the President of the International Court of Justice to appoint the Commissioner-General, who shall not take up his duties until the Party to which he is accredited has approved his appointment.

Article 5. Functions of delegates

The delegates of the Protecting Powers shall take note of violations of the Convention, investigate, with the approval of the Party to which they are accredited, the circumstances in which they have occurred, make representations locally to secure their cessation and, if necessary, notify the Commissioner-General of such violations. They shall keep him informed of their activities.

Article 6. Functions of the Commissioner-General

1. The Commissioner-General for Cultural Property shall deal with all matters referred to him in connection with the application of the Convention, in conjunction with the representative of the Party to which he is accredited and with the delegates concerned.

2. He shall have powers of decision and appointment in the cases specified in the present Regulations.

3. With the agreement of the Party to which he is accredited, he shall have the right to order an investigation or to conduct it himself.

4. He shall make any representations to the parties to the conflict or to their Protecting Powers which he deems useful for the application of the Convention.

5. He shall draw up such reports as may be necessary on the application of the Convention and communicate them to the Parties concerned and to their Protecting Powers. He shall send copies to the Director-General of the United Nations Educational, Scientific and Cultural Organization, who may make use only of their technical contents.

6. If there is no Protecting Power, the Commissioner-General shall exercise the functions of the Protecting Power as laid down in Articles 21 and 22 of the Convention.

Article 7. Inspectors and experts

1. Whenever the Commissioner-General for Cultural Property considers it necessary, either at the request of the delegates concerned or after consultation with them, he shall propose, for the approval of the Party to which he is accredited, an inspector of cultural property to be charged with a specific mission. An inspector shall be responsible only to the Commissioner-General.

2. The Commissioner-General for, delegates and inspectors may have recourse to the services of experts, who will also be proposed for the approval of the Party mentioned in the preceding paragraph.

Article 8. Discharge of the Mission of control

The Commissioners-General for Cultural Property, delegates of the Protecting Powers, inspector and experts shall in no case exceed their mandates. In particular, they shall take account of the security needs of the

High Contracting Party to which they are accredited and shall in all circumstances act in accordance with the requirements of the military situation as communicated to them by that High Contracting Party.

Article 9. Substitutes for Protecting Powers

If a Party to the conflict does not benefit or ceases to benefit from the activities of a Protecting Power, a neutral State may be asked to undertake those functions of a Protecting Power which concern the appointment of a Commissioner-General for Cultural Property in accordance with the procedure laid down in Article 4 above. The Commissioner-General thus appointed shall, if need be, entrust to inspectors the functions of delegates of Protecting Powers as specified in the present Regulations.

Article 10. Expenses

The remuneration and expenses of the Commissioner-General for Cultural Property, inspectors and experts shall be met by the Party to which they are accredited. Remuneration and expenses of delegates of the Protecting Powers shall be subject to agreement between those Powers and the States whose interests they are safeguarding.

CHAPTER II

SPECIAL PROTECTION

Article 11. Improvised refuges

1. If, during an armed conflict, any High Contracting Party is induced by unforeseen circumstances to set up an improvised refuge and desires that it should be placed under special protection, it shall communicate this fact forthwith to the Commissioner-General accredited to that Party.

2. If the Commissioner-General considers that such a measure is justified by the circumstances and by the importance of the cultural property sheltered in this improvised refuge, he may authorize the High Contracting Party to display on such refuge the distinctive emblem defined in Article 16 of the Convention. He shall communicate his decision without delay to the delegates of the Protecting Powers who are concerned, each of whom may, within a time-limit of thirty days, order the immediate withdrawal of the emblem.

3. As soon as such delegates have signified their agreement or if the

time-limit of thirty days has passed without any of the delegates concerned having made an objection, and if, in the view of the Commissioner-General, the refuge fulfils the conditions laid down in Article 8 of the Convention, the Commissioner-General shall request the Director-General of the United Nations Educational, Scientific and Cultural Organization to enter the refuge in the Register of Cultural Property under Special Protection.

Article 12. International Register of Cultural Property under Special Protection

1. An 'International Register of Cultural Property under Special Protection' shall be prepared.

2. The Director-General of the United Nations Educational, Scientific and Cultural Organization shall maintain this Register. He shall furnish copies to the Secretary-General of the United Nations and to the High Contracting Parties.

3. The Register shall be divided into sections, each in the name of a High Contracting Party. Each section shall be sub-divided into three paragraphs, headed : Refuges, Centres containing Monuments, Other Immovable Cultural Property. The Director-General shall determine what details each section shall contain.

Article 13. Requests for registration

1. Any High Contracting Party may submit to the Director-General of the United Nations Educational, Scientific and Cultural Organization an application for the entry in the Register of certain refuges, centres containing monuments or other immovable cultural property situated within its territory. Such application shall contain a description of the location of such property and shall certify that the property complies with the provisions of Article 8 of the Convention.

2. In the event of occupation, the Occupying Power shall be competent to make such application.

3. The Director-General of the United Nations Educational, Scientific and Cultural Organization shall, without delay, send copies of applications for registration to each of the High Contracting Parties.

Article 14. Objections

1. Any High Contracting Party may, by letter addressed to the Director-General of the United Nations Educational, Scientific and Cultural Organi-

zation, lodge an objection to the registration of cultural property. This letter must be received by him within four months of the day on which he sent a copy of the application for registration.

2. Such objection shall state the reasons giving rise to it, the only valid grounds being that:

(a) the property is not cultural property;

(b) the property does not comply with the conditions mentioned in Article 8 of the Convention.

3. The Director-General shall send a copy of the letter of objections to the High Contracting Parties without delay. He shall, if necessary, seek the advice of the International Committee on Monuments, Artistic and Historical Sites and Archaeological Excavations and also, if he thinks fit, of any other competent organization or person.

4. The Director-General, or the High Contracting Party requesting registration, may make whatever representation they deem necessary to the High Contracting Parties which lodged the objection, with a view to causing the objection to be withdrawn.

5. If a High Contracting Party which has made an application for registration in time of peace becomes involved in an armed conflict before the entry has been made, the cultural property concerned shall at once be provisionally entered in the Register, by the Director-General, pending the confirmation, withdrawal or cancellation of any objection that may be, or may have been, made.

6. If, within a period of six months from the date of receipt of the letter of objection, the Director-General has not received from the High Contracting Party lodging the objection a communication stating that it has been withdrawn, the High Contracting Party applying for registration may request arbitration in accordance with the procedure in the following paragraph.

7. The request for arbitration shall not be made more than one year after the date of receipt by the Director-General of the letter of objection. Each of the two Parties to the dispute shall appoint an arbitrator. When more than one objection has been lodged against an application for registration, the High Contracting Parties which have lodged the objections shall, by common consent, appoint a single arbitrator. These two arbitrators shall select a chief arbitrator from the international list mentioned an Article 1 of the

present Regulations. If such arbitrators cannot agree upon their choice, they shall ask the President of the International Court of Justice to appoint a chief arbitrator who need not necessarily be chosen from the international list. The arbitral tribunal thus constituted shall fix its own procedure. There shall be no appeal from its decisions.

8. Each of the High Contracting Parties may declare, whenever a dispute to which it is a Party arises, that it does not wish to apply the arbitration procedure provided for in the preceding paragraph. In such cases, the objection to an application for registration shall be submitted by the Director-General to the High Contracting Parties. The objection will be confirmed only if the High Contracting Parties so decide by a two-third majority of the High Contracting Parties voting. The vote shall be taken by correspondence, unless the Director-General of the United Nations Educational, Scientific and Cultural Organization deems it essential to convene a meeting under the powers conferred upon him by Article 27 of the Convention. If the Director-General decides to proceed with the vote by correspondence, he shall invite the High Contracting Parties to transmit their votes by sealed letter within six months from the day on which they were invited to do so.

Article 15. Registration

1. The Director-General of the United Nations Educational, Scientific and Cultural Organization shall cause to be entered in the Register, under a serial number, each item of property for which application for registration is made, provided that he has not received an objection within the time-limit prescribed in paragraph 1 of Article 14.

2. If an objection has been lodged, and without prejudice to the provision of paragraph 5 of Article 14, the Director-General shall enter property in the Register only if the objection has been withdrawn or has failed to be confirmed following the procedures laid down in either paragraph 7 or paragraph 8 of Article 14.

3. Whenever paragraph 3 of Article 11 applies, the Director-General shall enter property in the Register if so requested by the Commissioner-General for Cultural Property.

4. The Director-General shall send without delay to the Secretary-General of the United Nations, to the High Contracting Parties, and, at the request of the Party applying for registration, to all other States referred to in Articles 30 and 32 of the Convention, a certified copy of each entry in

the Register. Entries shall become effective thirty days after despatch of such copies.

Article 16. Cancellation

1. The Director-General of the United Nations Educational, Scientific and Cultural Organization shall cause the registration of any property to be cancelled:

(a) at the request of the High Contracting Party within whose territory the cultural property is situated;

(b) if the High Contracting Party which requested registration has denounced the Convention, and when that denunciation has taken effect;

(c) in the special case provided for in Article 14, paragraph 5, when an objection has been confirmed following the procedures mentioned either in paragraph 7 or in paragraph 8 of Article 14.

2. The Director-General shall send without delay, to the Secretary-General of the United Nations and to all States which received a copy of the entry in the Register, a certified copy of its cancellation. Cancellation shall take effect thirty days after the despatch of such copies.

CHAPTER III

TRANSPORT OF CULTURAL PROPERTY

Article 17. Procedure to obtain immunity

1. The request mentioned in paragraph 1 of Article 12 of the Convention shall be addressed to the Commissioner-General for Cultural Property. It shall mention the reasons on which it is based and specify the approximate number and the importance of the objects to be used, the route to be followed, the date proposed for the transfer, and any other relevant information.

2. If the Commissioner-General, after taking such opinions as he deems fit, considers that such transfer is justified, he shall consult those delegates of the Protecting Powers who are concerned, on the measures proposed for carrying it out. Following such consultation, he shall notify the Parties of the conflict concerned of the transfer, including in such notification all useful information.

3. The Commissioner-General shall appoint one or more inspectors, who shall satisfy themselves that only the Property stated in the request is

to be transferred and that the transport is to be by the approved methods and bears the distinctive emblem. The inspector or inspectors shall accompany the property to its destination.

Article 18. Transport abroad

Where the transfer under special protection is to the territory of another country, it shall be governed not only by Article 12 of the Convention and by Article 17 of the present Regulations, but by the following further provisions:

(a) while the cultural property remains on the territory of another State, that State shall be its depositary and shall extend to it as great a measure of care as that which it bestows upon its own cultural property of comparable importance;

(b) the depositary State shall return the property only on the cessation of the conflict; such return shall be effected within six months from the date on which it was requested;

(c) during the various transfer operations, and while it remains on the territory of another State, the cultural property shall be exempt from confiscation and may not be disposed of either by the depositor or by the depositary. Nevertheless, when the safety of the property requires it, the depositary may, with the assent of the depositor, have the property transported to the territory of a third country, under the conditions laid down in the present article;

(d) the request for special protection shall indicate that the State to whose territory the property is to be transferred accepts the provisions of the present Article.

Article 19. Occupied territory

Whenever a High Contracting Party occupying territory of another High Contracting Party transfers cultural property to a refuge situated elsewhere in that territory, without being able to follow the procedure provided for in Article 17 of the Regulations, the transfer in question shall not be regarded as misappropriation within the meaning of Article 4 of the Convention, provided that the Commissioner-General for Cultural Property certifies in writing, after having consulted that usual custodians, that such transfer was rendered necessary by circumstances.

CHAPTER IV

THE DISTINCTIVE EMBLEM

Article 20. Affixing of the emblem

1. The placing of the distinctive emblem and its degree of visibility shall be left to the discretion of the competent authorities of each High Contracting Party. It may be displayed on flags or armlets; it may be painted on an object or represented in any other appropriate form.

2. However, without prejudice to any possible fuller markings, the emblem shall, in the event of armed conflict and in the cases mentioned in Articles 12 and 13 of the Convention, be placed on the vehicles of transport so as to be clearly visible in daylight from the air as well as from the ground.

The emblem shall be visible from the ground:

(a) at regular intervals sufficient to indicate clearly the perimeter of a centre containing monuments under special protection;

(b) at the entrance to other immovable cultural property under special protection.

Article 21. Identification of persons

1. The persons mentioned in Article 17, paragraph 2 (b) and (c) of the Convention may wear an armlet bearing the distinctive emblem, issued and stamped by the competent authorities.

2. Such persons shall carry a special identity card bearing the distinctive emblem. This card shall mention at least the surname and first names, the date of birth, the title or rank, and the function of the holder. The card shall bear the photograph of the holder as well as his signature or his fingerprints, or both. It shall bear the embossed stamp of the competent authorities.

3. Each High Contracting Party shall make out its own type of identity card, guided by the model annexed, by way of example, to the present Regulations. The High Contracting Parties shall transmit to each other a specimen of the model they are using. Identity cards shall be made out, if possible, at least in duplicate, one copy being kept by the issuing Power.

The said persons may not, without legitimate reason, be deprived of their identity card or of the right to wear the armlet.

19. ICOM Code of Professional Ethics

I. PREAMBLE

The ICOM Code of Professional Ethics was adopted unanimously by the 15th General Assembly of ICOM meeting in Buenos Aires, Argentina on 4 November 1986.

It provides a general statement of professional ethics, respect for which is regarded as a minimum requirement to practise as a member of the museum profession. In many cases it will be possible to develop and strengthen the *Code* to meet particular national or specialized requirements and ICOM wishes to encourage this. A copy of such developments of the *Code* should be sent to the Secretary General of ICOM, Maison de l'Unesco, 1 rue Miollis, 75732 Paris Cedex 15, France.

For the purposes of Articles 2 para. 2, 9 para. 1(d), 14 para. 17(b), 15 para. 7(c), 17 para. 12(e) and 18 para. 7(d) of the ICOM *Statutes*, this *Code* is deemed to be the statement of professional ethics referred to therein.

1. DEFINITIONS

1.1. The International Council of Museums (ICOM)

ICOM is defined in Article 1 para. 1 of its *Statutes* as "the international non-governmental organization of museums and professional museum workers established to advance the interests of museology and other disciplines concerned with museum management and operations."

The objectives of ICOM, as defined in Article 3 para. 1 of its *Statutes* are:

"(a) To encourage and support the establishment, development and professional management of museums of all kinds;

(b) To advance knowledge and understanding of the nature, functions and role of museums in the service of society and of its development;

(c) To organize co-operation and mutual assistance between museums and between professional museum workers in the different countries;

(d) To represent, support and advance the interests of professional museum workers of all kinds;

(e) To advance and disseminate knowledge in museology and other disciplines concerned with museum management and operations."

1.2. Museum

A museum is defined in Article 2 para. 1 of the *Statutes* of the International Council of Museums as "a non-profit making, permanent institution in the service of society and of its development, and open to the public which acquires, conserves, researches, communicates and exhibits, for purposes of study, education and enjoyment, material evidence of people and their environment"

(a) The above definition of a museum shall be applied without limitation arising from the nature of the governing body, the territorial character, the functional structure or the orientation of the collections of the institution concerned.

(b) In addition to institutions designated as 'museums', the following qualify as museums for the purposes of this definition:

(i) natural, archaeological and ethnographic monuments and sites of a museum nature that acquire, conserve and communicate material evidence of people and their environment;

(ii) institutions holding collections of and displaying live specimens of plants and animals, such as botanical and zoological gardens, aquaria and vivaria;

(iii) science centres and planetaria;

(iv) conservation institutes and exhibition galleries permanently maintained by libraries and archive centres;

(v) nature reserves;

(vi) such other institutions as the Executive Council, after seeking the advice of the Advisory Committee, considers as having some or all of the characteristics of a museum, or as supporting museums and professional museum workers through museological research, education or training.

1.3. The Museum Profession

ICOM defines the members of the museum profession, under Article 2, para. 2 of its *Statutes*, as follows: " Professional museum workers include all the personnel of museums or institutions qualifying as museums in accordance with the definition in Article 2 para. 1 (*as detailed under para 1.2 above*), having received specialized training, or possessing an equivalent practical experience, in any field relevant to the management and operations of a museum, and privately or self-employed persons practising in one of the museological professions and who respect the *ICOM Code of Professional Ethics*."

1.4. Governing Body

The government and control of museums in terms of policy, finance and administration etc., vary greatly from one country to another, and often from one museum to another within a country according to the legal and other national or local provisions of the particular country or institution.

In the case of many national museums, the Director, Curator or other professional head of the museum may be appointed by, and directly responsible to, a Minister or a Government Department, whilst most local government museums are similarly governed and controlled by the appropriate local authority. In many other cases the government and control of the museum are vested in some form of independent body, such as a board of trustees, a society, a non-profit company, or even an individual.

For the purposes of this *Code*, the term "Governing Body" has been used throughout to signify the superior authority concerned with the policy, finance and administration of the museum. This may be an individual Minister or official, a Ministry, a local authority, a Board of Trustees, a Society, the Director of the museum or any other individual or body. Directors, Curators or other professional heads of the museum are responsible for the proper care and management of the museum.

II. INSTITUTIONAL ETHICS

2. BASIC PRINCIPLES FOR MUSEUM GOVERNANCE

2.1. Minimum Standards for Museums

The governing body or other controlling authority of a museum has an ethical duty to maintain, and if possible enhance, all aspects of the museum, its collections and its services. Above all, it is the responsibility of each governing body to ensure that all of the collections in their care are adequately housed, conserved and documented.

The minimum standards in terms of finance, premises, staffing and services will vary according to the size and responsibilities of each museum. In some countries such minimum standards may be defined by law or other government regulation and in others guidance on and assessment of minimum standards is available in the form of "Museum Accreditation" or similar schemes. Where such guidance is not available locally, it can usually be obtained from appropriate national and international organizations and experts, either directly or through the National Committee or appropriate International Committee of ICOM.

2.2. Constitution

Each museum should have a written constitution or other document setting out clearly its legal status and permanent, non-profit nature, drawn up in accordance with appropriate national laws in relation to museums, the cultural heritage, and non-profit institutions. The governing body or other controlling authority of a museum should prepare and publicize a clear statement of the aims, objectives and policies of the museum, and of the role and composition of the governing body itself.

2.3. Finance

The governing body holds the ultimate financial responsibility for the museum and for the protecting and nurturing of its various assets: the collections and related documentation, the premises, facilities and equipment, the financial assets, and the staff. It is obliged to develop and define the purposes and related policies of the institution, and to ensure that all of the museum's assets are properly and effectively used for museum purposes. Sufficient funds must be available on a regular basis, either from public or private sources, to enable the governing body to carry out and develop the work of the museum. Proper accounting procedures must be adopted and maintained in accordance with the relevant national laws and professional accountancy standards.

2.4. Premises

The board has specially strong obligations to provide accommodation giving a suitable environment for the physical security and preservation of the collections. Premises must be adequate for the museum to fulfil within its stated policy its basic functions of collection, research, storage, conservation, education and display, including staff accommodation, and should comply with all appropriate national legislation in relation to public and staff safety. Proper standards of protection should be provided against such hazards as theft, fire, flood, vandalism and deterioration, throughout the year, day and night. The special needs of disabled people should be provided for, as far as practicable, in planning and managing both buildings and facilities.

2.5. Personnel

The governing body has a special obligation to ensure that the museum has staff sufficient in both number and kind to ensure that the museum is able to meet its responsibilities. The size of the staff, and its nature (whether paid or unpaid, permanent or temporary), will depend on the size of the museum, its collections and its responsibilities. However, proper arrangements should be made for the museum to meet its obligations in relation to the care of the collections, public access and services, research, and security.

The governing body has particularly important obligations in relation to the appointment of the director of the museum, and whenever the possibility of terminating the employment of the director arises, to ensure that any such action is taken only in accordance with appropriate procedures under the legal or other constitutional arrangements and policies of the museum, and that any such staff changes are made in a professional and ethical manner, and in accordance with what is judged to be the best interests of the museum, rather than any personal or external factor or prejudice. It should also ensure that the same principles are applied in relation to any appointment, promotion, dismissal or demotion of the personnel of the museum by the director or any other senior member of staff with staffing responsibilities.

The governing body should recognize the diverse nature of the museum profession, and the wide range of specializations that it now encompasses, including conservator/restorers, scientists, museum education service personnel, registrars and computer specialists, security service managers, etc. It should ensure that the museum both makes appropriate use of such specialists where required and that such specialized personnel are properly recognized as full members of the professional staff in all respects.

Members of the museum profession require appropriate academic, technical and professional training in order to fulfil their important role in relation to the operation of the museum and the care for the heritage, and the governing body should recognize the need for, and value of, a properly qualified and trained staff, and offer adequate opportunities for further training and re-training in order to maintain an adequate and effective workforce.

A governing body should never require a member of the museum staff to act in a way that could reasonably be judged to conflict with the provisions of this *Code of Ethics*, or any national law or national code of professional ethics.

The Director or other chief professional officer of a museum should be directly responsible to, and have direct access to, the governing body in which trusteeship of the collections is vested.

2.6. Educational and Community Role of the Museum

By definition a museum is an institution in the service of society and of its development, and is generally open to the public (even though this may be a restricted public in the case of certain very specialized museums, such as certain academic or medical museums, for example).

The museum should take every opportunity to develop its role as an educational resource used by all sections of the population or specialized group that the museum is intended to serve. Where appropriate in relation to the museum's programme and responsibilities, specialist staff with training and skills in museum education are likely to be required for this purpose.

The museum has an important duty to attract new and wider audiences within all levels of the community, locality or group that the museum aims to serve, and should offer both the general community and specific individuals and groups within it opportunities to become actively involved in the museum and to support its aims and policies.

2.7. Public Access

The general public (or specialized group served, in the case of museums with a limited public role), should have access to the displays during reasonable hours and for regular periods. The museum should also offer the public reasonable access to members of staff by appointment or other arrangement, and full access to information about the collections, subject to any necessary restrictions for reasons of confidentiality or security as discussed in para. 7.3. below.

2.8. Displays, Exhibitions and Special Activities

Subject to the primary duty of the museum to preserve unimpaired for the future the significant material that comprises the museum collections, it is the responsibility of the museum to use the collections for the creation and dissemination of new knowledge, through research, educational work, permanent displays, temporary exhibitions and other special activities. These should be in accordance with the stated policy and educational purpose of the museum, and should not compromise either the quality or the proper care of the collections. The museum should seek to ensure that information in display and exhibitions is honest and objective and does not perpetuate myths or stereotypes.

2.9. Commercial Support and Sponsorship

Where it is the policy of the museum to seek and accept financial or other support from commercial or industrial organizations, or from other outside sources, great care is needed to define clearly the agreed relationship between the museum and the sponsor. Commercial support and sponsorship may involve ethical problems and the museum must ensure that the standards and objectives of the museum are not compromised by such a relationship.

2.10. Museum Shops and Commercial Activities

Museum shops and any other commercial activities of the museum, and any publicity relating to these, should be in accordance with a clear policy, should be relevant to the collections and the basic educational purpose of the museum, and must not compromise the quality of those collections. In the case of the manufacture and sale of replicas, reproductions or other commercial items adapted from an object in a museum's collections, all aspects of the commercial venture must be carried out in a manner that will not discredit either the integrity of the museum or the intrinsic value of the original object. Great care must be taken to identify permanently such objects for what they are, and to ensure accuracy and high quality in their manufacture. All items offered for sale should represent good value for money and should comply with all relevant national legislation.

2.11. Legal Obligation

It is an important responsibility of each governing body to ensure that the museum complies fully with all legal obligations, whether in relation to national, regional or local law, international law or treaty obligations, and to any legally binding trusts or conditions relating to any aspect of the museum collections or facilities.

3. ACQUISITIONS TO MUSEUM COLLECTIONS

3.1. Collecting Policies

Each museum authority should adopt and publish a written statement of its collecting policy. This policy should be reviewed from time to time, and at least once every five years. Objects acquired should be relevant to the purpose and activities of the museum, and be accompanied by evidence of a valid legal title. Any conditions or limitations relating to an acquisition should be clearly described in an instrument of conveyance or other written documentation. Museums should not, except in very exceptional circumstances, acquire material that the museum is unlikely to be able to catalogue, conserve, store or exhibit, as appropriate, in a proper manner. Acquisitions outside the current stated policy of the museum should only be made in very exceptional circumstances, and then only after proper consideration by the governing body of the museum itself, having regard to the interests of the objects under consideration, the national or other cultural heritage and the special interests of other museums.

3.2. Acquisition of Illicit Material

The illicit trade in objects destined for public and private collections encourages the destruction of historic sites, local ethnic cultures, theft at both national and international levels, places at *risk* endangered species of flora and fauna, and contravenes the spirit of national and international patrimony. Museums should recognize the relationship between the market-place and the initial and often destructive taking of an object for the commercial market, and must recognize that it is highly unethical for a museum to support in any way, whether directly or indirectly, that illicit market.

A museum should not acquire, whether by purchase, gift, bequest or exchange, any object unless the governing body and responsible officer are satisfied that the museum can acquire a valid title to the specimen or object in question and that in particular it has not been acquired in, or exported from, its country of origin and/or any intermediate country in which it may have been legally owned (including the nuseum's own country), in violation of that country's laws.

So far as biological and geological material is concerned, a museum should not acquire by any direct or indirect means any specimen that has been collected, sold or otherwise transferred in contravention of any national or international wildlife protection or natural history conservation law or treaty of the museum's own country or any other country except with the express consent of an appropriate outside legal or governmental authority.

So far as excavated material is concerned, in addition to the safeguards set out above, the museum should not acquire by purchase objects in any case where the governing body or responsible officer has reasonable cause to believe that their recovery involved the recent unscientific or intentional destruction or damage of ancient monuments or archaeological sites, or involved a failure to disclose the finds to the owner or occupier of the land, or to the proper legal or governmental authorities.

If appropriate and feasible, the same tests as are outlined in the above four paragraphs should be applied in determining whether or not to accept loans for exhibition or other purposes.

3.3. Field Study and Collecting

Museums should assume a position of leadership in the effort to halt the continuing degradation of the world's natural history, archaeological, ethnographic, historic and artistic resources. Each museum should develop policies that allow it to conduct its activities within appropriate national and international laws and treaty obligations, and with a reasonable certainty that its approach is consistent with the spirit and intent of both national and international efforts to protect and enhance the cultural heritage.

Field exploration, collecting and excavation by museum workers present ethical problems that are both complex and critical. All planning for field studies and field collecting must be preceded by investigation, disclosure and consultation with both the proper authorities and any interested museums or academic institutions in the country or area of the proposed study sufficient to ascertain if the proposed activity is both legal and justifiable on academic and scientific grounds. Any field programme must be executed in such a way that all participants act legally and responsibly in acquiring specimens and data, and that they discourage by all practical means unethical, illegal and destructive practices.

3.4. Co-operation between Museums in Collecting Policies

Each museum should recognize the need for co-operation and consultation between all museums with similar or overlapping interests and collecting policies, and should seek to consult with such other institutions both on specific acquisitions where a conflict of interest is thought possible and, more generally, on defining areas of specialization. Museums should respect the boundaries of the recognized collecting areas of other museums and should avoid acquiring material with special local connections or of special local interest from the collecting area of another museum without due notification of intent.

3.5. Conditional Acquisitions and other Special Factors

Gifts, bequests and loans should only be accepted if they conform to the stated collecting and exhibition policies of the museum. Offers that are subject to special conditions may have to be rejected in the long term interests of the museum and its public.

3.6. Loans to Museums

Both individual loans of objects and the mounting or borrowing of loan exhibitions can have an important role in enhancing the interest and quality of a museum and its services. However, the ethical principles outlined in paras. 3.1 to 3.5 above must apply to the consideration of proposed loans and loan exhibitions as to the acceptance or rejection of items offered to the permanent collections: loans should not be accepted nor exhibitions mounted if they do not have a valid educational, scientific or academic purpose.

3.7. Conflicts of Interest

The collecting policy or regulations of the museum should include provisions to ensure that no person involved in the policy or management of the museum, such as a trustee or other member of a governing body, or a member of the museum staff, may compete with the museum for objects or may take advantage of privileged information received because of his or her position, and that should a conflict of interest develop between the needs of the individual and the museum, those of the museum will prevail. Special care is also required in considering any offer of an item either for sale or as a tax-benefit gift, from members of governing bodies, members of staff, or the families or close associates of these.

4. DISPOSAL OF COLLECTIONS

4.1. General Presumption of Permanence of Collections

By definition one of the key functions of almost every kind of museum is to acquire objects and keep them for posterity. Consequently there must always be a strong presumption against the disposal of specimens to which a museum has assumed formal title. Any form of disposal, whether by donation, exchange, sale or destruction requires the exercise of a high order of curatorial judgement and should be approved by the governing body only after full expert and legal advice has been taken.

Special considerations may apply in the case of certain kinds of specialized institutions such as "living" or "working" museums, and some teaching and other educational museums, together with museums and other institutions displaying living specimens, such as botanical and zoological gardens and aquaria, which may find it necessary to regard at least part of their collections as "fungible" (i.e. replaceable and renewable). However, even here there is a clear ethical obligation to ensure that the activities of the institution are not detrimental to the long term survival of examples of the material studied, displayed or used.

4.2. Legal or other Powers of Disposal

The laws relating to the protection and permanence of museum collections, and to the power of museums to dispose of items from their collection vary greatly from country to country, and often from one museum to another within the same country. In some cases no disposals of any kind are permitted, except in the case of items that have been seriously damaged by natural or accidental deterioration. Elsewhere, there may be no explicit restriction on disposals under general law.

Where the museum has legal powers permitting disposals, or has acquired objects subject to conditions of disposal, the legal or other requirements and procedures must be fully complied with. Even where legal powers of disposal exist, a museum may not be completely free to dispose of items acquired where financial assistance has been obtained from an outside source (e.g., public or private grants, donations from a Friends of the Museum organization, or private benefactor), and disposal would normally require the consent of all parties who had contributed to the original purchase.

Where the original acquisition was subject to mandatory restrictions, these must be observed unless it can be clearly shown that adherence to such restrictions is impossible or substantially detrimental to the institution. Even in these circumstances, the museum can only be relieved from such restrictions through appropriate legal procedures.

4.3. De-accessioning Policies and Procedures

Where a museum has the necessary legal powers to dispose of an object, the decision to sell or otherwise dispose of material from the collections should only be taken after due consideration, and such material should be offered first, by exchange, gift or private treaty sale, to other museums before sale by public auction or other means is considered. A decision to dispose of a specimen or work of art, whether by exchange, sale or destruction (in the case of an item too badly damaged or deteriorated to be restorable) should be the responsibility of the governing body of the museum, not of the curator of the collection concerned acting alone. Full records should be kept of all such decisions and the objects involved, and proper arrangements made for the preservation and/or transfer, as appropriate, of the documentation relating to the object concerned, including photographic records where practicable.

Neither members of staff, nor members of the governing bodies, or members of their families or close associates, should ever be permitted to purchase objects that have been de-accessioned from a collection. Similarly, no such person should be permitted to appropriate in any other way items from the museum collections, even temporarily, to any personal collection or for any kind of personal use.

4.4. Return and Restitution of Cultural Property

If a museum should come into possession of an object that can be demonstrated to have been exported or otherwise transferred in violation of the principles of the Unesco *Convention on the Means of Prohibiting and Preventing the Illicit Import, Export and Transfer of Ownership of Cultural Property (1970)* and the country of origin seeks its return and demonstrates that it is part of the country's cultural heritage, the museum should, if legally free to do so, take responsible steps to co-operate in the return of the object to the country of origin.

In the case of requests for the return of cultural property to the country of origin, museums should be prepared to initiate dialogues with an open-minded attitude on the basis of scientific and professional principles (in preference to action at a governmental or political level). The possibility of developing bilateral or multilateral co-operation schemes to assist museums in countries which are considered to have lost a significant part of their cultural heritage in the development of adequate museums and museum resources should be explored.

Museums should also respect fully the terms of the *Convention for the Protection of Cultural Property in the Event of Armed Conflict (The Hague Convention, 1954),* and in support of this Convention, should in particular abstain from purchasing or otherwise appropriating or acquiring cultural objects from any occupied country, as these will in most cases have been illegally exported or illicitly removed.

4.5. Income from Disposal of Collections

Any moneys received by a governing body from the disposal of specimens or works of art should be applied solely for the purchase of additions to the museum collections.

III. PROFESSIONAL CONDUCT

5. GENERAL PRINCIPLES

5.1. Ethical Obligations of Members of the Museum Profession

Employment by a museum, whether publicly or privately supported, is a public trust involving great responsibility. In all activities museum employees must act with integrity and in accordance with the most stringent ethical principles as well as the highest standards of objectivity.

An essential element of membership of a profession is the implication of both rights and obligations. Although the conduct of a professional in any area is ordinarily regulated by the basic rules of moral behaviour which govern human relationships, every occupation involves standards, as well as particular duties and responsibilities that from time to time create the need for a statement of guiding principles. The museum professional should understand two guiding principles: first, that museums are the object of a public trust whose value to the community is in direct proportion to the quality of service rendered; and, secondly, that intellectual ability and professional knowledge are not, in themselves, sufficient, but must be inspired by a high standard of ethical conduct.

The Director and other professional staff owe their primary professional and academic allegiance to their museum and should at all times act in accordance with the approved policies of the museum. The Director or other principal museum officer should be aware of, and bring to the notice of the governing body of the museum whenever appropriate, the terms of the *ICOM Code of Professional Ethics* and of any relevant national or regional Codes of Policy Statements on Museum Ethics, and should urge the governing body to comply with these. Members of the museum profession should also comply fully with the *ICOM* Code and any other Codes or Statements on Museum Ethics whenever exercising the functions of the governing body under delegated powers.

5.2. Personal Conduct

Loyalty to colleagues and to the employing museum is an important professional responsibility, but the ultimate loyalty must be to fundamental ethical principles and to the profession as a whole.

Applicants for any professional post should divulge frankly and in confidence all information relevant to the consideration of their applications, and if appointed should recognize that museum work is normally regarded as a full-time vocation. Even where the terms of employment do not prohibit outside employment or business interests, the Director and other senior staff should not undertake other paid employment or accept outside commissions without the express consent of the governing body of the museum. In tendering resignations from their posts, members of the professional staff, and above all the Director, should consider carefully the needs of the museum at the time. A professional person, having recently accepted a new appointment, should consider seriously the professional commitment to the present post before applying for a new post elsewhere.

5.3. Private Interests

While every member of any profession is entitled to a measure of personal independence, consistent with professional and staff responsibilities, in the eyes of the public no private business or professional interest of a member of the museum profession can be wholly separated from that of the professional's institution or other official affiliation, despite disclaimers that may be offered. Any museum-related activity by the individual may reflect on the institution or be attributed to it. The professional must be concerned not only with the true personal motivations and interests, but also with the way in which such actions might be construed by the outside observer. Museum employees and others in a close relationship with them must not accept gifts, favours, loans or other dispensations or things of value that may be offered to them in connection with their duties for the museum (see also para 8.4 below).

6. PERSONAL RESPONSIBILITY TO THE COLLECTIONS

6.1. Acquisitions to Museum Collections

The Director and professional staff should take all possible steps to ensure that a written collecting policy is adopted by the governing body of the museum, and is thereafter reviewed and revised as appropriate at regular intervals. This policy, as formally adopted and revised by the governing body, should form the basis of all professional decisions and recommendations in relation to acquisitions.

Negotiations concerning the acquisition of museum items from members of the general public must be conducted with scrupulous fairness to the seller or donor. No object should be deliberately or misleadingly identified or valued, to the benefit of the museum and to the detriment of the donor, owner or previous owners, in order to acquire it for the museum collections nor should be taken nor retained on loan with the deliberate intention of improperly procuring it for the collections.

6.2. Care of Collections

It is an important professional responsibility to ensure that all items accepted temporarily or permanently by the museum are properly and fully documented to facilitate provenance, identification, condition and treatment. All objects accepted by the museum should be properly conserved, protected, and maintained.

Careful attention should be paid to the means of ensuring the best possible security as a protection against theft in display, working or storage areas, against accidental damage when handling objects, and against damage or theft in transit. Where it is the national or local policy to use commercial insurance arrangements, the staff should ensure that the insurance cover is adequate, especially for objects in transit and loan items, or other objects, which are not owned by the museum but which are its current responsibility.

Members of the museum profession should not delegate important curatorial, conservation, or other professional responsibilities to persons who lack the appropriate knowledge and skill, or who are inadequately supervised, in the case of trainees or approved volunteers, where such persons are allowed to assist in the care of the collections. There is also a clear duty to consult professional colleagues within or outside the museum if at any time the expertise available in a particular museum or department is insufficient to ensure the welfare of items in the collections under its care.

6.3. Conservation and Restoration of Collections

One of the essential ethical obligations of each member of the museum profession is to ensure the proper care and conservation of both existing and newly-acquired collections and individual items for which the members of the profession and the employing institutions are responsible, and to ensure that as far as is reasonable the collections are passed on to future generations in as good and safe a condition as practicable having regard to current knowledge and resources.

In attempting to achieve this high ideal, special attention should be paid to the growing body of knowledge about preventative conservation methods and techniques, including the provision of suitable environmental protection against the known natural or artificial causes of deterioration of museum specimens and works of art.

There are often difficult decisions to be made in relation to the degree of replacement or restoration of lost or damaged parts of a specimen or work of art that may be ethically acceptable in particular circumstances. Such decisions call for proper co-operation between all with a specialized responsibility for the object, including both the curator and the conservator or restorer, and should not be decided unilaterally by one or the other acting alone.

The ethical issues involved in conservation and restoration work of many kinds are a major study in themselves, and those with special responsibilities in this area, whether as director, curator, conservator or restorer, have an important responsibility to ensure that they are familiar with these ethical issues, and with appropriate professional opinion, as expressed in some detailed ethical statements and codes produced by the conservator/restorer/professional bodies.[1]

6.4. Documentation of Collections

The proper recording and documentation of both new acquisitions and existing collections in accordance with appropriate standards and the internal rules and conventions of the museum is a most important professional responsibility. It is particularly important that such documentation should include details of the source of each object and the conditions of acceptance of it by the museum. In addition specimen data should be kept in a secure environment and be supported by adequate systems providing easy retrieval of the data by both the staff and by other *bona fide* users.

6.5. De-accessioning and Disposals from the Collections

No item from the collections of a museum should be disposed of except in accordance with the ethical principles summarized in the Institutional Ethics section of this *Code*, paras. 4.1 to 4.4 above, and the detailed rules and procedures applying in the museum in question.

6.6. Welfare of Live Animals

Where museums and related institutions maintain for exhibition or research purposes live populations of animals, the health and well-being of any such creatures must be a foremost ethical consideration. It is essential that a veterinary surgeon be available for advice and for regular inspection of the animals and their living conditions. The museum should prepare a safety

1. 'The Conservator-Restorer : A Definition of the Profession': *ICOM News*, Vol.39, No.1, 1986, pp. 5-6.

code for the protection of staff and visitors which has been approved by an expert in the veterinary field, and all staff must follow it in detail.

6.7. Human Remains and Material of Ritual Significance

Where a museum maintains and/or is developing collections of human remains and sacred objects, these should be securely housed and carefully maintained as archival collections in scholarly institutions, and should always be available to qualified researchers and educators, but not to the morbidly curious. Research on such objects and their housing and care must be accomplished in a manner acceptable not only to fellow professionals but to those of various beliefs, including in particular members of the community, ethnic or religious groups concerned. Although it is occasionally necessary to use human remains and other sensitive material in interpretative exhibits, this must be done with tact and with respect for the feelings for human dignity held by all peoples.

6.8. Private Collections

The acquiring, collecting and owning of objects of a kind collected by a museum or by a member of the museum profession for a personal collection may not in itself be unethical, and may be regarded as a valuable way of enhancing professional knowledge and judgement. However, serious dangers are implicit when members of the profession collect for themselves privately objects similar to those which they and others collect for their museums. In particular, no member of the museum profession should compete with their institution either in the acquisition of objects or in any personal collecting activity. Extreme care must be taken to ensure that no conflict of interest arises.

In some countries and many individual museums, members of the museum profession are not permitted to have private collections of any kind, and such rules must be respected. Even where there are no such restrictions, on appointment, a member of the museum profession with a private collection should provide the governing body with a description of it, and a statement of the collecting policy being pursued, and any consequent agreement between the curator and the governing body concerning the private collection must be scrupulously kept. (See also para 8.4 below.)

7. PERSONAL RESPONSIBILITY TO THE PUBLIC

7.1. Upholding Professional Standards

In the interests of the public as well as the profession, members of the museum profession should observe accepted standards and laws, uphold the dignity and honour of their profession and accept its self-imposed disciplines. They should do their part to safeguard the public against illegal or unethical professional conduct, and should use appropriate opportunities to inform and educate the public in the aims, purposes and aspirations of the profession in order to develop a better public understanding of the purposes and responsibilities of museums and of the profession.

7.2. Relations with the General Public

Members of the museum profession should deal with the public efficiently and courteously at all times, and should in particular deal promptly with all correspondence and enquiries. Subject to the requirements of confidentiality in a particular case, they should share their expertise in all professional fields in dealing with enquiries, subject to due acknowledgment, from both the general public and specialist enquirers, allowing *bona fide* researchers properly controlled but, so far as possible, full access to any material or documentation in their care, even when this is the subject of personal research or special field of interest.

7.3. Confidentiality

Members of the museum profession must protect all confidential information relating to the source of material owned by or loaned to the museum, as well as information concerning the security arrangements of the museum, or the security arrangements of private collections or any place visited in the course of official duties. Confidentiality must also be respected in relation to any item brought to the museum for identification and, without specific authority from the owner, information on such an item should not be passed to another museum, to a dealer, or to any other person (subject to any legal obligation to assist the police or other proper authorities in investigating possible stolen or illicitly acquired or transferred property).

There is a special responsibility to respect the personal confidences contained in oral history or other personal material. Investigators using recording devices such as cameras or tape recorders or the technique of oral interviewing should take special care to protect their data, and persons investigated, photographed or interviewed should have the right to remain anonymous if they so choose, This right should be respected where it has been specifically promised. Where there is no clear understanding to the contrary, the primary responsibility of the investigator is to ensure that no information is revealed that might harm the informant or his or her community. Subjects under study should understand the capacities of cameras, tape recorders and other machines used, and should be free to accept or reject their use.

8. PERSONAL RESPONSIBILITY TO COLLEAGUES AND THE PROFESSION

8.1. Professional Relationships

Relationships between members of the museum profession should always be courteous, both in public and in private. Differences of opinion should not be expressed in a personalized fashion. Notwithstanding this general rule, members of the profession may properly object to proposals or practices which may have a damaging effect on a museum or museums, or the profession.

8.2. Professional Co-operation

Members of the museum profession have an obligation, subject to due acknowledgement, to share their knowledge and experience with their colleagues and with scholars and students in relevant fields. They should show their appreciation and respect to those from whom they have learned and should present without thought of personal gain such advancements in techniques and experience which may be of benefit to others.

The training of personnel in the specialized activities involved in museum work is of great importance in the development of the profession and all should accept responsibility, where appropriate, in the training of colleagues. Members of the profession who in their official appointment have under their direction junior staff, trainees, students and assistants undertaking formal or informal professional training, should give them benefit of their experience and knowledge, and should also treat them with the consideration and respect customary among members of the profession.

Members of the profession form working relationships in the course of their duties with numerous other people, both professional and otherwise, within and outside the museum in which they are employed. They are expected to conduct these relationships with courtesy and fair-mindedness and to render their professional services to others efficiently and at a high standard.

8.3. Dealing

No number of the museum profession should participate in any dealing (buying or selling for profit), in objects similar or related to the objects collected by the employing museum. Dealing by museum employees at any level of responsibility in objects that are collected by any other museum can also present serious problems even if there is no risk of direct conflict with the employing museum, and should be permitted only, if, after full disclosure and review by the governing body of the employing museum or designated senior officer, explicit permission is granted, with or without conditions.

Article 7 para 5 of the ICOM *Statutes* provides that membership of ICOM shall not be available, under any circumstances, to any person or institution that is dealing (buying or selling for profit) in cultural property.

8.4. Other Potential Conflicts of Interest

Generally, members of the museum profession should refrain from all acts or activities which may be construed as a conflict of interest. Museum professionals by virtue of their knowledge, experience, and contacts are frequently offered opportunities such as advisory and consultancy services, teaching, writing and broadcasting opportunities, or requests for valuations, in a personal capacity. Even where the national law and the individual's conditions of employment permit such activities, these may appear in the eyes of colleagues, the employing authority, or the general public to create a conflict of interest. In such situations all legal and employment contract conditions must be scrupulously followed, and in the event of any potential conflict arising or being suggested, the matter should be reported immediately to an appropriate superior officer or the museum governing body, and steps must be taken to eliminate the potential conflict of interest.

Even where the conditions of employment permit any kind of outside activity, and there appears to be no risk of any conflict of interest, great care should be taken to ensure that such outside interests do not interfere in any way with the proper discharge of official duties and responsibilities.

8.5. Authentication, Valuation and Illicit Material

Members of the museum profession are encouraged to share their professional knowledge and expertise with both professional colleagues and the general public (See para. 7.2 above)

However, written certificates of authenticity or valuation (appraisals) should not be given, and opinions on the monetary value of objects should only be given on official request from other museums or competent legal, governmental or other responsible public authorities.

Members of the museum profession should not identify or otherwise authenticate objects where they have reason to believe or suspect that these have been illegally or illicitly acquired, transferred, imported or exported.

They should recognize that it is highly unethical for museums or the museum profession to support either directly or indirectly the illicit trade in cultural or natural objects (See para. 3.2 above), and under no circumstances should they act in a way that could be regarded as benefiting such illicit trade in any way, directly or suspect illicit trade in any way, directly or indirectly. Where there is reason to believe or suspect illicit or illegal transfer, import or export, the competent authorities should be notified.

8.6. Unprofessional Conduct

Every member of the museum profession should be conversant with both any national or local laws, and any conditions of employment concerning corrupt practices, and should at all times avoid situations which could rightly or wrongly be construed as corrupt or improper conduct of any kind. In particular no museum official should accept any gift, hospitality, or any form of reward from any dealer, auctioneer or other person as an improper inducement in respect of the purchase or disposal of museum items.

Also, in order to avoid any suspicion of corruption, a museum professional should not recommend any particular dealer, auctioneer or other person to a member of the public, nor should the official accept any "special price" or discount for personal purchases from any dealer with whom either the professional or employing museum has a professional relationship.

20. Guidelines for Loans*

1. GENERAL

1.1 Both the Borrower and the Lender agree to abide by the guidelines for loans as set out below, although by mutual agreement sections of these guidelines may be added to, waived, or modified in writing.

1.2 The Lender reserves the right to recall the loans at any time if these guidelines are not respected, and disclaims any liability resulting from such action.

2. RESPONSIBILITIES AND EXPENSES

2.1 The Borrower accepts the responsibility to pay, promptly and upon demand, all agreed expenses relating to insurance, packing, customs, transport (including the expenses of any official who may be required to travel with the loan), exhibition and custody arising from the loan agreement.

2.2 Where requested by the Lender, the Borrower will accept responsibility for agreed costs incurred in the preparation of the loan.

2.3 The Borrower will exercise due care in the custody, handling, transport, unpacking and repacking of the loan.

2.4 The Borrower, upon unpacking, will acknowledge immediately the receipt of the loans.

3. CONDITION REPORTS

3.1 The Lender will prepare a condition report before packing and, where possible, will provide the Borrower with full documentation.

3.2 The condition report will specify any required environmental and travel

---

* Adopted by The International Council of Museums, June 1973

conditions for the loan, with full regard to the media of the work as well as to its physical condition.

3.3 The condition report will be forwarded to the Borrower prior to the removal of the loan so that he may satisfy himself that no undue risks are being accepted. Additional copies of the condition report will travel with the loan.

3.4 On receiving the loan, the Borrower will check the condition report and return one copy to the Lender within 48 hours of unpacking, noting any changes in the condition of the loan. The same procedure will be adopted on any occasion when the loan is transferred to another institution.

3.5 Any evident change in the condition of the loan, either in transit or during exhibition, will be reported immediately to the Lender.

3.6 Should the Lender consider that the loan should be examined by himself or an officer of the lending museum or its agent, then the expenses incurred with such an examination shall be borne by the Borrower.

4. INSURANCE

4.1 The Borrower agrees to provide or pay for insurance, or provide an indemnity, acceptable to the Lender.

4.2 The insurance or indemnity shall be "nail-to-nail", i.e., covering the loan from the time when it is removed from its location prior to its shipment to the Borrower, and until directly to the location specified in the Certificate of Insurance or Indemnity.

4.3 In the event of total loss, the policy of indemnity agreement should provide for coverage of the declared value as specified in the Certificate of Insurance or Indemnity.

4.4 In the event of partial loss or damage the policy or indemnity should provide for the cost of replacing or repairing the loan so damaged, and depreciation.

4.5 The policy may provides a waiver of subrogation against the Borrower.

4.6 When the Borrower provide the insurance or indemnity, he shall submit evidence to the Lender for approval by him prior to the removal of the loan.

4.7 If the Lender elects to arrange his own insurance cover, he will on demand submit to the Borrower evidence of insurance.

5. CUSTOMS FORMALITIES

5.1 Customs formalities should be cleared by the Lender at the premises of final packing, before dispatch. The Borrower is responsible for making every effort to ensure that Customs examination is made only on his premises on arrival. No loan should be unpacked for examination at any point on the journey, and the same procedure should apply in reverse for the return of the loan.

6. PACKING

6.1 The Lender shall prepare the loan shipment in packing considered to be safe and adequate for the purpose, and reserves the right to appoint his own packing agent should it be deemed necessary. The Borrower reserves the right to examine the packing before dispatch takes place.

6.2 On return, the loan shall be packed in exactly the same way as received and with the same cases, packages, pads and other furnishings when possible, unless a change is specifically authorized by the Lender. All packing materials should be stored during the loan period in a place fully conditioned to the same temperature and relative humidity levels as those under which the loan itself is stored or displayed.

7. TRANSPORT

7.1 The Borrower and the Lender shall mutually agree to the transport arrangements. The Lender reserves the right to specify the transport programme to be employed and to object to a specific contractor without stating his reasons. The vehicles and other equipment used for handling should be suitable for the specialized work involved, and where necessary they are to be fitted with approved security devices.

7.2 Both parties are responsible for ensuring that movements of the loan through ports of entry and exit are effected with speed and efficiency.

8. ESCORTS

8.1 When the Lender specifies that the loan be accompanied by a courier or escort, he may reserve the right of nomination.

8.2 Escorts should be experienced museum officials familiar with the modern packing and transport methods employed.

8.3 The escort will personally witness and oversee packing and unpacking, loading and unloading of the loan, and any transfer between different forms of transport.

9. PHYSICAL ENVIRONMENT

9.1 The Borrower undertakes to maintain constant and adequate protection of the loan from the hazards of fire and flood, exposure to excessive light levels or harmful radiations, extremes of temperature and relative humidity, insect attack and pollution. The Borrower will also notify the Lender of any unusual environmental exposure.

9.2 The Lender reserves the right to define specific conditions relating to item 9.1 above, and to require that the Borrower undertakes to maintain environmental conditions within pre-agreed limits. (Note: ICOM recommends that light sensitive loans should not be exposed to direct sunlight. Moderately light sensitive loans should only be exposed to ultra-violet filtered light at intensity levels not exceeding 150 lux, and for very light sensitive loans, not exceeding 50 lux. Relative humidity in normal circumstances should be maintained at 54% + 4%).

10. SECURITY

10.1 The Borrower must undertake to maintain constant and adequate protection of the loan to minimize the risk of theft or damage. The Lender may agree to the employment of a security system relying upon electronic devices either alone or in conjunction with physical invigilation.

10.2 The Lender or his authorized agent retains the right to inspect all environmental and security precautions during the period of the loan without prior warning.

10.3 The Borrower agrees that the loan will not in any way be treated, cleaned, repaired, remounted, reset or submitted to any scientific examination, except when such an action has been specifically authorized by the Lender, or is undertaken for the loan's immediate protection consequent to a mishap (see also paragraph 3.5).

11. PHOTOGRAPHY AND REPRODUCTION

11.1 The loan must not be individually photographed, filmed, televised or reproduced, without the prior consent of the Lender, although there is no objection to general views of an exhibition being taken for press and publicity purpose.

11.2 In the case of the Lender agreeing to the loan being filmed, photographed or televised, the Borrower will ensure that:

(a) lamps are not placed closer than two metres from the loan;

(b) the lamps used do not raise the surface temperature of the loan more than 3°C above room temperature;

(c) the loan is not touched or moved, except by the qualified employees of the Borrower.

11.3 In the case of the Lender agreeing to photographic reproduction of the loan, the Borrower will ensure that the ownership of the loan is indicated in such a form as the Lender may direct.

11.4 It is the responsibility of the Borrower to acquaint himself with any copyright ownership which may apply to the loan and to take the legally required action in the event of the loan being reproduced.

INDEX

Pl. 1. Nataraj : Customs confiscated, c. 11th/12th century A.D.

Pl. 2. Amarous couple : Sunga, c. 2nd century B.C.

Pl. 3. Yaksha : Sunga, c. 2nd century B.C.

Pl. 4. Indrani : Late Gupta, c. 6th century A.D.

Pl. 5. Vishnu : c. 6th century A.D.

Pl. 6. Vishnu : c. 11th century A.D.

Pl. 7. Vishnu : Chalukyan, c. 10th/11th century A.D.

Pl. 8. Stone head of Shiva, c. 10th/11th century A.D.

Pl. 9. Torso of a female deity, c. 7th/8th century A.D.

Pl. 10. Stone head, c. 12th/13th century A.D.

Pl. 11. T.C. plaque with Buddha in *Bhumisparsha Mudra*, inscribed, c. 7th/8th century A.D.